KINGSTON, ELLENVILLE AND SAUGERTIES DIRECTORY FOR 1873–1874

(NEW YORK)

Containing
the Names of the Inhabitants, a
BUSINESS DIRECTORY
or
Classification of the
VARIOUS TRADES, PROFESSIONS, ETC.

Together with
Much Miscellaneous Information

J. H. Lant

HERITAGE BOOKS
2022

HERITAGE BOOKS
AN IMPRINT OF HERITAGE BOOKS, INC.

Books, CDs, and more—Worldwide

For our listing of thousands of titles see our website
at
www.HeritageBooks.com

A Facsimile Reprint
Published 2022 by
HERITAGE BOOKS, INC.
Publishing Division
5810 Ruatan Street
Berwyn Heights, Md. 20740

Originally published by J. H. Lant
Kingston, N. Y.
1873

The ads on the covers and fly leaves
have been ommitted in this reprint.

— Publisher's Notice —
In reprints such as this, it is often not possible to remove
blemishes from the original. We feel the contents of this
book warrant its reissue despite these blemishes and
hope you will agree and read it with pleasure.

International Standard Book Number
Paperbound: 978-1-55613-189-9

INDEX TO ADVERTISEMENTS.

Allen J. H., ...28	Keller K. F., ...33
Auchmoody D. J., ...back cover	Kingsbury W. H., ...11
Barth A., ...35	Kirchner L., ...20
Baylor A. H., ...7	Kleisner J., ...13
Bond J. T., ...11	Larkin M. H., ...23
Bond J. T. Jr., ...11	Liscomb C. G., ...41
Booth Nathaniel, ...50	Loughran Bernard, ...39
Bostwick A., ...9	McBride B., ...19
Bradbury Daniel, ...5	McCausland J. & J., ...34
Brigham E. M., ...12	MacMonagle W. B., ...192
Burhans & Felten, ...1	Merrihew, Hommel & Dunwoody, ...10
Burhans Albert, ...front cover	Merritt C. M. & Son, ...26
Burhans J. S., ...3	Merritt J. O. & G. B., bottom every page, ...
Carley A. A., ...39	
Charlouis John I., ...19	Mick H. & Co., ...22
Constable & DeGarmo, ...41	Mills J. & Bro., ...40
Crouch H. C., ...10	Murphy Frank, ...38
Crosby A. A. & Co., ...front cover	Newwitter M., ...13
Cullen J. H., ...36	Norton J. C., ...21
Cunyes W. D. W., ...back outside cover	Nestell Frank M., ...1
Curtis J. P., ...4	O'Neil C. M. & Co., ...6
Decker B. P. & Bro., ...27	Ostrander T. P., ...37
Decker D. L., ...13	Payntar, Burhans & Oliver, ...24
Decker John T., ...1	Perez A., ...28
Derrenbacher John, ...29	Peters F. F., ...14
Derrenbacher J. & J. P., ...35	Pitts C. V. L., ...12
Deyo J. D., ...280	Reading J. P., ...37
Deyo John H., ...79	Rice A., ...16
Diamond J., ...27	Rice M., ...27
Dolson P. J., ...15	Ridenour & Sleight, ...19
Donaldson & Musson, ...17	Robson Wm., ...20
Donovan D. E., ...36	Roosa C. D., ...6
DuBois Lorenzo, ...2	Roosa Hiram, ...top every page.
Dummer A. O., ...8	Roosa Isaac I., ...4
Dunn A. Jr., ...front fly leaf	Roosa S., ...3
Dutcher & Holmes, ...39	Russell & Myers, ...41
Edmonston C. D., ...25	Ryan Joseph, ...18
Eltinge J. H. Jr., ...24	Safford & Carter, ...157
Finch J., ...8	Sahler, Reynolds & DuBois, ...6
Fitch S. & W. B., ...34	Samter Morris, ...32
Forbes A. J., ...3	Schoonmaker & Van Wagener, ...9
Forst Henry, ...35	Schreiber J. H., ...32
Forst Isidore, ...36	Seaman & Miller, ...32
Fredenburgh Wm. H., ...front paster	Sherwood V., ...front cover
Freilewell Martin, ...42	Short Lorenzo, ...33
Fries & Myer, ...2	Short M. E., ...40
Gage George A., ...15	Snyder M. B., ...front fly leaf
Gassen & Ellsworth, ...16	Stebbins J. R. & Co., ...front cover
Geisler B., ...42	Stephan F. & Co., ...29
Goetcheus & Larsen, ...31	Stokes James, Jr., ...5
Gokey William, ...22	Stow & Benson, ...21
Gross F. W., ...31	Sweeney James, ...26
Hallahan Michael, ...28	Tappen, Burhans & Webster, ...front paster.
Hale J. P., ...42	
Hale Wilbur L., ...100	Thompson Geo. & Sons, ...40
Hamilton Thomas, ...38	The Freeman, ...21
Heimer S. J., ...23	Tillson & Brink, ...22
Herdman James Jr., ...5	Turck & Burhans, ...15
Hoornbeek L. D. & Co., ...37	Van Gaasbeek A. E., ...18
Hume R. B. & J. W., ...9	Van Hoesen W. S. & Co., ...41
Hutchinson R. W., ...4	Westbrook C., ...back outside cover
Hyatt S. M., ...26	Westbrook Simon S., ...2
Jansen A. E., ...20	Willmott Edward, ...25
Johnston Thomas L., ...10	Wood Wm., ...31
Kelly & Cloonan, ...18	

- NOTE -

The original contained no pages 43 - 48, apparently because the ads did not sell as well as expected.

ADVERTISEMENTS.   1

BURHANS & FELTEN,

DEALERS IN

COAL

AND

LUMBER

Cor. East-Front and Main Sts., Kingston, N. Y.

Pine, Hemlock, Chestnut, Maple, Spruce, Cedar, and other Building Materials constantly on hand.

CORNS. BURHANS.   TITUS FELTEN.

J. TAYLOR DECKER,

PROPRIETOR OF

CONTINENTAL SALOON,

Fair St., 2d Door South of County Clerk's Office,
KINGSTON, N. Y.

Meals served at all hours in the finest style. Billiards, and the choicest of Wines, Liquors and Segars constantly on hand.

FRANK M. NESTELL,

Gas & Steam Fitter,

AND DEALER IN

Gas & Oil Fixtures,

Fair St., nearly opposite Music Hall, KINGSTON, N. Y.

ADVERTISEMENTS.

LORENZO DuBOIS,

Proprietor of CENTRAL BAKERY,

Grocer and Baker,

Corner of Prince St. and Hasbrouck Ave.,
KINGSTON, N. Y.

Groceries and Provisions of all kinds constantly on hand. Particular attention given to the Baking Business. Fancy Cakes for Donation Parties, &c., made to order. Goods delivered free to all parts of the city.

SIMON S. WESTBROOK,

GENERAL AUCTIONEER,

No. 32 Wall Street, Kingston, N. Y.

FRIES & MYER,

Dealers in

Groceries & Provisions,

Flour, Fish, Coarse and Fine Salt, Molasses and Syrups, Sugars, Teas, Coffee, Spices, Wood and Earthen Ware, Foreign & Domestic Dried Fruits, Notions, &c. All kinds of Country Produce bought, for which the Highest Market price will be paid.

No. 79 North Front Street,
KINGSTON, N. Y.

HENRY FRIES.   BENJ. S. MYER.

ADVERTISEMENTS.

J. S. BURHANS,
Dealer in

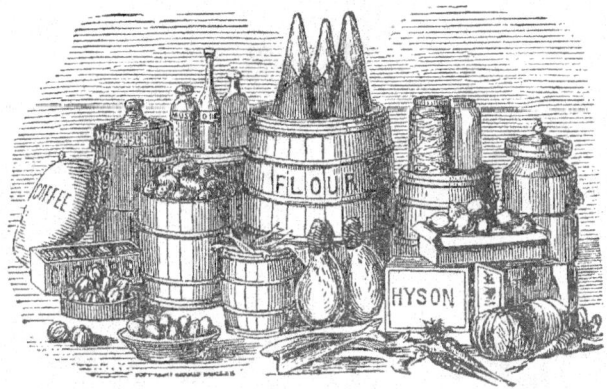

Domestic Dry Goods, Groceries,
Provisions, Flour, Feed, Paints, Oils, Clover and Timothy Seed,
HARDWARE, &c.,
East Front Street, corner of Pearl, Kingston, N. Y.

ALEXANDER J. FORBES,
Manufacturer of the Choicest Brands of

SEGARS

Union Avenue, bet. St. James and Elmendorf Sts., **Kingston, N. Y.**

SAMUEL ROOSA,
Carriage, Sign & Ornamental
PAINTER,
Residence—O'Neil Street, near Ten Broeck Avenue,
KINGSTON, N. Y.

Roman, Block, Gothic, Condensed Letters, German Text, &c. Particular Attention given to Plain Gold Leaf and Fancy Ornamental Lettering. All branches of Painting done in a good and workmanlike manner, with neatness and dispatch.

ADVERTISEMENTS.
J. P. CURTIS,

Carriage & Sleigh Manufacturer

Union Avenue, Kingston, N. Y.

☞ Road Wagons a specialty.   REPAIRING done promptly.

R. W. HUTCHINSON,
(Successor to S. VAN NAMEE,)

DENTIST

No. 12 Wall Street, Kingston, N. Y.

ISAAC I. ROOSA,

Livery & Boarding Stables,

Corner of Main and East Front Sts.,
OPPOSITE the CITY HOTEL,
KINGSTON, N. Y.

☞ First-Class Turnouts, with competent drivers, always on hand.

ADVERTISEMENTS. 5

JAMES STOKES, Jr.,
Dealer in

Crockery, Groceries,
PROVISIONS,
Flour, Feed,
HAY, OATS, &c.

Goods delivered free to any part of the city.

Cor. Union Ave. & St. James St.,
KINGSTON, N. Y.

JAS. HERDMAN, Jr.
PRACTICAL
Horse Shoer!

Particular attention paid to Shoeing Horses with bad or crippled feet. Also, Manufacturer of Sledge Hammers, Patent Stone Axes, &c. Orders promptly attended to, and executed with neatness & dispatch

Washington Av., corner North Front St., **Kingston.**

THE KINGSTON PRESS

Published every Thursday Morning, by
DANIEL BRADBURY, Editor and Proprietor,
Office—No. 30 Wall Street, KINGSTON, N. Y.

TERMS OF SUBSCRIPTION.—By Mail, or taken from the office, $2 a year, or $1,75 cents in advance; 25 cents additional will be charged when delivered by carrier. No paper discontinued until all arrearages are paid, unless at the publisher's option. Subscribers residing out of the county will be required to pay strictly in advance.

JOB WORK,
Executed with neatness and dispatch, and upon reasonable terms.

SHALER, REYNOLDS & DuBOIS,
Wholesale and Retail Dealers in American and Foreign

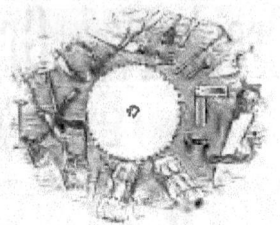

Hardware, Iron, Steel,

Shovels, Picks, House, Carriage and Harness Trimmings, Agricultural Implements, Leather Belting, &c.

Agents for Fairbanks Scales and DuPont's Sporting and Blasting Powder.

Cor. Wall & North Front Sts., Kingston, N. Y.
AND
ELLENVILLE, N. Y.

C. M. O'NEIL & CO.,
Wholesale and Retail Dealers in

Dry Goods, Crockery, Groceries,

Provisions, Flour, Grain, Feed and Farming Implements. Also, *Clover and Timothy Seed, Pine & Hemlock Lumber, Lath, Lime, Fertilizing Compost, &c.*

16 and 18 North Front Street, Kingston, N. Y.

C. M. O'NEIL.   S. W. HESTER.

C. D. ROOSA,
House, Sign & Decorative Painter,
PAPER HANGING, GLAZING, &c,
Dealer in
Paints, Oils, Varnishes, &c.
Fair St., near St. James, Kingston, N. Y.

ADVERTISEMENTS.

ULSTER COUNTY
DYE WORKS,

CONDUCTED BY

A. H. BAYLOR,

LATE OF STATEN ISLAND.

Offices for the Reception and Delivery of Goods :

JOHN H. DEYO, Garden St., Rondout, N. Y.,
DECKER & RADCLIFFE, 15 Wall St., Kingston, N. Y.,

AND AT THE

Dye House, on the Wilbur Road,

DYE AND FINISH

In the best manner, Ladies' and Gentlemen's Garments, Silks, Satins, Velvets, Ribbons, Crapes, Fringes, Gimps, Trimmings, Hosiery, Delaines, Feathers, &c. Also,

Cleanse and Re-Finish

Crape, Broche, Camel's Hair, Silk and Woolen Shawls,

LACE & MUSLIN CURTAINS,

Table Covers, Carpets, Rugs, &c.

MADE-UP GARMENTS, such as Coats, Pants, Vests, &c., can be Cleaned or Dyed in the best manner, without being ripped. All Dress Goods must be ripped.

☞ Parties residing at a distance from the City, can forward their Goods by Express, and have them returned in the same way.

ADVERTISEMENTS.

JEREMIAH FINCH,

Office—49 Wall Street, near Pearl St.,

KINGSTON, N. Y.

Choice Wines, Ales, Liquors & Cigars,
Bottled Liquors for Family and Medicinal use.

OYSTERS served in every style.

A. O. DUMMER,

Artist and Painter

IN

Oils, Water Colors and India Ink.

CRAYON PORTRAITS

MADE IN THE BEST STYLE.

OLD PHOTOGRAPHS copied and re-touched.
PICTURES from minature to full life-size.

Studio—No. 9 Wall Street,
KINGSTON, N. Y.

ADVERTISEMENTS.

Schoonmaker & Van Wagenen,

Manufacturer of all kinds of

FURNITURE,

TO ORDER,

As Cheap as any Furniture Store in the country.

Repairing and Upholstering,

Made a specialty. Neatly and substantially done. Also, Pictures Framed in every style. All work warranted to give satisfaction.

Pearl Street Avenue, near Green St., Kingston, N. Y.

R. B. & J. W. HUME,

Dealers in

Groceries & Provisions

Foreign and Domestic Fruit, Wood and Willow Ware, &c.,

No. 52 North Front Street, KINGSTON, N. Y.

Cash Paid for Country Produce.

A. BOSTWICK,

Livery & Boarding Stables,

Corner St. James and Pine Streets,

KINGSTON, N. Y.

Passengers taken to and from the Depot and Boats at reduced rates.

MERRIHEW, HOMMEL & DUNWOODY,

Wholesale and Retail Dealers in

DRY GOODS, GROCERIES

Provisions, Flour, Feed, Hay, and
Pine and Hemlock Lumber, Lath and Lime,

No. 19 and 21 Washington Avenue,

KINGSTON, N. Y.

JOHNSTON'S CITY MARKET.

T. L. JOHNSTON
DEALER IN
Beef, Pork, Veal
Mutton, Hams, &c.,
John St., Kingston.

THE KINGSTON ARGUS

STEAM POWER

JOB PRINTING HOUSE

29 Wall Street, (Wynkoop's Building,)
KINGSTON, N. Y.

First Class Cylinder Presses. Splendid Job Presses. Latest Styles of Type.

Plain and Ornamental Job Printing,

Of every description, executed with neatness, rapidity and accuracy.

The **ARGUS** has the Largest Circulation of any paper printed in Ulster County, and is the Best Advertising Medium.

H. G. CROUCH, Proprietor.

WATCHES AND JEWELRY

Made to Order and Repaired.

JOHN T. BOND,

Practical Watchmaker and Jeweler,

MAIN STREET,

Between Fair & East Front,

KINGSTON, N. Y.

JNO. T. BOND, Jr.,

PRACTICAL WATCH MAKER,

DIVISION STREET, RONDOUT, N. Y.

☞ Opposite O'Reilly's Blacksmith Shop. ☜

HILLSIDE

Greenkill Avenue, Kingston, N. Y.

School Year begins First Monday of September.

W. H. KINGSBURY, Principal.

ADVERTISEMENTS.

C. V. L. PITTS,

Wholesale and Retail Dealer in

CROCKERY,

Glass Ware,

Lamps,
    Fixtures, &c.

14 Wall Street,

KINGSTON, N. Y.

Hotels and Boarding Houses supplied on reasonable terms.

☞ *PICTURE FRAMES made to order.*

E. M. BRIGHAM,

HUDSON RIVER CEMENT WORKS

MANUFACTURER OF

Rosendale Cement.

MINER AND DEALER IN

LIME STONE BY THE CARGO.

General Office—**KINGSTON, N. Y.**

Branch Office—95 Liberty Street, New York City.

ADVERTISEMENTS. 13

M. NEWWITTER,
DEALER IN
Fancy Dry Goods

LADIES' & GENTLEMEN'S UNDER WEAR,
HAIR GOODS—real and imitation,
PERFUMERY,
Jewelry, Ribbons, &c.,
Division Street, nearly opp. Mansion House,
Next Door to A. Dunn, Jr., Jewelry Store,
RONDOUT, N. Y.

D. L. DECKER,
PRACTICAL
Horse Shoer,
Columbus Av., near Cedar,

CITY OF KINGSTON,
(Rondout,) N. Y.

JOBBING in all its branches promptly attended to.

J. KLEISNER,
Manufacturer of Improved
German Silver Reed Accordeons,
Wholesale and Retail Dealer in Pianos, Organs, Guitars, Violins, &c. A large stock of Sheet Music always on hand. All kinds of Instruments Tuned and Repaired at short notice. Italian Strings for sale. Pianos Tuned.

Mill Street, next door to Freeman Office, **RONDOUT, N. Y.**

ADVERTISEMENTS.
FREDERICK F. PETERS
DEALER IN

STOVES
FURNACES,
Kitchen Ranges, Pumps, Sinks, Lead Pipe,
AND ALL KINDS OF
HOUSEHOLD FURNISHING GOODS,
AND MANUFACTURER OF
Tin, Sheet Iron and Copper Ware,
ODD FELLOWS' HALL BUILDING,
No. 76 North Front Street, KINGSTON, N. Y.

ADVERTISEMENTS. 15

TURCK & BURHANS,
WHOLESALE AND RETAIL

Lumber Dealers

Yard on Garden St., opp. Rhinebeck Ferry,

RONDOUT, N. Y.

A general assortment of Pine, Spruce, Hemlock and Black Walnut. Pickets, Shingles and Lath constantly on hand. Also, Carpenters and Builders.

P. J. DOLSON,

House, Sign, Carriage & Ornamental

PAINTER,

Union Ave., Kingston, N. Y.

GRAINING, GILDING, GLAZING, PAPER HANGING AND KALSOMINING.

ALL ORDERS PROMPTLY ATTENDED TO.

GEO. A. GAGE,
Dealer in

Dry Goods & Groceries,

Wood and Willow Ware,

Flour, Meal and Country Produce, Tea, Coffee, Sugar, Spices, Butter, Cheese, &c.,

PRINCE ST., Wiltwyck,
CITY OF KINGSTON, N. Y.

ADVERTISEMENTS.

CASSEN & ELLSWORTH,
DEALERS IN
DRY GOODS & GROCERIES,
PROVISIONS,
BOOTS, SHOES, &C.,

Corner Union & Flatbush Avenues,

CITY OF KINGSTON, Ulster Co., N. Y.

The highest market price paid for all kinds of Country Produce. Goods delivered free to all parts of the city.

JOSEPH CASSEN. JAMES ELLSWORTH.

A. RICE,
Dealer in

Musical Instruments, Watches, Jewelry, Stationery, Confectionery, Pistols,

Guns, Toys, Pocket Cutlery, Perfumery, Cigars and Tobacco, &c.,

DIVISION STREET, RONDOUT, N. Y.
It is the Cheapest Place to buy.

REPAIRING OF ALL KINDS done at short notice.

ADVERTISEMENTS.

RONDOUT
Steam Planing & Saw Mill,

Powell Dock, Columbus Avenue,
RONDOUT, N. Y.

A large variety of IMPROVED WOOD-WORKING MACHINERY.

Planing, Matching, Beading,

Sawing, Turning, Re-Sawing and Scroll Work.

SAWING AND PLANING,

DONE AT SHORT NOTICE.

CARPENTERS, BOAT BUILDERS & REPAIRERS.

Particular attention is given to anything required in your line. We make a specialty of Sawing Knees with the Patent Band Saw.

☞ We are prepared to saw Lumber and Timber from the Log. Sawing of Building Timber a specialty.

PARTICULAR ATTENTION PAID TO

CUSTOM SAWING,

OF ALL KINDS.

☞ We are also prepared to receive LOGS IN QUANTITIES, and have ample room to store the same.

18   ADVERTISEMENTS.
A. E. VAN GAASBEEK,

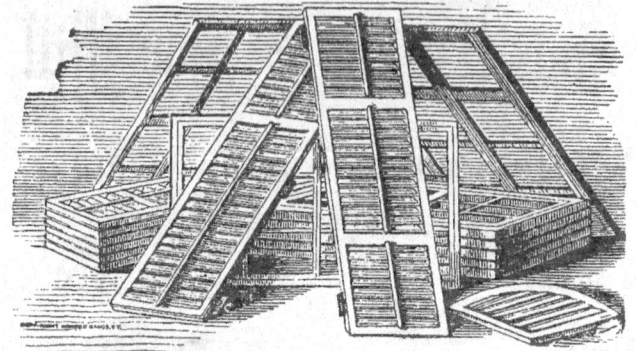

Carpenter, Builder and Contractor,
Sash, Blind and Door Manufacturer,
Union Ave., near City Hall, Rondout, N.Y.

JOSEPH RYAN,
Undertaker,

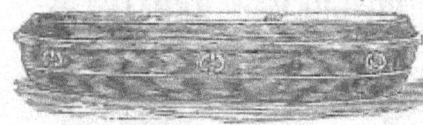

Has constantly on hand a large assortment of
Coffins and Caskets.

A First-Class Hearse furnished when desired. All orders promptly attended to, day or night.
Store opposite St. Mary's Church, Division St., Rondout, N.Y.

Kelly & Cloonan,
Meat Market,
Division St., above Union,
RONDOUT, N.Y.,
Dealers in all kinds of Meats kept in a first-class Market.

ADVERTISEMENTS. 19

C. P. RIDENOUR. J. D. SLEIGHT.

RIDENOUR & SLEIGHT,

Manufacturers of and Dealers in

FURNITURE,

UPHOLSTERY,

House Furnishing Goods

Window Shades & Fixtures, &c.

Undertaking promptly attended to. Also, Coffins, Caskets, Trimmings, Robes and Undertakers' Materials generally, always on hand at reasonable rates. Office & Principal Sales Room in

Ridenour's Building, 21 Wall St., Kingston, N. Y.
Manufactory & Sales Room at Sleight's Old Stand, opp. Kingston Tannery.

Prof. JOHN I. CHARLOUIS,

TEACHER OF

Pearl Street, opp. Rev. Dr. Hoes, Kingston, N. Y.

Instruction in the German, French, Italian, Spanish, Latin and Greek Languages. $15,00 a quarter for each language. Private Lessons, $2,00 a lesson. A quarter contains 24 lessons.

B. McBRIDE,

Wholesale and Retail Dealer in

Confectionery,

Parties Supplied at short notice.

OYSTERS, ICE CREAM, STATIONERY, &c.,

Union Avenue, near O'Neil Street,
KINGSTON, N. Y.

ADVERTISEMENTS.

ANDREW E. JANSEN,

Wholesale and Retail

Drug Warehouse

VOORHEES BUILDING,
East Front Street, cor. Albany Avenue,
KINGSTON, N. Y.

DEALER IN

DRUGS, MEDICINES,
CHEMICALS,

Perfumery, Fine Toilet Soaps, Fine Hair and Tooth Brushes, Fancy and Toilet Articles,

KEROSENE OIL,
LAMPS AND LANTERNS,
OF THE MOST APPROVED PATERNS.

Proprietor of Clay's Arnica Liniment, Irvine's Horse Liniment, Clay's Catechu Cordial, Irvine's Condition Powders, Strong's Enterprise Pills, French Chemical Blue. Also, Agents for all the Genuine and most Popular Patent Medicines of the day.

☞ Physicians' Prescriptions carefully compounded, and all orders carefully answered. Medicines warranted genuine and of the best quality.

TEETH AND DENTAL INSTRUMENTS.

ADVERTISEMENTS. 21

LIFE! FIRE! MARINE!

STOW & BENSON,

RONDOUT INSURANCE

AND

Real Estate Agents

MASONIC HALL BUILDING,
CITY OF KINGSTON, (Rondout,) N. Y.

Representing $46,692,944.

Also, NOTARIES PUBLIC.

DAN'L B. STOW. A. BENSON.

J. C. NORTON,

DENTIST

15 WALL STREET, KINGSTON, N. Y.

The Freeman

Printing & Publishing Association.

PLAIN AND ORNAMENTAL

JOB PRINTING.

Publishers of the DAILY AND WEEKLY FREEMAN,
MILL STREET, - **RONDOUT, N. Y.**

ADVERTISEMENTS.

WM. GOKEY,
Ship Builder,
AND
BOAT REPAIRER,

Columbus Avenue, Rondout, N. Y.

MATERIALS OF ALL SORTS FURNISHED FOR ALL KINDS OF VESSELS.

☞ Vessels of 200 tons burden, and under, taken out.

H. MICK & CO.,
DEALERS IN ALL KINDS OF
Salt & Fresh Meats, Butter, Eggs,
AND VEGETABLES,

Cor. Wall and St. James Sts., Kingston, N.Y.

TILLSON & BRINK,
Manufacturers of

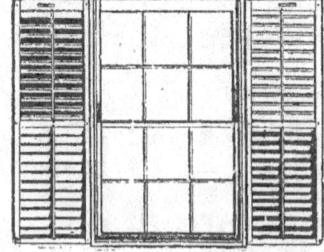

Sash, Blind, Door,

Door Frame, Window Frame and Moulding.

Also, Scroll Sawing and Turning, and as cheap as any establishment in the State.

Union Avenue, Kingston, N. Y.
(NEAR ELMENDORF STREET.)

JOHN D. TILLSON.   JAMES J. BRINK

ADVERTISEMENTS. 23

MICHAEL H. LARKINS,
Dealer in

Groceries & Provisions
DIVISION STREET,
Cor. of Meadow St., RONDOUT, N. Y.

—o—

WINES, LIQUORS,
Pork, Fish, Flour, Feed, Salt, Butter, Cheese, Eggs,

Crockery, Glass Ware,
KEROSENE OIL,
Soap, Candles, Oil Lamps, &c.

S. J. HEIMER,

LADIES
HAIR DRESSING,

Division St., between Abeel & Union,
CITY OF KINGSTON, (Rondout,) N. Y.

Braids, Curls, Switches, Frizettes, Puffs, &c., of every description. Ladies' Combings worked up in any manner desired. A good assortment of HUMAN AND IMITATION HAIR constantly on hand. Hair Jewelry made to order. Feeling confident of giving good satisfaction in every case, solicits a share of patronage.

ADVERTISEMENTS.
PAYNTAR, BURHANS & OLIVER,
Wholesale and Retail Dealers in

HARDWARE,
Iron, Steel, Nails, Cutlery, Wagon Materials,

Horse Powers, Agricultural Tools,
Circular Saws, Belting, Cordage, Powder, Fuse, &c.,

A. B. PAYNTAR,
J. BURHANS, JR.,
G. N. OLIVER.

Cor. Crown & North Front Streets,

KINGSTON, N. Y.

J. H. ELTINGE, Jr.,
(Successor to Dr. J. W. DuBois,)

Wholesale and Retail Dealer in

DRUGS, PAINTS,
OILS, GLASS,
Patent Medicines,
CHEMICALS, &C.

Proprietor of
Perrine's Peruvian Bitters, and Perrine's Sure Cure,

Corner of Washington and Hurley Avenues,
KINGSTON, N. Y.

ADVERTISEMENTS. 33

NEW CITY GALLERY!

No. 33 Division Street, opposite Mill,
RONDOUT, N. Y.

LORENZO SHORT,

Photography,

IN ALL ITS BRANCHES,

From the Bon Ton Tintype to the various sizes of Carte De Visite, the Rembrant Shadow Pictures, &c. Special attention given to out-door work. Views of Buildings, Steamboats, Landscapes, etc., etc.,—size from 8x10 to 18x22. Large assortment of **FRAMES** in stock. Frames made to order, Photographs colored in Oil, Ink, Crayon or Water Colors.

FRANK MURPHY,
PROPRIETOR OF

Mansion House Stables,
RONDOUT, N. Y.

Boarding Stables, and Horses and Carriages to let at all hours, and on reasonable terms.

K. F. KELLER,
DEALER IN FINE

Watches & Jewelry,
ABEEL STREET,
3 Doors from Division St., RONDOUT, N. Y.

REPAIRING of all kinds, neatly done.

ADVERTISEMENTS.

BUY AT HEADQUARTERS.

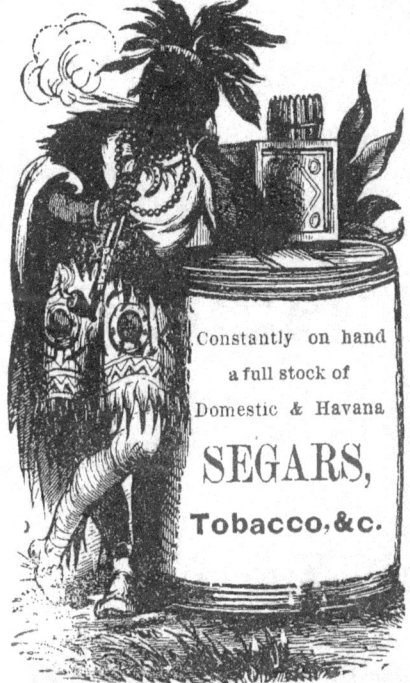

C. D. EDMONSTON'S

RONDOUT, N.Y.

TOBACCO

AND

SEGAR

Manufactory,

GARDEN STREET,

Opposite Rhinecliff Ferry,

RONDOUT, N. Y.

Constantly on hand a full stock of Domestic & Havana SEGARS, Tobacco, &c.

Trade Supplied at Lowest Cash Prices.

Centre Market,

Edward Willmott,
Proprietor,
Abeel St., opposite Hone,
RONDOUT, N. Y.,
Dealers in all kinds of Meats kept in a first-class Market.

ADVERTISEMENTS.
JAMES SWEENEY,

WHOLESALE DEALER IN

North River Blue Stone,

WILBUR,
Ulster Co., N. Y.

New York Office—229 BROADWAY, Room 17.

C. M. MERRITT & SON,
Dealers in all kinds of

GROCERIES,
And Provisions, Flour, &c.

16 Wall St., Kingston, N.Y.
C. M. MERRITT. CHAS. MERRITT.

The Highest Market Price Paid for Country Produce.

S. M. HYATT,
MANUFACTURER OF

Ground Lime,
SOUTH RONDOUT, N. Y.

ADVERTISEMENTS. 27

B. P. DECKER & BRO.,

No. 39 and 41 Division Street, Rondout, N. Y.

Dealers in Parlor, Bed-Room and Office

FURNITURE,

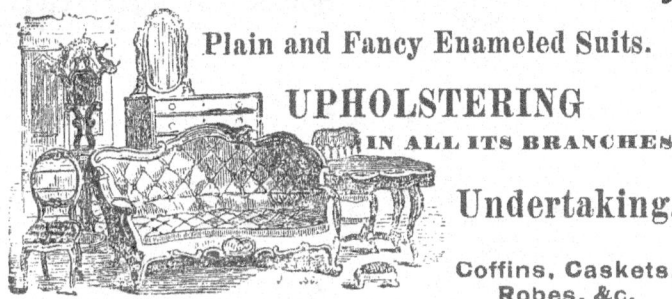

Plain and Fancy Enameled Suits.

UPHOLSTERING
IN ALL ITS BRANCHES,

Undertaking.

Coffins, Caskets, Robes, &c.

Carriages and Hearse for Funerals.

J. DIAMOND,
Wholesale and Retail Dealer

Teas, Coffees, Spices and Fine Groceries.

LIQUOR AT DISTILLERY PRICES.

Imported Wines, Brandies and Bitters at Importers' Prices.

No. 27 GARDEN STREET, RONDOUT, N. Y.

M. RICE,

Baker & Confectioner

DIVISION STREET,

Above Union Street, **RONDOUT, N. Y.**

—o—

Bread, Pies and Cakes

Made to order for Parties and Weddings, at short notice.

ADVERTISEMENTS.

MICHAEL HALLAHAN,

Wholesale Dealer in all kinds of

North River Blue Stone,

WILBUR,

Ulster County, N. Y.

Mechanics' & Traders' Exchange, Box No. 5,
No. 24 MURRAY ST., NEW YORK CITY.

J. H. ALLEN,

GROCER,

AND DEALER IN
Notions, Medicines, Crockery, &c.

PIERPONT ST., near Hone, RONDOUT, N. Y.

Particular attention paid to supplying Families with everything in our line.

A. PEREZ,

HAIR DRESSER & WIG MAKER,

Mansion House Building,
(RONDOUT,) CITY OF KINGSTON, N. Y.

☞ Constantly on hand and made to order, WIGS, SWITCHES, CURLS, FRONTS, etc. Combings made up from 50 to 75 cts. per oz.
HAIR CUTTING A SPECIALTY.

ADVERTISEMENTS. 29

JOHN DERRENBACHER,

Abeel and Dock Streets,

RONDOUT, N. Y.

Wholesale Dealer in

FLOUR,

FEED,

Grain and Oats.

---o---

F. STEPHAN & CO'S,

LAGER BEER BREWERY,

SOUTH RONDOUT, N. Y.

OFFICE AND DEPOT AT

JOHN DERRENBACHER'S

Flour and Feed Store,

RONDOUT, N. Y.

ADVERTISEMENTS.

NATHANIEL BOOTH,

WHOLESALE DEALER IN

NORTH RIVER BLUE STONE,

WILBUR P. O.,

Kingston, Ulster Co., N. Y.

---

36 Pine Street, Room 1, New York.

LAWRENCE KIRCHNER,

DEALER IN

Groceries, Provisions, Flour, Feed,

Oats, Hams, Lard, Ropes and Crockery, and in fact everything kept in a first-class Grocery, BOOTS, SHOES, &c.,

Abeel Street, cor. Ravine St., Rondout, N. Y.

N. B.—Particular attention paid to supplying Boats.

WILLIAM ROBSON,
SHIP-WRIGHT & CAULKER

**Ship Yard opp. D. & H. C. Co.'s Coal Dock,
SOUTH RONDOUT, N. Y.**

Constantly on hand the best of Timber, Pitch, Tar, Oakum, Cotton, Spikes, Iron, &c.

GOETCHEUS & LARSEN

House, Sign and Boat

PAINTERS,

GRAINING,

Kalsomining, Paper Hanging, &c.,

GARDEN STREET,

Next Door East to A. A. Crosby & Co's Hardware Store,

RONDOUT, N. Y.

ALL ORDERS PROMPTLY ATTENDED TO.

B. F. GOETCHEUS.   C. LARSEN.

WILLIAM WOOD,

AGENT FOR THE DANFORTH

Non-Explosive Petroleum Fluid,

The best artificial light that has yet been produced.

ALSO, THE LATEST STYLES OF

Lamps, Burners, Chimneys, &c.

Portable Gas Lamps.

Store on the Dock, Sleightburgh Ferry House, Rondout, N. Y.

F. W. GROSS,

MANUFACTURER OF

Ground Lime,

Cor. Hasbrouck Avenue & Ravine Sts.,

RONDOUT, N. Y.

ADVERTISEMENTS.

SEAMAN & MILLER,

Wholesale and Commission Merchants in

CANNED FRUITS,

Foreign and Domestic Nuts,

COUNTRY PRODUCE,

OYSTERS in their Season,

KEROSENE, BUCKWHEAT FLOUR, MAPLE SYRUP, &c.

FERRY STREET, RONDOUT, N. Y.

L. S. SEAMAN.   H. S. MILLER.

JOHN H. SCHREIBER,

Rectifier and Wholesale Dealer in

Brandies, Wines, Whiskies,

CROCKERY, GLASS,

Wood and Willow Ware, Groceries, &c.,

At the Old Store of T. Murray & Co.,

Garden and Ferry Streets, RONDOUT, N. Y.

MORRIS SAMTER,

Manufacturer of, and Wholesale and Retail Dealer in

IMPORTED AND DOMESTIC

Segars, Chewing and Smoking Tobacco, Smoker's Articles,

&c.

21 Garden St., RONDOUT, N. Y.

ADVERTISEMENTS.

J. & J. McCAUSLAND,

SHIP BUILDERS,

RONDOUT, N. Y.

Steam Floating Docks,

Capable of Lifting Vessels of 400 Tons Measurement.

Steam Saw Mill, Ship-Smith Shop,

And all the facilities for

BUILDING AND REPAIRING VESSELS.

Located on the West Side of the Rondout Creek, a short distance above the Coal Company's Dock.

S. & W. B. FITCH,

Wholesale Dealers in all kinds of

North River Blue Stone.

ALSO, IN THE

LIGHT BLUE BASALT ROCK

For Statuary, Pillars, Water Tables, Sills, &c.

KINGSTON,

Ulster County, N. Y.

ADVERTISEMENTS. 35

J. & J. P. DERRENBACHER,

DEALERS IN, WHOLESALE AND RETAIL,

GROCERIES, FLOUR, FEED,

Oats, Corn, Pork, Fish, Teas,

Coffees, Sugars, Vegetables, Fruits,

CANNED GOODS,

BOOTS, SHOES,

Crockery, Wood and Willow Ware, &c.

Dock, Ravine and Abeel Sts., RONDOUT, N. Y.

HENRY FORST,
Dealer in all kinds of
French & Canadian

HORSES.

Fancy and Work Horses constantly on hand.

Abeel St., opp. Hone St.
RONDOUT, N. Y,

AMBROSE BARTH,
DEALER IN
Cigars, Tobacco & Smokers Materials
ALSO,
ALL KINDS OF CONFECTIONERY,
Corner of Abeel and Hone Streets,
RONDOUT, N. Y.

ADVERTISEMENTS.

D. E. DONOVAN,

WHOLESALE DEALER IN

NORTH RIVER BLUE STONE,

Ulster County, N. Y.

New York Office—19 Park Place, Room 4.

ISIDORE FORST,
DEALER IN

Dry & Fancy Goods

Ladies' and Gents' Furnishing Goods, Hosiery and Notions,

Abeel Street, opposite Hone, Rondout, N. Y.

J. H. CULLEN,
DEALER IN

Groceries & Provisions,

Corner of Ann and Meadow Streets,
RONDOUT, N. Y.

Teas, Coffees, Spices, **WINES, LIQUORS,**
XX AND XXX ALE, Pork, Fish, Flour, Feed, Salt, Butter, Cheese, Eggs Crockery, Wood and Willow Ware, &c.

ADVERTISEMENTS.

JOHN P. READING,
MANUFACTURER OF

LEMON BISCUIT,
GINGER SNAPS,
AND CRACKERS,

Hasbrouck Avenue, near Mill Street,

CITY OF KINGSTON, (Rondout,) N. Y.

T. P. OSTRANDER,

DENTIST

Dental Rooms—Garden St., opposite Post Office,
RONDOUT, N. Y.

L. D. HOORNBEEK & CO.,
WHOLESALE
Grocers & Commission Merchants,

FERRY STREET, RONDOUT, N. Y.

L. D. HOORNBEEK.   GEO. C. PRESTON.

ADVERTISEMENTS.

HAMILTON HOUSE,

THOMAS HAMILTON, Proprietor.

Division Street, opposite Abeel St.,
KINGSTON, (Rondout,) N. Y.

EXTENSIVE LIVERY,
CONNECTED WITH THE HOUSE.

STEAM
KINDLING WOOD MANUFACTORY

THOMAS HAMILTON, Proprietor,

Has always on hand and for sale

Hard and Soft Kindling Wood by the Barrel or Load.

I have also connected with this business WOOD for sale, by the Cart or Boat Load.

YARDS—Ann Street, near Mill Street,
OFFICE—AT THOS. HAMILTON'S HOTEL,
Division Street, opposite Abeel Street,
KINGSTON, (Rondout,) N. Y.

ADVERTISEMENTS.   39

B. LOUGHRAN,

Practical Plumber, Steam and Gas Fitter,

Dealer in Plumbers Materials of all descriptions, Chandeliers and Gas Fixtures.

☞ Agent for the STAR GAS MACHINE. Country Houses fitted up with all the conveniences of city dwellings with both Gas & Water All goods and work warranted.

106 North Front Street,
KINGSTON, N. Y.

DUTCHER & HOLMES,

Manufacturers of and Wholesale and Retail Dealers in

ALL KINDS OF

FURNITURE!

Canal Street, near Main Street, ELLENVILLE, N. Y.

☞ UNDERTAKING in all its branches, a specialty.

CARLEY'S
Hair Restorative,

A Valuable Restorative. An Excellent Dressing.

☞ This Restorative is free from all injurious substances, does not color the Hair, but acts so as to restore the vigor of the scalp, rendering the Hair healthy and soft, and creating in all cases a new growth. It cures every case where the Hair is falling out. It removes Dandruff, renders the skin clean, and leaves no sticky substances on the Hair.

PRICE, $1,00 PER BOTTLE.

PUT UP BY

A. A. CARLEY,
Fashionable Hair-Dresser,
ELLENVILLE, Ulster Co., N. Y.

ADVERTISEMENTS.

J. MILLS & BRO.,

P. O. Box 3, Wilbur, Ulster Co., N.Y.

STONE SAWING,
PLANING, POLISHING

AND

STONE CUTTING

IN ALL ITS BRANCHES.

Contracts for furnishing Dress Stone for any kind of Buildings promptly attended to. Orders by Mail attended to as promptly and as thoroughly as when ordered in person.

GEO. THOMPSON & SONS,

PACKERS AND DEALERS IN

Hams, Shoulders, Pork,

FISH AND BEEF,

MORE'S CORNER, Hunter St., RONDOUT, N. Y.

GEO. THOMPSON.   A. S. THOMPSON.   J. S. THOMPSON.

M. E. SHORT,

Confectioner & Baker

WHOLESALE AND RETAIL,

**Corner Pierpont and Russell Streets,
below New School House,
RONDOUT, N. Y.**

Confectionery a specialty. Parties supplied at short notice.

ADVERTISEMENTS.

Terwilliger House

CONSTABLE & DeGARMO, Proprietors,
Corner of Canal and Market Streets,
ELLENVILLE, N. Y.

☞ Horses and Carriages to Let. Omnibus to and from all trains.

C. G. LISCOMB,
DRUGGIST,

Main St., in Schoenfeld's Building, Saugerties, N. Y.

Dealer in Drugs, Medicines, Chemicals, Perfumery, Toilet Soaps, Segars, Tobacco, &c. Physicians Prescriptions carefully compounded.

RUSSELL & MYERS,
WHOLESALE DEALERS IN
North River Blue Stone,

Flagging, Curb, Gutter, Bridge, Sills, &c.,
ALWAYS ON HAND,

JEREMIAH P. RUSSELL, }
WILLIAM E. MYERS. } **SAUGERTIES, N. Y.**

SAUGERTIES
VARIETY IRON WORKS,

Post Street, Saugerties, N. Y.

WM. S. VAN HOESEN & CO., Proprietors.
----o----

Manufacturers of Wagon Thimble Skains, Pumps, Stone Crushers, Mill Gearing, &c. Work of all kinds done to order in the best manner, and with dispatch.

ADVERTISEMENTS.

BERNARD GEISLER,
UNION MEAT MARKET

Foot of Canal Street, near the Glass Works,
ELLENVILLE, N. Y.

☞ Dealer in ALL KINDS OF MEAT kept in a First-Class Market.

HALE'S

Livery and Exchange Stables,

HORSES AND CARRIAGES TO LET.

ELLENVILLE,
Ulster Co., N. Y.

Horses kept on Livery by the Day, Week or Month.

MARTIN FREILEWEH,
Manufacturer of the Celebrated

Srpuce Beer,
AND SALOON KEEPER,

Canal Street, near Market, Ellenville, N. Y.

KINGSTON DIRECTORY.

ABREVIATIONS.—Ab., above; al., alley; av., avenue; bel., below; b. or bds., boards; b. or bet., between; c. or cor., corner; ct., court; ft., foot; h., house; R. R., Railroad; la., lane; opp., opposite; n., near; r., rear; rd., road; sq., square; tp., turnpike; N., North; E., East; W., West; S., South.

AARON D., tailor, h Garden and Ferry.
Aaron L., clothing, Lackawanna, h do.
AARON SAMUEL, groceries and liquors, South Rondout.
Abbey A. A., carpenter, h Staple n Union av.
Abbey A. A., bar tender, h Staple.
Abbey D. B., book keeper, h Point rd.
Abbey D. J., grocer, Flatbush av n Prince, h do.
Abbey H. L., (S. Abbey & Son,) h Pearl av cor Washington av.
Abbey S. & Son, flour, feed, &c., Ferry.
Abbey S., (S. Abbey & Son,) h Abruyn cor Grove.
Abbey S. L., clerk, bds Abruyn cor Grove.
Abrams Simon, peddler, h Third av n Elm.
Achart Josiah, pilot, Chester cor Hasbrouck av.
Ackerly A. Rev., h Henry cor Oak.
Ackerman Ira, hostler, h Wall cor St. James.
Ackert J. C., bar tender, Eagle Hotel.
ACKERT J. S., groceries, crockery, &c., St. James cor E Front, h Maiden Lane n E Front.
Ackley R., mail agt., bds Hamilton House.
Acley C. F., h Abeel opp Wurts.
Adams Chas., capt., h Hasbrouck av n Newkirk av.
Adams G., brewer, bds Sutton House.
Adams G. R., lawyer, Garden over Market.
Adams F. M., h Fair n St. James.

HIRAM ROOSA'S Accidental, Life, Fire, Marine

Adams K. W. Mrs., h Fair n St. James.
AGAR C., books, stationery, wall paper, book binding, Savings Bank Building opp Court House, h Elmendorf n R. R.
Ahlhaem Philip, mate, h Hasbrouck av n R. R.
Albrecht S., laborer, h Bond n Chester.
Alcock Wm., watchmaker, 26 Wall.
Alderman John, laborer, h Third av n Elm.
Aldrich S., bootmaker, Abeel, h Union n Wurts.
Aldridge Wm., tanner, h Union av n Cedar.
Allen Abram, h Holmes n Hone.
Allen A. J., carpenter, h Abruyn n Grove.
Allen Bros., ship builders, Columbus av ft Abruyn.
Allen Daniel, ship builder, h Chestnut n Abruyn.
Allen Geo. E., confectioner, &c., Pierpont n Hone.
ALLEN J. H., grocer, Pierpont n Hone, h do.
Allen John Jr., boatman, h Rogers n Division.
Allen J. S., h Point rd.
Allen M. S., clerk, bds Pierpont n Hone.
Alliger C. D., plows, &c., h Union n Wurts.
Alliger Edwin, clerk, bds Abeel n Post.
Alliger Hasbrouck, h Union n Wurts.
Alliger J., mason, h Cedar n Prospect.
Alliger John B., teller, h Abeel ab Post.
Allington Thomas, h German.
Altenburg Chas., laborer, h Dock.
Ament F., teacher, h Spring opp Russell.
AMERICAN HOTEL, (P. L. Osterhoudt, pro.,) Union av cor St. James.
American Express Co., D. C. Reid, agt., 34 Garden and 83 N Front.
Amy Ferris, clerk, h Henry cor Prospect.
Angove Josiah, miner, h Third av cor Elm.
Anderson George F., clerk, h Wurts n Pierpont.

J. O. & G. B. MERRITT, Laces and

Insurance and Real Estate Agency, Rondout, N. Y.

Anderson John, h Ann ab Meadow.
Anderson Nathan, h Abeel ab Division.
Anderson Rachel Mrs., h Wurts n Pierpont.
Apgar B., carpenter, h Prospect cor Van Buren.
Appleton Louis, mer. tailor, &c., 15 Garden, h do.
Archambauld Francis, blacksmith, h Meadow n R. R.
Arhoudt August, h Spring ab Ravine.
Arnold E. H. Mrs., h Union av opp Staple.
Arnold Frederick, boatman, h Germain n Ravine.
Arnold J. J., barber, Savings Bank Building.
Arnold Wm., caulker, h Hone cor Abeel.
Ashley Edward, shoemaker, h Abeel.
Ashtown Albert, sawyer, h Hasbrouck av n Bridge.
Atchison John, h Ravine ab Pine.
Atkins & DeGraff, millinery, &c., Fair cor John.
Atkinson James, laborer, h Garden n Ferry.
Atkinson John, clerk, h Hasbrouck av cor Union.
Atkinson Sisters, milliners, 5 Mansion House Block.
Atkinson Thos., blacksmith, Hurley av cor Taylor, h
 opp do.
Atler Alex., h Union n Wurts.
AUCHMOODY D. J.. photographer, Garden and Fer-
 ry, h Port Ewen.
Auchmoody W. W., teamster, h Wall cor St. James.
Austin John, laborer, h Flatbush av n Prince.
Avery G. W., agt., h Union av cor Flatbush av.
Avery Joseph, shoemaker, h Cedar n Union av.
Ayemiller M., h Newkirk av n Chambers.
Ayres S. F., upholsterer, h Elmendorf cor R. R.

BACHARCH L., junk, Garden and Ferry, h do.
Bachman Adolph, segar maker, bds John cor Fair.
Badgley David, laborer, h Ravine n R. R.
BAHRET JACOB, carpet weaver, Division ab Union,
 h Division n Union.

Embroideries, No. 5 Wall St., Kingston.

HIRAM ROOSA'S Agency represents a Combined

Bailey Geo., waiter, Excelsior House.
Bailey John, laborer, h Hudson.
Bailey Nancy Mrs., h O'Neil n Union av.
Bailey Richard, engineer, h Coardts n Point rd.
Baird R. G., dress maker, h Garden cor Hasbrouck av.
Baker F., laborer, h Ravine cor Vine.
Baldwin E. M., book keeper, h Cedar n Prospect.
Baldwin Henry, printer, h Elmendorf n Tremper.
Baldwin James W. Mrs., h Fair cor Maiden Lane.
Baldwin R. N. Mrs., h Fair n St. James.
Ball A., tinsmith, bds Pearl cor Wall.
Ballard D. M., grocer, bakery, &c., 5, 7 and 9 Washington av, h 5 do.
Ballard Geo., painter, bds E Front n Henry.
Ballard J., painter, Van Buren cor Furnace, h do.
Ballard J., veterinary surgeon, h E Front n Henry.
Balzer Eliza, h Tompkins n Union.
Banker J., upholsterer, h Washington av cor N Front.
Banks James, h Hasbrouck av bel Garden.
Barber Dudley, engineer, h Mapleton.
Barber H. E., capt., h Spring n Wurts.
Barber Jacob, boatman, h Hasbrouck av n Stuyvesant.
Barber John S., h Pierpont cor Russell.
Barber A. M., h Hone cor Pierpont.
Barnes A. N., (John R. Stebbins & Co.,) h Adams.
Barnes Geo., Rev., h Fair S of John.
Barnes James, h 7 Wall.
Barnes Nelson, watchman, h Cross n Ann.
Barnett A. Jr., teas, &c., St. James n Pine, h Wilbur.
Barnett Wm., h Hurley av.
Barnhart Hiram H., car driver, h Hurley av.
Barrett Andrew, engineer, Hone n Hunter.
Barrett J., weaver, h 43 Division.
Barrett Thos., laborer, h Abeel.

J. O. & G. B. MERRITT, Ladies'

Capital of $50,000,000. Rondout, N. Y.

KINGSTON DIRECTORY. 53

Barringer T. B., teacher, h Elmendorf n R. R.
Barry Garrett, h Division n Rogers.
Barry James, grocer, h Mapleton.
Barry John, h Division n Rogers.
Barry Patrick, h Division ab Cross.
Barry Thos., laborer, h Cross n Hasbrouck av.
BARTH AMBROSE, tobacco, confectionery, &c., Abeel cor Hone, h Hunter n Ravine.
Barth F. M., clerk, bds Hunter.
Barth V., h Spring ab Ravine.
Bartholomew A. Mrs., h Bowery n Union av.
Bartlett E. C., engineer, h Ravine n Vine.
Bartlett Geo., laborer, bds Ravine n Vine.
Bartlett Joseph, brakeman, h Jarrold n Point rd.
Bartlett J., switch tender, h Garden and Ferry.
Bartof J., h German n Ridge.
Basch C., grocer, Hasbrouck av cor St. Mary.
Basch Julius, peddler, h Newkirk av n Hasbrouck av.
Basch Stephen, laborer, h Second av n R. R.
Basten Geo., physician, h Garden,
Basten Lewis, clerk, bds Union.
Basten P. C., mill wright, h Tompkins cor Mill.
Baster Chas., clerk, h Mill.
Battle Patrick, saloon, h Livingston.
Baxter Thos., laborer, h Tompkins n Union.
BAYLOR A. H., dyer and scourer, Wilbur Plank rd., n Greenkill av.
Beadle Andrew, h Liberty n Union av.
Beadle W. D., h E Front cor Henry.
Beadle W. R., carpenter, h E Front cor Henry.
Bear Edward, clerk, h Union n Abeel.
Bear E., clothing, Lackawana, h Union n Abeel.
Beatcher C., clerk, h Hunter bel Hone.
Beatty B. Mrs., h Hurley av.

5*

Undergarments, 5 Wall St., Kingston.

HIRAM ROOSA Insures Vessels and Cargoes

Beck Henry, soda water, h Ann cor Cross.
Beck John, laborer, h Point rd n Livingston.
Beck Michael, laborer, h St. Mary n Chambers.
Beck Wm., mason, h Greenkill av.
Becker Chas., bar tender, Grand Central.
Becker L., h Hudson.
Becker Mary Mrs., saloon, h Main n Fair.
Becker Wallace, printer, Journal Office.
Beddington C., painter, h Wall cor St. James.
Bedford N., mason, h E Front cor Henry.
Beekman Sophia Mrs., h 39 N Front.
Beekman Thomas, carpenter, h Lucas av cor Washington av.
Belfe & Becker, painters, Cedar n Union av.
Bell H. T., gardener, h Greenkill av n Pine.
Beltar George, coachman, Metzger's Hotel.
Benathton Thomas, blacksmith, h Bowery n Union av.
Benjaman Geo., clerk, h Pierpont n Hone.
Benjamin Warren, clerk, bds Union av n toll gate.
Bennett Geo. W., foreman, h Hunter n Ravine.
Bennett J., tailor, h Washington av n N Front.
Benson & Hart, groceries, &c., 10 Wall.
Benson A., sec. R. S. B., h Maiden Lane cor Wall.
Benson Gilbert, carpenter, h Tompkins n Union.
Benson Levi, h Fair n St. James.
Benson Wm., (B. & Hart,) h Fair n St. James.
Berger John, wagon maker, bds Freileweh Hotel.
Bergin Martin, laborer, h Cedar n Union av.
BERNARD & FIERO, lawyers, Main n Fair.
Bernard Reuben, (B. & Fiero,) h Pearl cor Fair.
Bernstein Abram, book keeper, h 86 N Front.
Bernstein Isaac, mer. tailor and clothier, Wall cor N Front, h 86 N Front.

J. O. & G. B. MERRITT, Cloths and

of all kinds. Rondout, N. Y.

Berry Gilbert, toys, &c., 81 N Front, h Green n Maiden Lane.
Berry N. E., clerk, bds Green n Maiden Lane.
Berry W. H., civil engineer, bds Green n St. James.
Berrygan M., laborer, h DeWitt.
Bertsche Wm., brewer, h Spring n Hone.
Best & Wilson, hats, caps, &c., 74 N Front.
Best Eugene M., book keeper, City Hotel.
Best R. E., (B. & Wilson,) bds Kingston Hotel.
Betchie Mrs., h Hunter n Hone.
Betts Edward, clerk, h Hone n Holmes.
Betts G. B., pilot, h Abruyn cor Union.
Beutell A., carpenter, bds St. James n E Front.
Beutell E. M., carpenter, bds St. James n E Front.
BEUTELL H. M., stair builder, E Front n Liberty, h Linderman n Wall.
Beutz Geo., laborer, h Chambers n Ravine.
Bevier C. H. Mrs., h Green opp Maiden Lane.
Beyer E., laborer, h Hasbrouck av n R. R.
Beyer Geo., laborer, h Ravine n R. R.
Beyer Michael, laborer, h Pine n Ravine.
Bickley A. W., lawyer, Abeel cor Post.
Bird W. S., carriage trimmer, h St. James n E Front.
BISHOP CHAS. E., restaurant, Dock, h Ravine cor Pine.
Bishop Jane Mrs., h Ravine opp Pine.
Bishop S., h German n Ravine.
Bishop Wm., laborer, h Ravine n Vine.
Blackley L. Mrs., h Post n Spring.
Blackwell, Gross & Co., pros. Excelsior Iron Works, Albany av cor Union av.
Blackwell J. H. Mrs., Pine n St. James.
Blackwell P. H., teamster, h Union av n Henry.
Blackwell T. F., (B. Gross & Co.,) h Albany av cor Union av.

Cassimeres, No. 5 Wall St., Kingston.

Get an Accidental Policy at

KINGSTON DIRECTORY.

Blanchard H. H., tel. manager, Mansion House, bds Post cor Abeel.
Blanshan M., carpenter, h Oak n Bowery.
Blauvelt Augustus Rev., bds Garden cor Flatbush av.
Bleecker E. Miss, h E Front opp John.
Block Henrietta, dry goods, Division ab Union.
Blodgett C. Mrs., h Mason n Wurts.
Bloom Wm. E., h Albany av cor Union av.
Bloss Henry, butcher, bds Division cor Abeel.
Blum R., toys, Division ab Union, h do.
Bodell Robert, captain, h Bowery n Union av.
Bodenwager Ernest, butcher, bds Freileweh's Hotel.
Bodie Frank, cooper, h Union n Wurts.
Bogardus C. Mrs., h Union av opp Staple.
Bogardus Elliott, h Mapleton.
Bogardus Isaac, tanner, h Summer.
Bogart A. E. Mrs., h 17 N Front.
Bogart E. Mrs., h Union av n Greenkill av.
Bogart John, surveyor, h Union av bel St. James.
Bogart John T., clerk, h Hone.
Boice Geo., cooper, h Abeel.
Boice J. G., market, h Cross n Ann.
Boice John J., life ins., 4 Music Hall, h Maiden Lane cor E Front.
Boice Malisa, h 35 N Front.
Boice Matthew, American Express, h Liberty n Union av.
Bold K., farmer, h Pearl av n Green.
Bolles J. E., sewing machines, Garden n Hasbrouck av.
BOND J. T., watch maker and jeweler, Main n E Front, h Wall cor Linderman av.
BOND J. T. JR., jeweler, Division ab Union, h Wall n Bowery.
Bonds Thomas, miner, h Third av n Point rd.
Bonesteel Anna M. Mrs., h Hurley av.

J. O. & G. B. MERRITT, Flannels and

HIRAM ROOSA'S Agency, Rondout, N. Y.

Bonesteel C., cigar maker, bds Hurley av.
Bonesteel George, teamster, h Hurley av.
Bonesteel Hattie, Mrs., h N Front n Green.
Bonesteel R., Miss h 45 N Front.
Bonesteel Robert, bookkeeper, bds Maiden la cor Wall.
Bonesteel R. G., ice, h Union av cor Bowery.
Bonner Neily, boatman, h Lackawanna.
BONNER W., auditor of N. Y. K. & S. R. R., h Rogers cor Adams.
Booth J. A., stone, h Wilbur.
BOOTH NATHANIEL, North River blue stone, Wilbur.
Booth Thomas, h Wilbur.
Borley Francis, h Hasbrouck av n Meadow.
BOSTWICK A., livery, St. James cor Pine, h do.
Bostwick James, dept. county clerk, h St. James cor Pine.
Boss John G., fish, &c., Sleightburg Ferry, h Cross n Ann.
Boss Joseph, h German n Ravine.
Boules Thomas, boatman, h Garden cor Hasbrouck av.
Bow James, laborer, h Hasbrouck av n R. R.
Bowen A. J., painter, h Smith av n Garden.
Bower Fred., barber, Abeel opp Hone, h opp do.
Bower Paul, h German n Ravine.
Bowers Albert, gardener, h Post n Union.
Bowls J., tanner, h Washington av n N Front.
Bowman Eugene, carpenter, h Prince cor Grand.
Bowman E. M., carpenter, h Hasbrouck av n Union av.
Bowman Joseph, carpenter, h Union av n toll gate.
Bowman J. Merton, printer, Argus Office.
Boyce Alanson, clerk, h Columbus av n Cedar.
Boyce James M., butcher, Columbus av n Cedar, h do.
Boyce J. J., ins. agt., h Maiden Lane n E Front.
Boyd James, saloon, h Meadow n Hasbrouck av.

Blankets, No. 5 Wall St., Kingston.

Boyd John, (R. Jones & Co.,) h Hunter.
Boyle Aaron, h Division cor Meadow.
Boyle Patrick, laborer, h Point rd n First av.
Boyle Wm., (pro. Central House,) Hasbrouck av n Point rd.
Bradbury Daniel, editor, &c., Kingston Press and Post Master, h Hurley av.
Bradshaw George H., blacksmith, Union av n Liberty, h do.
Brady Andrew, peddler, h DuBois av Maple av.
Brady Charles, laborer, h Catherine cor Tompkins.
Brady Miles, laborer, h DeWitt.
Brady Richard, laborer, h Hasbrouck av n R. R.
Brady Thomas, boatman, h DeWitt.
Brady Thomas, h Division cor Pierpont.
Brady W. C., machinist, h Hasbrouck av n R. R.
Bragaw John A., club house, Main n E Front.

BRANDOW E. D.,
lawyer, 17 Garden, h Sleightburg.

Brannan Mary, grocer, Division ab Union.
Bratton M., laborer, h Washington av n Lucas av.
Branchle V., saloon, Division cor Newkirk av.
Braudes Henry, laborer, h Third av n Point rd.
Braun Jacob, shoemaker, h Ann ab Meadow.
Bray Charles, cashier F. N. B., h Union av n Point rd.
Bray John S., foreman, h Crown n N Front.
BREED H. P., supt. N. Y. K. & S. R. R., h Adams Woolsey's Row.
Breitenbucher A. Jr., butcher, h Washington av.
Breitenbucher Edward, confectioner, Abeel opp Hone, h do.
BREITENBUCHER JACOB, butcher, Abeel cor Hone, h Spring.

J. O. & G. B. MERRITT, Notions and

operative Plan at H. ROOSA'S Agency, Rondout.

Brennan Edward, h Division ab Meadow.
Brennan James, laborer, h Abeel.
Brennan James, carpenter, h Hunter n Ridge.
Brennan P. J., clerk, h Staples n Union av.
Brenshell John, h Ravine cor German.
Brewer Bela, tailor, h Spring cor Ravine.
Bridenbecker Louis, butcher, h Union av cor Chester.
Briggs A. R., lime, Wilbur bds Elmendorf.
Briggs George B., (J. Weber & Co.,) h Division ab Abeel.
Briggs Wm., farmer, h E Front n Greenkill av.
Briggs Wm. F., clerk, N Front cor Crown.

BRIGHAM E. M.,

cement manufacturer, h Union av n St. James.
Brill C. F., h Fair cor Bowery.
Brim John, h Spring ab Ravine.
Brink Adam, tanner, h Hurley av.
BRINK EDWARD, architect and carpenter, E Front n St. James, h do.
Brink George M., cigar maker, h Prospect n Liberty.
Brink James, h Wilbur.
Brink J. J., (Tillson & B.,) bds Elmendorf n Union av.
Brink J. A., carpenter, h E Front n Bowery.
Brink J. A., laborer, h Wall n Bowery.
Brink O., h Division n Cross.
Brinkman F., grocer, Hasbrouck av n R. R., h do.
BRINNIER J. M., saloon, Union av n Cedar, h do.
Brislien John, blacksmith, h Prospect n Union.
Britt Andrew, teamster, h Ten Broeck av cor Downs.
Britt Edgar, laborer, h E Front cor Bowery.
Britt P. W., farmer, h Smith av cor Elmendorf.
Broas R. H., billiards, &c., Wall opp Court House, h do.

Trimmings, No. 5 Wall St., Kingston.

Brocker Nicholas, h Pierpont cor Russell.
Brocker Peter, saloon, Pierpont cor Russell.
Broder B. Mrs., h Post n Union.
Brodery Mrs., h Meadow cor Ann.
Brodhead & Pine, grocers, &c., Wall cor Main.
Brodhead B. L., cashier, h John cor Wall.
Brodhead Charles, h St. James cor E Front.
Brodhead D. E. (B. & Pine,) h Main n Wall.
Brodhead E., miller, h E Front n Henry.
Brodhead J. D., teamster, h Prospect.
Brodhead J. F., coopers' tools, Mason n Wurts, h do.
Brodhead James, teamster, h Prospect n Liberty.
Brodhead J. C., h Fair n St. James.
Brodhead N. E., cashier, h Pine cor Henry.
Brodhead Thomas, boatman, h Post n Union.
Brodhead Thomas, Mrs., h Fair n St. James.
Brofee James, laborer, h Meadow n Ann.
Bronder John, clerk, h Hone.
Bronder Peter, grocer, Ulster Market, h Hone ab Pierpont.
Brooks Matthew, h German n Ravine.
Brophy Michael, h Van Deusen av.
Brower J. F. & Co., grocers, &c., Washington av n Depot.
Brower J. F., (J. F. Brower & Co.,) h Lucas av.
Brower O., measurer, h Plank rd.
Brower O. Z., measurer, h Wilbur.
Brown Bostey, blacksmith, h Hunter.
Brown C., laborer, h Wilbur.
Brown Frederick, laborer, h Ravine n R. R.
Brown Francis, capt., h Point rd n Flatbush rd.
Brown Geo., supt., h Albany av n Ten Broeck av.
Brown John, h Hunter.
Brown John Jr., h Hunter n Hone.

J. O. & G. B. MERRITT, Dry Goods and

Real Estate Agency, Rondout, N. Y.

Brown John, boatman, h Ann n Meadow.
Brown J. P., physician, Union av n Albany av, h do
Brown John, h German n Ravine.
Rrown John A., blacksmith, Dock, h Hunter.
Brown John, blacksmith, h Hunter.
Brown L. W., tel. operator, bds R. R. House.
Brown Narcissa, h R. R. n Chester.
Brown S., bds Kingston Hotel.
Brown Wm., laborer, h Meadow n Ann.
Bruce Sarah E., h Abeel cor Wurts.
Bruck John, saloon, German cor Ravine.
Bruker B., German n Ridge.
Bruyn Augustus H., h Pearl cor Fair.
Bruyn Charles D., pres., h Fair next P. O.
Bruyn C. Mrs., h Albany opp Tremper.
Buchanan John, boatman, h Pine n Ravine.
Buchanan James S., ship carpenter, h Hudson.
Buck John, Mrs., h Newkirk av n Chambers.
Buckbee S. V. R., tool manuf., Washington n Locust av, h St. James n Prospect.
Budington E. W., cement manuf., Albany av cor Union av, h do.
Budington H. J., bookkeeper, bds E Front n John.
Budington Walter J., h Hunter n Ravine.
Bug George, billiards, Garden and Ferry, h Chester n Union av.
Bullen Charles, h Spring ab Ravine.
Bullen Samuel, h Spring ab Ravine.
Bulmer Thad., tinman, bds Union av n Elmendorf.
Bunnatt Thomas, laborer, h Chestnut cor Ponkhockie.
Bunting Abram, laborer, h Hurley av.
Bunting J. S., carman, h Ann n Mill.
Bunton A. N., cigars, bds Hurley av.
Burger & Wells, grocers, St. James n Pine.

Carpets, No. 5 Wall St., Kingston.

Burger Abram, farmer, h N Front n Crown.
Burger A., musician, &c., E Front opp Main, h Main n E Front.
Burger Benjamin, h Union av cor O'Neil.
Burger D., h Spring ab Ravine.
BURGER ISRAEL, grocer, shoes, &c., Ferry n Division h Sleightburg.
Burger James, mason, h Wall cor St. James.
Burger Joseph, h German n Hone.
Burger Mary Mrs., h 19 N Front.
Burger Peter, h 87 Hasbrouck av.
Burger Robert R., keg maker, h Prince n Union av.
Burger S. D., mason, h Henry cor Furnace.
Burgess Thomas, h Abeel.
Burgevine Charles, florist, Lucas av, h do.
Burgevine V., florist, hd Pearl av, h n do.

BURHANS & FELTEN,
coal and lumber, E Front cor Main.

BURHANS ALBERT,
carpenter and builder, sash, blind and door manufac., Hoffman n Union av, h do.

Burhans A. N., carpenter, h Ravine n Hasbrouck av.
Burhans Arthur, carpenter, h Third n R. R.
Burhans Ann Miss, h Green cor Main.
Burhans Charles, cashier, h Pearl n E Front.
Burhans Cornelius, (B. & Felten,) h Pearl n E Front.
Burhans Daniel, engineer, h Union av n Albany av.
Burhans F., carpenter, h Ten Broeck n Elmendorf.
Burhans F., cigar maker, bds Union av n Pearl.
Burhans Gilbert, foreman, h Abruyn n Point rd.

Burhans George, carpenter, h Bond n Chester.
Burhans Henry, carpenter, h Ponkhockie n Union.
Burhans Isaac, carpenter, h Hone n Holmes.
Burhans Jacob, Jr., (Paynter, B. & Oliver,) h Albany av.

BURHANS J. S.,
general merchandise, E Front cor Pearl, h Pearl cor E Front.

Burhans Lewis, carpenter, bds Union av n Flatbush av.
Burhans M. Mrs., h Union av n Flatbush av.
Burhans N. H., (Turck & B.,) h Ponkhockie n Union.
Burhans Peter, carpenter, h Staple n Union.
Burhans R. P., (Tappen B. & Webster,) bds E Front n John.
Burk M. A., Mrs., h Point rd n Livingston.
Burk Sebree, carman, h Point rd n Livingston.
Burke James, h Ann ab Union.
Burke James, laborer, h Chestnut cor Ponkhockie.
Burke John, h Lucas av.
Burke Michael, stone cutter, h Union av bel Grand.
Burke Thomas, boots and shoes, Division n Garden, bds Hamilton's Hotel.
Burmingham John, laborer, h Washington av n Depot.
Burmingham M., laborer h Washington av n Depot.
Burns D., laborer, h Union n Cedar.
Burns John, harness maker, h 36 Howland av.
Burns John, h Division ab Union.
Burns John, shoemaker, h Hasbrouck av n Garden.
Burns J., shoemaker, Dock, h do.
Burns Jane, Mrs., h Mason n Hone.
Burns John, laborer, h Post n Union.
Burns John, laborer, h Ravine n R. R.
Burns Michael, h Division ab Union.
Burns Patrick, blacksmith, h Wilbur Plank rd.

Bargains, No. 5 Wall St., Kingston.

HIRAM ROOSA'S Insurance Agency has

Burns Thomas, shoemaker, h Hone cor Hunter.
Burns Thomas, laborer, h Post cor Union.
Burns Thomas, boatman, h Abruyn n Grove.
Burnett A. Mrs., h Green n Pearl.
Burnett Robert, pilot, h Spring n Hone.
Bush Frederick, laborer, h Hanraty n Point rd.
Bush Jacob, carpenter, h Ten Broeck av n Downs.
Bush Martin, foreman, bds City Hotel.
Bush Matthew, student, Savings Bank Building.
Bush Simon, carpenter, h Wall n St. James.
Bussemer L., cabinet maker, h Elmendorf cor R. R.
Butler Edward, laborer, h Cross n Ann.
Butler E., shoemaker, Dock, h do.
Butler E. K. Mrs., h Newkirk av n DuBois av.
Butler M. J., clerk, h Cross.

CABLE PAUL, tinsmith, h 19 N Front.
Caddy Benjamin, carpenter, h Hudson.
Caddy William, h Wilbur rd cor Hudson.
Cadwell J. W., dress maker, 7 Wall.
Cahill John, h Hudson.
Cahill M. Mrs, h Cedar n Union av.
Caffrey Charles, laborer, h DeWitt.
Callahan Daniel, carpenter, bds Hamilton House.
Callahan Walter, boatman, h Wilbur rd n Hudson.
Campbell Alex., capt., h Suydam, cor Division.
Campbell Christopher, laborer, h Ravine n R. R.
Campbell James, h Division n Spring.
Cane Schuyler, cooper, h Hasbrouck av n Cross.
CANFIELD P. A., stoves, &c., Garden and Ferry, h Holmes n Hone.
Canfield P. A. Jr., clerk, bds Holmes n Hone.
Canfield S. G., book keeper, bds Holmes n Hone.
Cansear Louis, wagon maker, h Hasbrouck av n Newkirk av.

J. O. & G. B. MERRITT, Black Alpacas

Never had any Disputed Claims.

CANTINE PETER, surrogate, Fair cor Main.
Caprice John, boatman, h Cross n Hasbrouck av.
Cardwell James, h Spring c Ravine.
Carey John, laborer, h Greenkill av n Union av.
Carey Patrick, grocer, &c., Abeel n Wilbur.
Carle Conrad, hostler, h Wall n St. James.
Carle David, grocer, Division and Canal.
Carle F. Mrs., h Wall n St. James.
Carle Jacob, clerk, Division and Canal.
Carle P. A., laborer, h Elmendorf n Bruyn av.
Carl Albert, clerk, h Albany av cor Union av.
Carl Herbert, clerk, 17 Garden, bds Grand n Union.
Carl Peter, carpenter, h Bowery n Union av.
Carlos J. W., clerk, Garden cor Hasbrouck av.
Carney E. A., laborer, h Liberty n Prospect.
CARPENTER & FOWLER, lawyers, Fair n Main.
Carpenter G. A., clerk, h Henry n Prospect.
Carpenter O. P., grocer, Union av cor O'Neil, h Fair n R. R.
Carpenter O. P., lawyer, h Fair n St. James.
Carr Albert, clerk, h Wall n St. James.
Carr Charles, printer, Daily Freeman.
Carr V. W., salesman, h Washington av cor N Front.
Carr William, laborer, h St. Mary n Hasbrouck av.
Carrol M., mason, h Wilbur Plank rd.
Carroll James, mason, h Union cor Post.
Carson Catherine, h Ravine ab Pine.
Carter C. P., (Safford & C.,) h Bowery n Union av.
Carter Enoch, tinsmith, h Meadow n R. R.
Carter M. A., Mrs., h Newkirk av n Hasbrouck av.
Carter Robert P., printer, Courier.
Casey John, grocer, h Washington av n Depot.
Casey M., stone cutter, h Washington av n Depot.
Casey P., grocer, Washington av n Depot, h do.

and Brilliantines, 5 Wall St., Kingston,

Cashin E., grocer, Garden cor Hasbrouck, h do.
Cashin John, clerk, Garden cor Hasbrouck av.
Cassidy Barney, farmer, h O'Reilly cor Prince.
Cassidy John, h Ravine cor German.
Castle John N., captain, h Pierpont n Hone.
Castor J. Mrs., saloon, Canal, h do.
Caswell Caroline, Mrs., h Main cor Green.
Caswell F. B., printer, Argus office.
Cator G., clerk, h St. James n Prospect.
Cator Jacob, clerk, h Elmandorf n Smith av.
Cator J. P., salesman, h Newkirk av n Hasbrouck av.
Catlin S. Mrs., h Prospect n Liberty.
Cavanagh B., saloon, Abeel, h do.
Cavanagh Edward, laborer, h Abeel.
Cavanagh L., blacksmith, h Cedar n Union.
Cedan John, shoemaker, Dock n Ravine.
Cearney S., teamster, h Prospect n St. James.
Ceasar Paul, boatman, h Flatbush av n Union av.
Chalker A. P., physician, Division cor Mill.
Chambers Jacob, boots and shoes, h Union av n Elmendorf.
CHAMPLIN C. R. N., lawyer and notary public, Murray's Building, Garden, h Ponkhockie n Chestnut.
Champlin Mary Mrs., Wall n Bowery.
Chandler Charles E., clerk, h Point rd n Livingston.
Chapman C. E., sewing machines, 68 N Front.
CHARLOUIS JOHN I., Prof., teacher of modern languages, h Pearl opp Rev. Dr. Hoes.
Chatfield Clark, surveyor, h Union n Hasbrouck av.
Chatfield, architect, Garden over Market.
Chidester Abram, foreman, h O'Neil cor Tremper.
Chipp Elizabeth Mrs., h John cor Crown.
Chipp Howard, lawyer, 30 Wall, h Main cor Fair.
Chipp Howard, Jr., lawyer, 30 Wall, h Main cor Fair.

J. O. & G. B. MERRITT, Choice Dress

HIRAM ROOSA, Agent at Rondout, N. Y.

KINGSTON DIRECTORY. 67

CHIPP J. DEYO, justice peace and ins. agt., Eagle Hotel, Main, h E Front bet St. James and Liberty.
Chipp Warren, vegetables, &c., Wall n St. James, h do.
CITY HOTEL, (M. D. Perrine, pro.,) E Front opp Main.
CITY HOTEL, (P. J. O'Pray, pro.,) Canal cor Ferry.
Claffy Thomas, boatman, h Wilbur.
Clark Frank, mason, h Cedar n Prospect.
Clark F. S., drover, h N Front n Crown.
Clark John, mason, h Sterling.
Clark L., boatman, h ft Chambers.
Clark Lewis, h E Front N of John.
Clark M., laborer, h Cedar n Union.
Clark Wm., h Russell.
CLAY C. S., ins. and real estate, 28 Wall, h E Front n John.
Clear Julia, Mrs., h Union av cor Liberty.
Clearwater A. T., (Van E. & C.,) h E Front cor Cedar.
Clearwater I., carpenter, h E Front cor Cedar.
Clearwater I., carpenter, h Hurley av.
Clearwater John, laborer, h Wilbur.
Clearwater William, laborer, h old Wilbur rd.
Clearwater William, laborer, h Meadow n R. R.
Clearwater Mrs., h Cottage Hill, Wilbur.
Clemens Robert, h Hunter n Hone.
Clemmer John, carpenter, h Third av n R. R.
Cloonan & Co., soda water manuf., Spring n Division.
Cloonan E., (Cloonan & Co.,) h Division cor Spring.
Cloonan Lawrence, h Division cor Union.
Cloonan M., (Kelly & C.,) h St. Mary's.
Cloonan Michael, h Division cor Cross.
Cloonan Richard, h Division n Union.
Cloonan Peter, constable, h Division ab Union.
Cloonan Thomas, grocer, Division cor Union, h do.

Goods, No. 5 Wall St., Kingston.

If not convenient to call, send your application by

KINGSTON DIRECTORY.

Close Thomas, laborer, h Abeel.
Clow C. G., clerk, bds Mason.
Coady Patrick, laborer, h Wilbur.
Cobbold & Epps, blacksmiths, Van Buren n Prospect.
Cobbold Thomas, (C. & Epps,) h Prospect cor Liberty.
Cockburn Howard, lawyer, Savings Bank Building.
Cockburn William, boarding, Fair n Bowery, h do.
Cockburn William, clerk, bds Fair n John.
Cocoley John, boatman, h Abeel.
Cocoley K., laborer, h Abeel.
Cody Moses, laborer, h Catherine n Cedar.
Coe Warren C., bar tender, h Wall cor St. James.
Coen E. A. M. Mrs., h Lord.
Coen S. C. Mrs., h Lord.
Coffee J., cigar manuf., E Front n St. James, h E Front n Henry.
Coffee James, cigar maker, bds E Front n Henry.
Coffee P., stone cutter, h Orchard av.
Cogan James, painter, h Bowery n Pine.
Cogswell James, saloon, Sleightburg.
Cohen A., & Corn, clothing, &c., 47 and 94 N Front.
Cohen A., (A. Cohen & Corn,) h 47 N Front.
Cohen Lewis, pictures, &c., h Mason n Hone.
Con Abram W., h Washington av ab Hurley av.
Colburn E., dentist, 9 Wall, h Flatbush av.
Cole C. C., h Fair cor John.
Cole D. W., chief clerk P. O., h Fair cor John.
Cole E., farmer, h Mapleton.
Cole Elias, mason, h Smith av cor Grand.
Cole J. W., h 11 Washington av.
Cole Martin, clerk, h Union n Wurts.
Cole Patrick, carman, h Jarrold n Point rd.
Cole Robert, printer, h St. James cor Wall.
Cole Simon A., brewer, h Grand n Union av.

J. O. & G. B. MERRITT, Kid Gloves,

Mail to HIRAM ROOSA, Insur. Agent, Rondout.

Coleman Charles, butcher, bds Union av cor Orchard.
Coleman P., h Holmes n Hone.
Colfax Robert, clerk, h Elmendorf n Bruyn.
Colligan Catherine Mrs., h Post.
Colligan David, clerk, h German.
COLLIGAN HENRY, saloon and horse dealer, Abeel n Ravine, h German.
Colligan Jane, confectioner, Abeel W of Wurts.
Collins James, laborer, h Cedar n Union.
Collins Patrick, cooper, h Tompkins n Union.
Colloten B., grocer, &c., Prospect cor Union, h do.
Collum John, laborer, h Ann cor Union.
Colvill George, ice, h Holmes n Hone.
Colvill R., grocer, Hone cor Hunter, h do.
Comback M. Mrs., h Furnace n Bowery.
Comer Thomas, clerk, h Point rd.
Conklin Charles, captain, h Pierpont opp Russell.
Conklin E. D., ship carpenter, h Esther.
Conklin Harris, captain, h Chester n Union av.
Conklin M. T., printer, Argus office.
Conklin Thomas, h Pierpont ab Ravine.
Conklin W. L., law student, bds Downs n Ten Brœck av.
Conlan John, tailor, h Washington av n Depot.
Conlan Patrick, bar tender, Mansion House.
Conlan William, saloon, Columbus av cor Prospect, h do.
Conley John, boatman, h Abeel.
Conn John, h German cor Ridge.
Conn Joseph, h Pine n Hudson.
Connor John, laborer, h Ravine n R. R.
Connors B. Mrs., h Division ab Pierpont.
Connors B. Mrs., h Union cor Tompkins.
Connors Edward, laborer, h Point rd.
Connors M. J., bookkeeper, h Hone cor Pierpont.
Connors M. Mrs., h Ravine cor Chambers.

No. 5 Wall Street, Kingston.

Insure with no other Agent.

Connors Patrick, engineer, h Cedar n Catherine.
Connolly David, h Taylor.
Connolly Edward, boatman, h Ridge.
Connolly John, h Division ab Rogers.
Connolly Michael, laborer, h Taylor.
Conoway John, blacksmith, bds Wilbur Hotel.
Conrad Charles, h Ravine n Hunter.
Conrad T., clerk, Sutton House.
Conroy D., (Scully & C.,) h 13 N Front.
Conroy E. Mrs., h E Front.
Conroy James, carriage manuf., Wilbur Plank rd h do.
Conroy John, h Ann ab Meadow.
Constantine Amos, laborer, h Newkirk av n Division.
Conway John, laborer, h Catherine n Cedar.
Conway John, blacksmith, Wilbur.
CONWELL M., grocer, Abeel cor Hone, h do.
Conwell P., clerk, bds Dock n Ravine.
Conwell Stephen, grocer, h Abeel cor Hone.
Conwell Stephen, Jr., clerk, bds Abeel cor Hone.
Coogan Michael, laborer, h 25 Washington av.
Coogan P. Mrs., hotel, 13 N Front, h do.
Coogan P., machinist, bds 13 N Front.
Cook Albert, laborer, h Summer n Susan.
Cook George, (pro. Western Hotel,) Washington av n Depot.
Cook James, bar tender, h Division n Holmes.
Cook John, laborer, h Chambers n Ravine.
Cook John, laborer, h Newkirk av n Chambers.
Cook Peter, Jr., hostler, h E Front n Cemetery.
Coons Eliza, Mrs., h Flatbush av n Union av.
Coons H. H., harness, &c., Main n E Front, h do.
Coons Jacob, hostler, h Taylor.
Coons Theodore, clerk, bds Kingston Hotel.
Cooper Asa, cigar maker, bds Western Hotel.

J. O. & G. B. MERRITT, Gent's

HIRAM ROOSA, Gen'l Ins. Agent, Rondout, N. Y.

Cooper Charles G., clerk, h Green cor Lucas av.
Cooper C., laborer, h Wilbur Plank rd.
Cooper Egbert, bds 45 N Front.
Cooper Gilbert, Mrs., h 36 N Front.
Cooper James M., lawyer, Savings Bank Building.
Cooper James, Rev., h Wurts cor Pierpont.
Cooper Thomas, cooper, h Oak n Bowery.
Cooper William, clerk, bds N Front n Crown.
Corbin J. G., grocer, Hasbrouck av cor Meadow, h do.
Corcoran John, h Division ab Holmes.
Corcoran M., laborer, h Union n Cedar.
Cordts J. H. & Co., brick manuf., hd Livingston.
Corn Isidor, (A. Cohen & C.,) h 94 N Front.
Cornford Harry, marble cutter, bds St. James n E Front.
Cornell Elizabeth, Mrs., h 106 N Front.
CORNELL FREIGHT & TOWING LINE, ft Division.
Cornell Thomas, steamboats, &c., h Wurts cor Spring.
Cornett John, clerk, bds 21 Garden.
Cornwell Charles, h German n Ridge.
Costello Charles J., music teacher, h Main n Fair.
Costello James, boatman, h Hanraty n Point rd.
Costello John H., saloon, Garden and Ferry, h do.
Costello John, laborer, h Cross n Ann.
Costello M., saloon, Division ab Union, h do.
Costello M. h Mrs., Hanraty n Point rd.
Costello Peter, boatman, h Newkirk n Chambers.
Coughline B. Mrs., h DeWitt.
Coughlan Patrick, machinist, h Ravine n Point rd.
Cousins H. C., (Horvers & C.,) h Cedar n Union av.
Coutant A. K., carpenter, h Abruyn n Chesnut.
Coutant E. B., machinist, h Henry n Oak.
Coutant Stephen, millwright, h Abruyn cor Chestnut.
Covel C. C., physician, Union n Pine Grove, h do.

Furnishing Goods, 5 Wall St., Kingston.

HIRAM ROOSA'S Accidental, Life, Fire, Marine

Cowell George, carpenter, h Third n Elm.
COYKENDALL GEORGE, freight agent, Cornell Dock, bds Spring and Wurts.
Coykendall S. A., freighter, h Spring n Wurts.
Cragan M., stone cutter, Wilbur Plank rd, h do.
Cramer J., carpenter, Catherine n Foundry, h hd Grove.
Crane Henry M., bookkeeper, bds Columbus av cor Abruyn.
Crane Michael, engineer, h Abruyn n Grove.
Crane Patrick, laborer, h Catherine n Cedar.
Crane P., laborer, h Cedar n Catherine.
Crane Walter B., lumber, Abruyn cor Columbus av, h Abruyn cor Grove.
Crapser Morgan, car driver, h Taylor.
CRISPELL & SMITH, physicians, Lackawanna next Mansion House.
Crispell A., (C. & Smith,) h Chestnut.
Crispell G. D., physician, Fair cor Pearl, h do.
Crispell H. S., clerk, h Chestnut.
Crispell John, wagon maker, h Taylor.
Crispell M. J. Mrs., h Flatbush av n R. R.
Cromie Thomas, cutter, h Hone cor Wurts.
Cronin Margaret, h Division ab Cross.
Crook Henry, painter, h Oak n Bowery.
Crook Peter, h Fair n St. James.
Crook Peter, laborer, h E Front.

CROSBY A. A. & CO.,
hardware, iron, steel, &c., Division cor Garden.
CROSBY, MERRITT & CO., dry goods and carpets, 7 Wall.
Crosby A. A., (A. A. Crosby & Co.,) h Abeel bet Post and Wurts.

J. O. & G. B. MERRITT, Gloves and

Insurance and Real Estate Agency, Rondout, N. Y.

Crosby E., (Crosby M. & Co.,) h Fair ab Pearl.
Crosby Robert, coachman, h Liberty n Union av.
Crosbier William, boatman, h Abeel.
Crossman N., saloon, Garden cor Ferry, h do.
Crossman W. H., cabinet, h 45 N Front.
Crouch H. G., (pro. Kingston Argus,) h Green n St. James.
Crow Michael, laborer, h Ann n Union.
Crowell James, laborer, h Ann n Union.
Crowly Daniel, h Wilbur.
Cuddy Edward, laborer, h Union n Division.
Cuddy John, laborer, h Garden cor Prince.
CULLEN JAMES H., grocer and liquors, Ann cor Meadow, h do.
Cullen Philip, grocer, h Ann cor Meadow.
Cullen Thomas, carpenter, h DeWitt.
Cullen Samuel, h Pine, (Rondout.)
Cumberland A., hostler, Hamilton House.
Cummings & Kiernan, brewery, Hurley av cor Washington av.
Cummings Julia, h Ann cor Cross.
Cummings James, (C. & Kiernan,) h Hurley av.
Cummings John, cigar maker, h Furnace n E Front.
Cummings J. T., bookkeeper, h Wilbur.
Cummings John, h Wilbur.
Cummings J. V., bookkeeper, h Wilbur.
Cunniff M. J., marble cutter, h Division opp Rogers.
Cunniff M., shoemaker, h Division opp Rogers.
Cunningham John, laborer, h Second av n Point rd.
Cunningham John, laborer, h Hanraty n Point rd.
Cunningham Michael, laborer, h Garden n Flatbush av.
Curley Jas., dry goods, h Hasbrouck av cor Union.
Curran Michael, h Division ab Holmes.
Curren John, clerk, bds Division cor Meadow.

Hosiery, No. 5 Wall St., Kingston.

HIRAM ROOSA'S Agency represents a Combined

Curtis Charles, teacher, h Elmendorf n R. R.
Curtis Frank, printer, Daily Freeman.
Curtis J. A., (N. & J. A. Curtis.) h Main n E Front.
CURTIS J. P., carriage manufac., Union av n O'Neil, h Union av n Henry,
CURTIS N. & J. A., drugs and seeds, 3 Music Hall.
Curtis Nathan, (N. & J. A. Curtis,) h Pearl bet Fair and E Front.

DAGAN WILLIAM, laborer, h Ravine n Vine.
Daglish Thomas, bds Albany av. opp Maiden Lane.
DAILY AND WEEKLY FREEMAN, H. Fowks, ed., &c., Mill.
Dale Patrick, h Division ab Union.
Daley Patrick, carpenter, h Tompkins n Columbus av.
Daly P., books, &c., Division n Ferry, h Lackawana.
Daly James, h Union av bel Grand.
Dalton James, contractor, h Orchard av.
Dalton Michael, h Cross n Chambers.
Dalzell William, h Hunter.
Dangler Simon, barber, Union av bel St. James, h do.
Dann Jasper, shoemaker, h Maiden Lane n Pine.
Darling William W., mason, h Hurley av.
Dales Henry, boot maker, h St. James n Prospect.
Daguhen John, h Ann cor Cross.
Daugherty Mary, h Ann ab Meadow.
Daven John, h Ann cor Meadow.
David Patrick, laborer, h Newkirk n Maple av.
Davis & De Graff, boots, shoes, &c., Savings Bank Building opp Court House.
Davis Anthony, laborer, h Cedar n Prospect.
Davis A. Miss, h Pine.
Davis D. W., teamster, h Ponkhockie n Union.
Davis Edward D., coal, &c., Furnace n Liberty, h Prospect cor Cedar.

J. O. & G. B. MERRITT, Laces and

Davis Hiram, barrel heads, Van Buren n Sterling, h E Front cor Bowery.
Davis Isaac F., grocer, Union av n O'Neil, h do.
Davis J. E., agent, h Second av.
Davis John J., laborer, h Wall n St. James.
Davis J. L., clerk, 7 Wall.
Davis J. S., contractor, h hd Chestnut.
Davis L. D., h Hunter n Ravine.
Davis L. G. H., boots and shoes, 21 Garden, h do.
Davis Oscar, clerk, 5 Wall.
Davis P. J., mer. tailor, 5 Music Hall, h John n E Front.
Davis Silas H., (D. & De Graff,) h Green n Lucas av.
Davis Simon, carpenter, h Elmendorf n R. R.
Davis Theodore, printer, Kingston Press.
Davis T. D., clerk, Grand.
Davis Wm. B., physician, St. James cor E Front, h do.
Davidson & Krauser, tobacconists, John n Wall.
Davidson David, (D. & Krauser,) bds N Front n Green.
Davison E., keeper of alms house, Flatbush av.
Davison George P., clerk, Hamilton House.
Day Benjamin, h Maiden Lane n E Front.
Day Thomas F., clerk, h Cedar.
Day T. F., boatman, h Cedar n Prospect.
Day Thomas, boatman, h Union n Post.
Dean Cornelius, gardener, h n Grove.
DEAN J. J. Rev., h Wurts n Mason.
Deats Abram, laborer, h Garden cor Smith av.
Deats John, h Newkirk av n Hasbrouck av.
DECATUR R. W. fish, oysters, vegetables &c., John n Wall, h John cor Crown.
Decatur R. W. Jr., clerk, bds Crown cor John.
Decker & Radcliff, dry goods, notions, &c., Wall.
Decker A. H., (Decker & Radcliff,) h Fair n John.

Embroideries, No. 5 Wall St., Kingston.

DECKER B. P. & BRO., furniture, undertaking and livery, 39 and 41 Division.
Decker B. P., (B. P. Decker & Bro.,) h Pierpont n Wurts.
Decker C. S., cigar box manuf., Elmendorf n R. R., h do.
DECKER D. L., blacksmith, Columbus av n Cedar, h n opp do.
Decker G. M., printer, Daily Freeman.
Decker Isaac, machinist, h Union av n Elmendorf.
DECKER J. TAYLOR, continental saloon, Fair S of Main, h do.
Decker Jane, Mrs., h Holmes n Wurts.
Decker J. M., printer, Daily Freeman.
Decker Moses, h Mapleton.
Decker Morris, printer, h n Bond.
Decker Nelson, boatman, h Newkirk av n Chambers.
Decker P. M. G. Mrs., h Abeel opp Wurts.
Decker Wm., (B. P. Decker, & Bro,) h Wurts n Pierpont.
Dederick Addison E., carpenter, h Prince opp Smith av.
Dedrick E. P., cabinet Maker, bds Kingston Hotel.
Dee David, laborer, h Newkirk av n Maple av.
Dee Michael, laborer, h Abeel.
DeGraff Charles T., clerk, h Fair cor John.
DeGraff J., (D. & De Graff,) h Pearl n Wall.
DeGraff Nellie, Mrs., h Bowery cor Oak.
DeGroff W. H., foreman, h Pierpont n Wurts.
Doihl Augustus, laborer, h Wilbur.
DELAFIELD WALTER, Rev., h Green n St. James.
DeLamater Garritt, printer, bds Hurley av.
DeLamater H., laborer, h Cedar n Prospect.
DeLamater Isaac L., teamster, h 19 N Front.
DeLamater J. Mrs., h Green junc. Crown.
DeLamater J., foreman, h Hurley av.

of all kinds. Rondout, N. Y.

DeLamater S. Mrs., h Pine cor Wilbur Plank rd.
DeLamater Tjerick, blacksmith, h Union av n R. R.
DeLamater William G., clerk, h Wall cor Pearl.
DeLaMontanye John, Mrs., h Maiden la cor Pine.
DeLaMontanye J. D. W., clerk, h Maiden la c Pine.
DeLaMontanye James, clerk, Fair n Main.
Delanoy D. M., printer, Argus office.
Delanoy E. & Son, grocers, Cedar n Prospect.
Delanoy Joseph M., boatman, h Union av n O'Reilly.
Delanoy Matthew W., fisherman, n Prince ab Union av.
Delaney Eliza, h Washington av cor N Front.
Delaney James, h Division cor Union.
Delaney Mrs., h Division ab Meadow.
Delavergne Isaac, clerk, h Pierpont n Hone.
Delany James, laborer, h Cross n Chambers.
Delany Mary E. Mrs., h Union av n Flatbush av.
Delany Patrick, laborer, h Henry n Union av,
Delany Thomas, mason, h Union av n Cedar.
DELAWARE & HUDSON CANAL CO., Dock.
Delaware & Hudson Canal Co., Light Boat Dock.
DeLilley J. P., barber, h Henry n Furnace.
DeLilley Thomas, laborer, h R. R. n Chester.
Dempsey M. Mrs., h Ann ab Meadow.
Dempaey Thomas, h Garden ab Prince.
Dempsey William, pilot, bds Mansion House.
Demsky Peter, h Hunter n Ridge.
Denike Isaac, grocer, &c., Wilbur, h do.
Denniston J. O. Rev., bds Fair n Bowery.
Dennis George, teamster, h Washington av n Depot.
Dennis John B., book binder, h Furnace n Bowery.
Dennis Wm. H., harness maker, h Hunter n Ravine.
De Puy B. L., h Mill.
De Puy Lewis, clerk, h John n Fair.
De Puy Rachel C. Mrs., h Union n Wurts.

7*

Undergarments, 5 Wall St., Kingston.

Get an Accidental Policy at
KINGSTON DIRECTORY.

Dermody Patrick, laborer, h Hasbrouck av bel Prince.
Derrenbacher C. Mrs., h German cor Ravine.
DERRENBACHER J. & J. P., grocers, &c., Dock cor Ravine.

DERRENBACHER JOHN,
flour, feed, &c., Abeel n Ravine, h Abeel n Hone.
Derrenbacher Jacob E., clerk, h Hone n Pierpont.
Derrenbacher J. P., (J. & J. P. Derrenbacher,) h Abeel n Hone.
Derrenbacher John P. Jr., saloon, Ravine n Abeel, h do.
Derrenbacher John D., bookkeeper, h Abeel n Hone.
Derrenbacher J. E., bookkeeper, h Hone ab Pierpont.
Derrenbacher William, clerk, bds Abeel n Hone.
Desmond D. J., saloon, Division ab Union, h do.
Desmont Mary, h Division opp Holmes.
Detis John, baker, Hone cor Union, h do.
Deudney A. L., millinery, 26 Garden.
Deudney Henry A., clerk, h Abruyn cor Union.
DeVeau S., shoes, &c., Division ab Garden, h Wurts, n Holmes.
DeVeau W., ferry house, Sleightburg.
DeVine John, boiler maker, h Prospect n Liberty.
Devlin William, blacksmith, h Pine n Ravine.
Dewire Henry, mason, h Union n Post.
Dewey A., butcher, h St. James n Union av.
Dewey A., carman, h Henry n Union av.
Dewey Steuben, laborer, h Henry n Union av.
Dewey S. A. Mrs., h Prospect n St. James.
DeWitt & Gillespie, grocers, 12 Wall.
DeWitt D. M. Hon., h Pearl av n Washington.
DeWitt E. A. Miss, h Wall n Maiden la.
DeWitt Eugene, clerk, bds Fair n Henry.

J. O. & G. B. MERRITT, Cloths and

HIRAM ROOSA'S Agency, Rondout, N. Y.

DeWitt Harry, cook, h R. R. n Chester.
DeWitt J. C. Mrs., h Main n E Front.
DeWitt J. L., (De W. & G.,) h Fair n Henry.
DeWitt John S., h E Front n John.
DeWitt Newkirk, clerk h 20 N Front.
DeWitt R. Mrs., dressmaker, h Prospect n Liberty.
DeWitt William, h Catherine n Hasbrouck av.
Deyo A. A. Jr., h Pearl n Wall.
Deyo A. E., carman, h Ponkhockie cor Union.
DEYO C. W., county clerk, Main cor Fair, h Pearl cor E Front.
Deyo Elvin, clerk, bds Adams.

JOHN H. DEYO,
Dealer in Domestic, Foreign and Fancy

DRY GOODS,
LADIES' AND GENTS' FURNISHING GOODS,
17 Garden St., City of Kingston, (Rondout,)
OPPOSITE R. DEYO'S.
☞ Agency of the Ulster County Dye Works.

Cassimeres, No. 5 Wall St., Kingston.

Life Insurance on the Stock, Mutual or Co-

Deyo Henry, laborer, h Newkirk av n Chambers.
DEYO JOHN H., dry goods, gents' furnishing, &c., 17 Garden, Hasbrouck Block,h Wurts 3d ab Pierpont.
Deyo John, laborer, h Union av n Cedar.
Deyo L. Miss, h E Front n Bowery.
Deyo M., clerk, h Abeel.
Deyo Mary, h Hurley av.
Deyo Richard, grocer, crockery, &c., Garden and Ferry, h Adams.
Deyo R. H., clerk, h E. Front n St. James.
Dezutter Joseph, tailor, Division ab Union.
Diamond George V., student, h Garden cor Flatbush av.
Diamond Hugh, liquors, h Henry n Union av.
Diamond Hugh, Jr., clerk, h Garden cor Flatbush av.
DIAMOND J., grocer, liquors, &c., 27 Garden, h Garden cor Flatbush av.
Diamond James, laborer, h Third n Elm.
Dibblee Francis, Mrs., h Albany av cor Tremper av.
Dickerson Charles H., waiter, Excelsior House.
Diehl Charles, saloon, Garden opp Ferry, h do.
Diehl Frederick, wagon maker, Union av cor Elmendorf.
Diehl William, laborer, h Newkirk av n Chambers.
Dille Jacob, mason, Ten Brœck av n Grand.
Dillon J., (McE. & D.,) h Chestnut.
Dillon Patrick, laborer, h Meadow n Chambers.
Dillon Philip, laborer, h Hanraty n Point rd.
Dimmack S. G., h E Front n St. James.
Dimmick William, h Mapleton av.
Dingeee John, fruit, &c., St. James n Prospect, h do.
Dippold M., leather, &c., Division opp Abeel, h do.
Disbrow D. A., general store, Union av cor St. James, h do.

J. O. & G. B. MERRITT, Flannels and

operative Plan at H. ROOSA'S Agency, Rondout.

Dish George, boatman, h Garden cor Smith av.
Dittus Leonard, saloon, Abeel W of Wurts, h do.
Dobbs Samuel, slate roofer, h Ann n Union.
Dockstader J. S., clerk, bds Fair n N Front.
Dodge A., hardware, &c., Garden and Ferry, h Hone bet Spring and Pierpont.
Dodge D. G., gen. merchandise, 9 N Front, h do.
Dodge E. T., clerk, bds 9 N Front.
Dofeldecker John, cooper, h n Chestnut.
Doggan Thomas, laborer, h Ravine n Hasbrouck av.
Dohnken William, carpenter, h Hunter n Ravine.
Dolan M., shoemaker, Abeel, h do.
Dolan Philip, teamster, h Union n Wurts.
Dolkey Augustus, laborer, h Chambers cor Newkirk.
Doll John, T., pattern maker, h St. James n Prospect.
DOLSON PETER J., painter, Union av n Elmendorf, h do.
Dolton John, laborer, h Abeel.
Donahue Patrick, laborer, h Cross n Division.

DONALDSON & MUSSON,
planing, sawing timber, &c., Powell Dock, Columbus av.

Donaldson E. L., (D. & Musson,) h Abruyn n Union.
Donaldson Thomas, h Ravine opp Spring.
Donaldson William, carpenter, h Ten Broeck av n Downs.
DONNELLY & SOILBERGER, stoves, &c., Ferry cor Division.
Donnelly J., shoemaker, Dock n Ravine.
Donnelly James, h Division ab Cross.
Donnelly John, mason, h Division n Rogers.
Donnelly Michael, h Division cor Cross.

Blankets, No. 5 Wall St., Kingston.

Donnolly Peter, (D. & S.,) h Adams.
Donnelly Peter, boatman, h Meadow n Chambers.
Donnelly Thomas, laborer, h Chambers n Union.
DONOVAN D. E., North River blue stone, Wilbur, h Washington av cor Love la.
Dooley Andrew, laborer, h Cedar n Union.
Dooley Michael, laborer, h Smith av n Garden.
Dooley Patrick, laborer, h Cross n Division.
Doran Patrick, h Abeel n Ravine.
Dorcy James, laborer, h Union cor Tompkins.
Dorcy Michael, laborer, h Ann cor Meadow.
Dorcy Michael, gas maker, h Cross n Railroad.
Dorcy William, laborer, h Abeel.
Doremus F. H., clerk, bds Pierpont n Wurts.
Dorn Catherine Mrs., h Catherine n Cedar.
Dorn James, boatman, h Catherine n Tompkins.
Dorne Michael, foreman, h Union n Cement Works.
Dorren A. L., clerk, h Chester n Union av.
Doudney William, clerk, bds Hamilton House.
Dougherty Elizabeth, h Spring cor Russell.
Dougherty James, Rev., h Wall cor Pearl.
Dougherty M. Mrs., h Division opp Abeel.
Douglas Ann, h Washington av cor N Front.
Douglas A. T., physician, Garden, h Spring n Hone.
Douglas Eliza, milliner, Division ab Union.
Douglas John, clerk, h Prospect cor Union.
Douglas John, carpenter, h Abeel.
Douglas William, sup't., h Cross n Chambers.
Dow William, bookkeeper, h Tremper av n Downs.
Downey John, h Garden n Ferry.
Doyle B., h Catherine, n Hasbrouck av.
Doyle Eliza, Mrs., h Abeel.
Doyle S. W., mason, h Henry n Prospect.
Doyle William, laborer, h Cedar n Union.

Real Estate Agency, Rondout, N. Y.

Drake A. T., agent, h Wall n Bowery.
Drake Henry, foreman, h hd Staple.
Drake J., small beer manuf., Pine cor Wilbur Plank rd.
Draper James, moulder, h Newkirk av n Hasbrouck av.
Drautz George, stoves, &c., Hone n Abeel, h do.
Drennan James, h Division ab Union.
Dressel G. & Co., brewers, Holmes cor Wurts.
Dressel G., (G. D. & Co.,) h Wurts n Holmes.
Dreyfus B., h Hasbrouck av n St. Mary.
Dreyfus Charles, drover, h Abeel W of Wurts.
Dreyfus Edward, clothier, 19 Garden, h 2 Wurts.
DuBois & Freer, blacksmiths and carriage manufacs., St. James n Prospect.
DuBois & Shelightner, blacksmiths, Henry cor Fair.
DuBois A. E., clerk, bds Fair n N Front.
DuBois Charles, carriage maker, h Bowery n Oak.
DuBois C. D., restaurant, Washington av cor Hurley av, h Washington av n N Front.
DuBois C. Mrs., h St. James n R. R.
DuBois Elijah, pres. First Nat. Bank, h E Front n John.
DuBois E., blacksmith, h E Front n Henry.
DuBois George, capt., h Wilbur rd cor Hudson.
DuBois G., h German n Hone.
DuBois Henry J., boatman, h Hudson.
DuBois H., teamster, h E Front n Cedar.
DuBois Hiram, bds Western Hotel.
DuBois Jacob, captain, h Chester n School House.
DuBois Jacob H., lawyer, John cor Wall, h John n E Front.
DuBois J., liniment, Washington av n Hurley av, h do.
DuBois J., painter, h Pine.
DuBois James, bds Mansion House.
DuBois J., stone cutter, h Old Wilbur rd.

Trimmings, No. 5 Wall St., Kingston.

Losses Equitably Adjusted and Promptly Paid

DUBOIS JOSIAH, Jr., justice peace, Garden, h Newkirk av opp DuBois av.
DuBois John, carriage manuf., h Bowery n Oak.
DuBois J. D., ship carpenter, h Pierpont n Hone.

DUBOIS LORENZO,
baker, grocer, &c., Prince cor Hasbrouck av.
DuBois L. Mrs., h O'Neil n Union av.
DuBois P. J., h Union av cor Bowery.
DuBois Peter, captain, h Wurts cor Union.
DuBois Peter Jr., clerk, 15 Wall.
DuBois R. D., h St. James n Union av.
DuBois R. W., h Hurley av.
DuBois S. M. Mrs., h Wurts n Pierpont.
DuBois S. V., foreman, h Elmendorf c Ten Broeck av.
DuBois Thomas, laborer, h Flatbush av n Union av.
DuBois William, teamster, h Van Deusen av.
Duffy Bernard, grocer, &c., Cedar n Union, h do.
Duffy Luke, laborer, h Ann n Union.
Duffy Michael, clerk, h Mill n Prospect.
Duffy Patrick Mrs., h Hasbrouck av n R. R.
Duffy Patrick, laborer, h Ann n Union.
DuFlon J. E., tobacconist, Green n Pearl av, h do.
Dulan John, laborer, h Chestnut n Ponkhockie.
Duley Patrick, h Ann cor Meadow.
DUMMER A. O., artist, 9 Wall, h do.
Dumond Alexander, laborer, h Liberty n Prospect.
Dumond A. M., clerk, 16 and 18 N Front.
Dumond G., laborer, h Washington av n Depot.
Dumond George P., gas fitter, h E Front n St. James.
Dumond James, stage driver, h r 108 N Front.
Dumond John P., h E Front n St. James.
Dumond W. P., laborer, h E Front.

J. O. & G. B. MERRITT, Dry Goods and

At HIRAM ROOSA'S Agency, Rondout, N. Y.

Dumont Peter, h Albany av opp Maiden la.
Duncan John, mason, h Union av cor Dederick.
Duncan John W., laborer, h Garden n Flatbush av.
Duncan L., harness maker, h Henry n Fair.
DUNN ANDREW, Jr., jeweler, Newkirk Building, Division, bds Pierpont cor Adams.
Dunn Catherine, saloon, Wilbur.
Dunn C. Mrs., h Hasbrouck av n Garden.
Dunn Charles Mrs., h Prospect n Union.
Dunn Dennis, caulker, h German n Ravine.
Dunn George W., h Adams cor Pierpont.
Dunn James, h Division ab Cross.
DUNN JOHN, boat builder, Dock, h German n Ridge.
Dunn John, h Division cor Cross.
Dunn John Mrs., h Union cor Ann.
Dunn Michael, soda water, h Ann cor Union.
Dunn Michael, h Division n Spring.
Dunn, h Wilbur.
Dunwoody F. G. Mrs., h N Front n opp Green.
Dunwoody J. E., (M., H. & D.,) N Front opp Green.
Durham A. Mrs., h Pearl cor Wall.
Durham A. K., carriage trimmer, h Fair n St. James.
Durham E. A., (Van W. & D.,) h Union av cor Grand.
Durham L. B., clerk, bds Wall cor Pearl.
Dwyer Dennis, saloon, h Division n Cross.
Dwyre Michael, h Division n Rogers.

EAGAN FRANK, laborer, h Ann n Meadow.
EAGLE HOTEL, (H. W. Winnie, pro.,) Main bet E Front and Fair.
Earles Mrs., h Hone cor Pierpont.
Eaman J. H. Mrs., h E Front n John.
Eastman O. L., clerk, bds Hone n Pierpont.
Echart John, cooper, h Abeel.

Carpets, No. 5 Wall St., Kingston.

Eck George L., butcher, h Hunter.
Eckert C. M., bookkeeper, bds Pine n St. James.
Eckert Daniel, cabinet maker, h Albany av n Maiden la.
Eckert N. S., clerk, h Pine n St. James.
Eddy William, upholsterer, bds Hamilton House.
Edginger E. G., printer, Daily Freeman.
Edict Robert, conductor, h Hasbrouck av n Newkirk av.
Edler Aaron, peddler, h Hone cor Union.
Edmonds C. L., confectioner, &c., 10 Garden, h do.
EDMONSTON C. D., tobacconist, Garden opp Rhinecliff Ferry, h do.
Edmonston Thomas H., cigar maker, h Garden opp Ferry.
Edwards Leonard, teacher, h Chestnut n Abruyn.
Edwards M., laborer, h Cross n Chambers.
Edwards William, h Hudson.
Egan Alice, sewing machines, bds Abeel cor Wurts.
Egan W. Mrs., h Abeel.
Ehelrs F., miller, h Tompkins n Union.
Eichenberg Morris, carpenter, h Union av n Greenkill.
Eichler Adolph, liquors, h Chester n Union av.
Eisenla Christian, saloon, Union av bel Grand, h do.
Eighmey David B., engineer, h Grand n Esther.
Eighmey E. A., Mrs., h Esther.
Eighmey Herbert, carpenter, h Esther.
Eighmey Henry P., ship carpenter, h Grand n Esther.
Eisner Joseph, Rabbi, h 64 N Front.
Eldridge Ralph, clerk, h German cor Ravine.
Elerson George, engineer, h Hasbrouck av n Newkirk av.
Elley J., foreman, h Union av n Greenkill av.
Elley J. Mrs., confectionery, &c., Union av n Greenkill av.
Elliott Mary, Mrs., h Prospect cor Liberty.
Elliott O. F., carpenter, h Elmendorf n Tremper av.

Never had any Disputed Claims.

Ellis N., (E. Sampson & Co.,) h Union n Wurts.
ELLSWORTH & SCHEPMOES, grocers, &c., E Front cor Liberty.
Ellsworth E., baker, h Furnace n Henry.
Ellsworth James, (Gassen & E.,) h Furnace n Bowery.
Elmendorf A., clerk, h E Front n Liberty.
Elmendorf George, blacksmith, Washington av ab Hurley av, h 32 N Front.
Elmendorf James, clerk, bds 20 N Front.
Elmendorf J., carpenter, h Flatbush av n Prince.
Elmendorf Nicholas Mrs., h junc. Green and Crown.
Elmendorf S., teamster, h Greenkill av.
Elting David, carpenter, h Liberty n Prospect.
Elting E., watchmaker, 27 Wall.
Elting Jacob, clothier, 50 N Front, h N Front cor E Front.
Elting Louis, clothing, &c., 96 and 98 N Front, h do.
Elting M. Mrs., h St. James n Prospect.
Elting R., physician, bds Mansion House.
ELTINGE EDGAR, physician, St. James cor Fair, h do.
ELTINGE J. H. Jr., druggist, Washington av cor Hurley av, h Maiden Lane.
Emmet George, tinsmith, h Hasbrouck av n Point rd.
Emmet Peter, laborer, h Pine n Ravine.
Enderly Simon, mason, h E Front n Liberty.
Englert John, saloon, Divison ab Abeel, h do.
ENGLISH & SCHERMERHORN, merchant tailors, Savings Bank Building opp Court House.
English Edmond, (E. & Schermerhorn,) h Pearl n Wall.
English Mary, Mrs., h Division ab Union.
English Oliver, machinist, h Tompkins n Columbus av.
Ennis Richard, clerk, bds Abeel n Wurts.
ENNIST ALONZO, dry goods, groceries, &c., Washington av opp Hurley av h Green n John.

Bargains, No. 5 Wall St., Kingston,

Your best interest will dictate to Insure with

Ennist E. B., (Crosby, M. & Co.,) h Bowery cor Union av.
Ennist Edward, mason, h Pine n St. James.
Ennist Stephen, boatman, h Liberty n E Front.
Enright Daniel, laborer, h Henry.
Eppenstein Louis, shoemaker, h Abeel n Hone.
Epps William, blacksmith, h Prospect cor Liberty.
Ertelt Frank, saloon, Ravine cor Vine.
Esray G. C., associate ed., h Sleightburg.
Evans Andrew, h Division ab Union.
Evans E. Miss, h E Front n John.
Evans P., h Division ab Union.
Everett George E., freight agent, h Mapleton.
Everett (J. H.) & Treadwell (J. C.,) flour, feed, &c., 3, 5 and 7 N Front.
Everson Charles S. Mrs., h Hunter n Hone.
EVERSON MORGAN, ship builder, Sleightburg.
Everson Jefferson, ship carpenter, h Pierpont n Holmes.
Every Eli, Rev., h Union av n Flatbush.
EWEN G. W., fine groceries, wines and liquors for medicinal use, Main cor E Front, bds City Hotel.
EXCELSIOR HOUSE, (Peter Weaver,) Garden and Ferry streets and Hasbrouck av.
Extram Frederick, h Division ab Union.

FALLEN JOHN, laborer, h Abeel.
Fallon John, boatman, h Hasbrouck av n Newkirk av.
Fallon Thomas, boatman, h Ann cor Union.
Falnnery E., hostler, Hamilton House.
Farless Thomas A., real estate, Wall cor John, bds Fair n Bowery.
Farrand William D., h Pine n St. James.
FARRELL JOHN, pumps and sewing machine repairer, E Front next City Hotel, h Prospect c Liberty.
Farrell John, h Division ab Union.

J. O. & G. B. MERRITT, Black Alpacas

HIRAM ROOSA, Agent at Rondout, N. Y.

Farrell R. Mrs., h Division ab Cross.
Farrer John, machinist, h Liberty n Prospect.
Fassett E. H. Mrs., milliner, 22 Wall, h do.
Fassett Frederick A., clerk, bds St. James n Fair.
Fatter Jacob, tailor, h Lucas av.
Fay Ambrose, expressman, h Union av cor Elmendorf.
Featherly A. T., (O'Donnell & F.,) h St. James n Fair.
Feeney B., h Division ab Union.
Feeney John, laborer, Chestnut n Ponkhockie.
Feeney K., h Wilbur.
Feeney Patrick, boatman, h Meadow n Ann.
Feeney Thomas, boatman, h DeWitt.
Felder Henry, mason, h Cedar n Prospect.
Fellon Pat., boatman, h Hasbrouck av n Newkirk av.
Felten Chester, clerk, 7 Wall.
Felten Titus, (B. & Felten,) h Bowery n Union av.
Felter C. S., mason, h Fair n St. James.
Ferguson A., carpenter, h Washington av n N Front.
Ferguson M., laborer, h Division cor Union.
Ferguson Wm., h Division ab Union.
Field E., boatman, h E Front n Henry.
Fields A., carpenter, h Cedar cor Union.
Fiero J. Newton, (Bernard & F.,) h Pine n Maiden Lane.
FINCH JEREMIAH, saloon, 49 Wall n Pearl, h do.
Finch Wm. B. & Son, insurance agts., Fair n John.
Finch Wm. B., (Finch & Son,) bds John cor Wall.
Finch Wm. H., (Finch & Son,) bds John cor Wall.
Finger G., clerk, h Elmendorf n Union av.
Finley George, laborer, h Susan n Pine Grove av.
Finley John, boatman, h Russell.
Finley John, h Hunter n Hone.
Finley Mary, Mrs., h German n Ravine.

and Brilliantines, 5 Wall St., Kingston.

If not convenient to call, send your application by

Finley P., laborer, h Union n Cedar.
Finley William, h Hone cor Hunter.
Finley William, teamster, h Ford.
Finney E., h Wilbur.
First Abram, dry goods, &c., h Union n Wurts.
FIRST NATIONAL BANK OF RONDOUT, Garden cor Division.
FISHER & STONE, merchant tailors, 35 Wall.
Fisher A. C., painter, h Pearl av n Washington av.
Fisher Charles A., bookkeeper, bds Chester n R. R.
Fisher C. J., machinist, h Chester n R. R.
Fisher David, (F. & Stone,) h Union av next Foundry.
Fisher Ida, saloon, Garden n Ferry, h do.
Fisher J. O., (Hageman & Fisher,) h Pearl av.
Fisher Lewis, peddler, h Chambers n Stuyvesant.
Fisher John, laborer, h Pine n Ravine.
Fisher L., h Ann ab Union.
Fisher N. S., pay master, h Adams n Rogers.
FISHER W. L., ticket agent, h Pearl n Washington av.
Fisher, h Hunter n Hone.
Fisher, h Pierpont ab Ravine.
Fisk A. B. Mrs., h Cedar, n Union av.
Fisk Charles W., carpenter, h Esther.
Fisk L. L. & Bro., carpenters, &c., Hasbrouck av n Cross.
Fisk L. L., (L. L. Fisk & Bro.,) h Hasbrouck av n Cross.
Fitch Elizabeth, Mrs., h Hunter n Abeel.
Fitch Owen, laborer, h DeWitt.
FITCH S. & W. B., North River blue stone, Wilbur.
Fitch W. B., (S. W. B. Fitch,) h Albany av opp Academy.
Fitzgerald (F. H.,) & Johnson, grocers, Washington av n Depot, h n do.

J. O. & G. B. MERRITT, Choice Dress

Mail to **HIRAM ROOSA**, Insur. Agent, Rondout.

Fitzgerald Garrett, laborer, h Chestnut.
Fitzgerald John, laborer, h Union n Division.
Fitzgerald M., clerk, h Cross.
Fitzgerald Wm., laborer, h Chestnut n Poukhookie.
Flaherty James, laborer, h Prospect n Union.
FLANNIGAN JAMES, grocer, flour, feed, oats, crockery, wood and willow ware, stabling, &c., Dock n Ravine, h do.
Flannagan K. Mrs., h Cross n Chambers.
Flannagan Patrick, boatman, h Ann n Meadow.
Flannery John, boatman, h Abeel.
Flannery K., saloon, Wilbur rd n Hudson.
Flannery Patrick, laborer, h Cross n Ann.
Flannery William, boatman, h Post n Spring.
Flatow A., watch maker, bds Division ab Mill.
Flatow Harriet, Mrs., h Division n Spring.
Fleaury J., tailor, h Green cor Pearl av.
Flemming J. D., clerk, bds Washington av n Pearl.
Flemming Patrick, laborer, h Tompkins n Union.
Flemming Robert, h Hunter n Ravine.
Flemming R.J., coachman, h Washington av n Pearl av
Fletcher George, grocer and saloon, Union av n Greenkill av, h do.
Flick Lawrence, saloon, Ravine ab Abeel, h do.
Flick Michael, saloon, Division opp Holmes.
FLINTOFF WM., stoves and tinware, Union av n Elmendorf, h do.
Flood James, laborer, h Wilbur.
Flynn James, boatman, h Dock.
Flynn N., cabinet maker, h Washington av n N Front.
FLYNN P. J., grocer and liquors, Division cor Meadow, h do.
Fogerty Catherine Mrs., h Ravine n Hasbrouck av.
Folant & Budington, coal and lumber, Union av cor Henry.

Goods, No. 5 Wall St., Kingston.

Folant John P., (F. & Budington,) h Saugerties rd.
Folant James R., book keeper, h E Front n St. James.
Folant S. O., clerk, bds Spring cor Wurts.
Folant William H., salesman, bds Saugerties rd.
Foley J. Mrs., h Division ab Cross.
Foley John, h Ravine n Hasbrouck av.
Foley Thomas, laborer, h Ann n Meadow.
Foley Thomas, saloon, Garden n Ferry, h do.
FORBES ALEX. J., segar manufac., Union av bet St. James and Elmendorf, h do.
Forbes Joseph, student, bds Union av n St. James.
Forde William, shoemaker, Abeel W of Wurts, h do.
Forrest James, saloon, Division opp Holmes.
Forrest J., shoemaker, Columbus av, h Division.
Forst Abram, fancy goods, Abeel W of Wurts, h Union.
Forst Carl, butcher, h Union W of Wurts.
FORST HENRY, horse dealer, Abeel opp Hone, h do.
FORST ISIDORE, dry goods and fancy goods, Abeel opp Hone, h Union West of Wurts.
Forst Morris, clerk, 84 N Front.
Forstal P., h Division cor Cross.
Forsyth Alexander, captain, h Pierpont cor Ravine.
Forsyth Isaac, boatman, h Ravine cor Pierpont.
Forsyth James, boatman, h Abeel W of Wurts.
Forsyth J. F., student, h Pearl cor Fair.
Forsyth S. B., lawyer, h Pearl cor Fair.
Forsyth Mary, Mrs., h Pearl cor Fair.
Fort A. E. Mrs., h Garden cor Flatbush av.
Fort B., laborer, h Ann n Union.
Foss Fritz, laborer, h Hasbrouck av n Point rd.
Foster A., fruits, &c., Division cor Lackawanna.
Fowkes Horatio, editor, &c., h Hasbrouck av cor Stuyvesant.
Fowl John, coachman, h Hasbrouck av n Union.

J. O. & G. B. MERRITT, Kid Gloves,

HIRAM ROOSA, Gen'l Ins. Agent, Rondout, N. Y.

Fowler Charles A., (Carpenter & F.,) h Maiden Lane cor Green.
Fowler Douglas, engineer, h Abeel n Post.
Fowler L. Frank, agent, h Lackawanna.
Fowler O. G., engineer, h Adams n Pierpont.
Fox B. Mrs., saloon, Division ab Holmes.
Fox Ernest, painter, h Ravine cor German.
Fox George, boatman, h Columbus av.
Fox Herman, painter, h Union n Ann.
Fox Jacob, clerk, bds Abeel n Ravine.
Fox Jacob, saloon, South Rondout.
Fox Jacob, saloon, Garden n Division, h do.
Fox John, blacksmith, h E Front n Greenkill av.
Fox Michael, painter, h Pierpont opp Russell.
Fox Michael, laborer, h Meadow n Ann.
Fox Peter, clerk, bds Pierpont cor Holmes.
Fox Teressa, Mrs., h Cross n Chamber.
Fraley Henry, boatman, h Meadow n Chambers.
Fraley Solomon, farmer, h Green cor Pearl av.
Frame M. F., clerk, bds Crown.
Frame S., grocer, Crown n N Front, h n opp do.
Frank E. Mrs., h Furnace n Bowery.
Frank Morris, h Hasbrouck av ab Garden.
Frank Myer, junk, Abeel W of Wurts, h do.
Fraser R. J., laborer, h Newkirk av n DuBois av.
Fraulie J., laborer, h Union n Cedar.
Freas George, h Division cor Pierpont.
FREDENBURGH WM. H., gen. insurance and real estate, Main n Fair, h E Front cor Centre.
Fredenburgh William, clerk, h Green cor Pearl.
Fredenburg M., h Pine n St. James.
Frederick Adam, grocer, Newkirk av n Hasbrouck av.
Freer D., sash maker, bds Elmendorf n Tremper av.
Freer David, blacksmith, h Union n Post.

No. 5 Wall Street, Kingston,

Freer G. T., blacksmith, bds Prince cor Hasbrouck av.
Freer Jacob R., h Prince cor Hasbrouck av.
Freer J. D., car driver, h Taylor.
Freer John, laborer, h Old Wilbur rd.
Freer J. R., mason, h E Front n Henry.
Freer Mary, Miss, dress making, h N Front n Crown.
Freer Robert, blacksmith, h Elmendorf n Tremper.
Freer W. H., tobacconist, 20 Wall, bds Fair n N Front.
FREILEWEH G. J., butcher, 19 N Front, bds Freileweh's Hotel.
Freileweh Jacob, (pro. Freileweh Hotel,) 5, 7 and 9 Green.
French Mrs., h Hunter n Ridge.
Frey David, carpenter, h Spring n Hone.
Frey E. D., watch maker, bds Spring n Hone.
Frick Charles, h Division ab Holmes.
FRICKEL PETER, saloon and hardresser, Union av n Cedar, h do.
Frier Michael, laborer, h Ann cor Union.
FRIES & MYER, grocers, 79 N Front.
Fries Frederick, laborer, h St. Mary.
Fries H., (F. & Myer,) h Pearl av cor Washington av.
Frisselle & Rosa, dentists, John cor Wall, and Garden n Division.
Frisselle M. M., (F. & Rosa,) h Fair n St. James.
Fuller E., laborer, h Greenkill av.
Fulton Frank, barber, h O'Neil n Union av.
Fuller J., stone cutter, h Oak n Bowery.

GAGE EDWIN N., clerk, bds Grand cor Prince.
GAGE GEO. A., dry goods and groceries, Prince n Union av, h Prince cor Grand.
Gage Henry E., clerk, bds Grand cor Prince.
Gage James, machinist, h Meadow n Hasbrouck av.

Gage William, dock builder, h Hone n Union.
Gaibed John, laborer, h Ravine cor Chambers.
Gakin Matthew, h Wilbur.
Gallagher A. A., stoves, 109 N Front.
Gallagher John, hostler, bds Dock n Ravine.
Gallagher John, h Dock n Ravine.
Gallagher Michael, laborer, h Vine n Ravine.
Gallagher P. S., (A. A. Crosby & Co.,) h Adams n Pierpont.
GALLAGHER P., stoves & tinware, 109 N Front, h n do.
Gallagher Patrick, laborer, h Post n Spring.
Gallagher Peter, h Dock n Ravine.
Gallagher Thomas, h Division ab Union.
Gannon Mrs., h Division ab Meadow.
Garratt G., laborer, h Old Wilbur rd.
GASSEN & ELLSWORTH, dry goods, groceries, &c., Union av cor Flatbush av.
Gassen Joseph, saloon, Union av cor Flatbush av, h do.
Gates T. B., lawyer, h Manor pl.
Gay Charles, h Russell.
Geary Charles, brewer, h Union n Wurts.
Geary Daniel, laborer, h Abruyn n Church.
Geary William, carpenter, h Mason n Hone.
Geethlein Peter, h Ann ab Meadow.
Geil Lazarus, grocer, Abeel W of Wurts, h do.
Geisler John, saloon, Division n Abeel, h do.
Geldart J., grainer, h Meadow n Hasbrouck av.
Gelhart R. G., watchmaker, 27 Wall.
Gelley J. A. Mrs., h 76 N Front.
Gelsonal Thomas, blacksmith, h Catherine.
Geoghegan Daniel, h Wilbur rd.
Gerber Richard, (Strump & G.,) h N Front n Green.
Gerlauch F., h Hudson.

Furnishing Goods, 5 Wall St., Kingston.

Gerrett John, tailor, bds Freileweh Hotel.
Gesiler C. Mrs., h Ann n Meadow.
Gesiler Michael, boatman, bds Ann n Meadow.
Gessler John, wagon maker, h Chambers cor Cross.
Gibson A. & Sons, soap and candles, 11 N Front.
Gibson A., (A. Gibson & Sons,) h Green n Lucas av.
Gibson Jason, (A. Gibson & Sons,) h Green c Lucas av.
Gibson R. A., (A. Gibson & Sons,) h Green c Lucas av.
Gidley M. Mrs., h E Front n Cedar.
Giere Ernst, tailor, Prospect n Bowery, h do.
Gilcrist John, salesman, bds City Hotel.
Gile L., junk, Dock, h n Abeel.
Gill David, carpenter, h Prospect n Union.
Gill James, carpenter, Mill n Prospect.
Gill John, mason and builder, h Chestnut n Union av.
Gill Peter, builder, h Prince n Union av.
Gillen B., laborer, h O'Neil n Union av.
Gillen Helen Mrs., h Columbus av n Prospect.
Gillespie James, clerk, bds 13 N Front.
Gillispie W. Scott, (DeW. & G.,) h Fair n Henry.
Gillett G. M., h Pearl n Green.
Gillikan Charles, h Wilbur.
Giliss James, carpenter, bds Abeel.
Gillman A., h Division n Spring.
Gilmore W. M. Jr., (R. & G.,) h 47 Division.
Gilpatrick P., laborer, h Wilbur.
Gippert A., physician, h Abeel W of Wurts.
Gitty William, h Spring ab Ravine.
Glass Jacob, oysters, &c., 27 Washington av, h do.
Glaman J. P., h Pine n Ravine.
Glancy B., h Division cor Meadow.
Glennon James, grocer, Dock n Ravine, h do.
Glennon Luke, boatman, h Hanraty n Point rd.
Glosser Isaac, h Union cor Division.

Gloud E., boatman, h Newkirk av n DuBois av.
Godkins Frederick, carpenter, h Bowery n Prospect.
Goeller George, music teacher, h Pierpont n Hone.
Goeringer Joseph, teamster, h Hone ab German.
GOETCHEUS & LARSEN, painters, Garden next door East to A. A. Crosby & Co's hardware store.
Goetcheus B. F., (G. & Larsen,) h Wilbur.
Goetcheus William, h Ravine n German.
GOKEY WM., ship builder, Columbus av ft Prospect, h Abruyn cor Union.
Golden Anthony, carpenter, bds Union n Division.
Golden Peter, carriage maker, h Flatbush av cor Hasbrouck.
Golden Wm., grocer, Union n Division, h do.
Goldsmith Alexander, clerk, bds 86 N Front.
Goldsmith A. Marshall, watchmaker, bds Union av n R. R.
GOLDSMITH ELIZABETH, jewelry, Union av n R. R.
Goldsmith H., watchmaker, h Union av n R. R.
Goldstein B. & Bro., dry goods, &c., Division ab Union, h do.
Goodrich Chauncey, carpenter, h Livingston n Point rd.
Goodrich N. Mrs., h Pierpont n Hone.
Goodsell John, carpenter, h Ponkhockie cor Chestnut.
Gorey Thos., boatman, h Hasbrouck av n Stuyvesant.
Gorham C. R., mail agt., bds Excelsior House.
Gorman Mary Mrs., h Cross n R. R.
Gorman Peter, laborer, h Cross n Division.
Gorseline A. Mrs., h 72 N Front.
Gosman M. Mrs., h Hasbrouck av n Newkirk av.
Gosman Misses, h Maiden Lane n Fair.
Gottstien Frederick, shoemaker, Division cor Union.
Gould A., wagon maker, bds Mill.
Grady John, h Division cor Cross.

Hosiery, No. 5 Wall St., Kingston.

Graffe Joseph, milk depot, Abeel opp Hone.
Graham B., h Catherine n Hasbrouck av.
Grand Central Hotel, (B. Schwalbach, pro.,) Union av cor Pine Grove av.
Graney J., laborer, h Ann n Ravine.
Graney James, laborer, h Ann n Meadow.
Granger Mary E., h St. James cor R. R.
Grant J. F., horse medicines, Crown n N Front.
Grant R. W., hostler, h Liberty n Furnace.
Gratts Charles, laborer, h Pine n Ravine.
Gray James, laborer, h Meadow n Ann.
Gready A. P., Rondout station agt., bds Newkirk av, opp DuBois.
Green E., shoes, Wall n Pearl, h Pearl cor Wall.
Green Van Kuren, book keeper, h Prospect n St. James.
Greenman Jeremiah, h Union av cor Point rd.
Gregory Henry, laborer, h First av n R. R.
Gregory Jas., contractor, h Hasbrouck av n Meadow.
Gregory John, miner, h Ravine n Vine.
Gregory J., laborer, h Newkirk av n Hasbrouck av.
Gregory Joseph, foreman, h Hasbrouck av n Meadow.
Gregory John, laborer, h Second av n R. R.
Gregory Thomas, laborer, h Second av n R. R.
Grenell Z. Jr., Rev., h Albany av cor Union av.
Grey Mary E. Mrs., h Henry.
Grice Edward, shoemaker, h Chambers cor Cross.
Grice Joseph, caulker, h Wilbur rd cor Hudson.
Griffiths F. H., book keeper, h Hone cor Pierpont.
Griffiths George R., clerk, bds Pine n St. St. James.
Griffiths James, Mrs., h Pine n St. James.
Griffin J. Mrs., h Green junc. Crown.
Griffin Patrick, laborer, h Abruyn n Church.
Griffin Susan, h Union av n St. James.

of all kinds. Rondout, N. Y.

Griggs Thomas, printer, Daily Freeman.
Grimes James, boots, &c., Lackawanna, h Union.
Grimes John, boatman, h Henry.
Grimes John, boatman, h Division ab Union.
Grimes Owen, laborer, h Hudson.
Grimes Patrick, h Abeel W of Hone.
Grimes Peter, boatman, h Post.
Grimes R. Mrs., h Tompkins n Columbus av.
Grommeyer Frank, carpenter, bds Union n Hone.
Grommeyer Henry, laborer, h Union n Hone.
Gronbach Fred., baker, Abeel W of Hone, h do.
Gropeman William, h Ravine opp Pine.
GROSS F. W., lime mill, Hasbrouck av cor Ravine.
Gross J. A., (Blackwell, G. & Co.,) h Prospect cor Liberty.
Gross S. A. Mrs., h Smith av n Garden.
Groves Betsey, Mrs., h Ravine ab Pine.
Gschwind Michael, laborer, h Ravine n R. R.
Grube G., cooper, h Hunter n Hone.
Gue A. Miss, h E Front n Bowery.
Guinan Daniel, laborer, h Hanraty n Point rd.
Gulchen John, laborer, h Ann n Union.
Gunther Goorge, barber, bds Garden n Hasbrouck av.
Gurray Laughlin, boatman, h Hasbrouck av n Stuyvesant.

HAAS H., shoemaker, Abeel bel Hone, h Abeel n Wurts.
Haddew M. Mrs., h Henry n Union av.
Hadigiken Patrick, laborer, h Ann cor Union.
Hadgken John, laborer, h Post cor Union.
Haefer Wm., h Ravine n Hasbrouck av.
Haenamrnn Fred., butcher, Division ab Meadow, h do.
Hagan John, laborer, h Pine n Ravine.

Embroideries, No. 5 Wall St., Kingston.

Get an Accidental Policy at

KINGSTON DIRECTORY.

Hagan Peter, boatman, h Ann n Union.
HAGEMAN & FISHER, job printers, Division c Mill.
Hageman J. P., (H. & Fisher,) h Pearl av.
Haggarty Joseph, laborer, h Abeel.
Haggerty John, laborer, h Columbus av.
Haines Storm, painter, h Summit cor S Sterling.
Hale W. D., book keeper, bds Union av cor Chester.
HALE WILBUR L., growsirees and kole, Union av, cor Chester, h do.

WILBUR L. HALE,
Dealer in

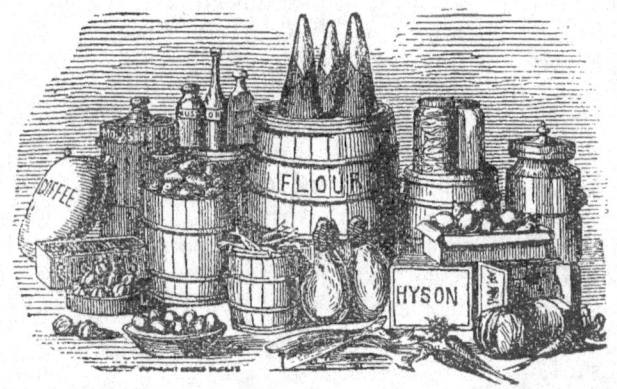

Growsirees, Prouvizuns, Kole, &c.,
Corner of Union Avenue and Chester Street,
NEAR TOLL GATE, WILTWYCK, N. Y.

Haley James, boatman, h Union n Chambers.
Haley John, h Wilbur.
Haley John, boatman, h Abeel.

J. O. & G. B. MERRITT, Ladies'

HIRAM ROOSA'S Agency, Rondout, N. Y.

Haley Martin, millinery, Division n Holmes.
Haley Michael, boatman, h Abeel.
Haley Patrick, laborer, h Abeel.
Hall H. Mrs., h E Front n Henry.
Hall Henry, laborer, h Catherine n Cedar.
HALL THOS. R., glue, &c., Greenkill av, h Fair n Bowery.
Hall W. F., printer, Daily Freeman.
Hallahan D. P., salesman, h Wilbur.
HALLAHAN MICHAEL, north river bluestone, Wilbur, h do.
Hallenbeck W. Scott, clerk, h 28 Wall.
Hallett B. F., finisher, bds St. James cor Albany av.
Hallett C., finisher, bds St. James cor Albany av.
Hallett D., finisher, h St. James cor Albany av.
Hallinon C., laborer, h Catherine.
Halloran D., stoves, &c., Hasbrouck av n Garden, bds Hamilton's Hotel.
Hamblen C. E., clerk, h Hone cor Spring.
Hamblin Wm. H., variety, Main cor Fair.
Hamburger Urban, bridge builder, h Union av bel Grand.
Hamilton Charles, carpenter, h Hunter n Ravine.
Hamilton Henry, carpenter, h Mason n Wurts.
HAMILTON HOUSE, (Thos. Hamilton, pro.,) Division opp Abeel.
Hamilton James, h Division cor Rogers.
Hamilton Jesse, farmer, St. James n E Front.
Hamilton Peter, supt. livery, bds Hamilton House.
Hamilton Robert, livery, bds Hamilton House.
Hamilton Thomas, (Hamilton House,) Division opp Abeel.
Hammond Edward, boatman, h DeWitt.
Hammond J. D., boatman, h Lucas av.

Undergarments, 5 Wall St., Kingston.

Hammond Thomas, laborer, h DeWitt.
Hammond William, Mrs., h Ann cor Union.
Hanaford A., mason, h Mill.
Hanna David, carpenter, h Greenkill av.
Hannly James, Mrs., h Hanraty n Point rd.
Hannon James, laborer, h Catherine cor Tompkins.
Hanratty F., dry goods, Division n Mill, h Division cor Rogers.
Hardenbergh Charles, bookkeeper, h Pierpont n Hone.
Hardenbergh Jacob, Mrs., h Crown cor John.
Hardenbergh T. R., printer, Journal office.
HARGRAVES JAMES, ale brewer, Wilbur Plank rd h do.
Hargraves John, birch beer manuf., h Greenkill av n Prospect.
Hargraves Joseph, carpenter, h Cedar cor Prospect.
Hargraves Robert, laborer, h Henry n Sterling.
HARLEY W. H. G., hairdresser, Fair n John, h Bowery bet E Front and Furnace.
Harlow Wm. P., printer, h Union av n opp Cedar.
Harman Thomas, engineer, h Union n Post.
Harmon James, laborer, h Chambers.
Harney Barney, h Division cor Meadow.
Harney Patrick, boatman, h Hanraty n Point rd.
Harper W. H., captain, h Abruyn opp Church.
Harris E. Mrs., h Hurley av.
Harris E. H., laborer, h Liberty n Furnace.
Harris Jacob, tailor, h Grand cor Esther.
Harris M. L., laborer, h Greenkill av.
Harris Wm., oysters, &c., h Hasbrouck av n Stuyvesant.
Harris Wm., oysters, Ulster Market.
Harrison Frank, h Pierpont n School House.
Harrison John, h Pine n Hudson.

J. O. & G. B. MERRITT, Cloths and

operative Plan at H. ROOSA'S Agency, Rondout.

Hart Abram, laborer, h Ten Brœck av n Downs.
Hart G. A., (Benson & H.) h Fair n Bowery.
Hart William, laborer, h Point.
Harvers Jacob, painter, h Cross n R. R.
Harvey James, laborer, h Lackawana.
Hasbrouck Abram, clerk, bds Garden and Mill.
Hasbrouck A. Bruyn, Hon., Green n John.
Hasbrouck Alexander, h Van Buren n Prospect.
Hasbrouck Alfred H., printer, Daily Freeman.
Hasbrouck Augustus, (Hasbrouck Bros.,) h Rogers n Wurts.
Hasbrouck Augustus, painter, h Union av n St. James.
HASBROUCK BROTHERS, grocers, Columbus av ab Tompkins.
Hasbrouck B. M. Mrs., h Crown n John.
Hasbrouck C., farmer, h Greenkill av n Prospect.
Hasbrouck David S., night ed., h Union av cor Chestnut.
Hasbrouck Frank, clerk, h Crown n John.
Hasbrouck George W., clerk, bds Union n Wurts.
Hasbrouck Henry, blacksmith, h Fair cor Bowery.
Hasbrouck Jacob, cement maker, h Oak cor Bowery.
Hasbrouck J. D., h Union av cor Chestnut.
Hasbrouck Jansen, banker, h Garden & Mill.
Hasbrouck J. M., clerk, bds Union av cor Chestnut.
Hasbrouck Jerry, clerk, bds Prospect n St. James.
Hasbrouck Jacob M., county treas., John n Wall.
Hasbrouck J. H., carpenter, h Cedar n Prospect.
Hasbrouck J. W., publisher, h Staple n Union av.
Hasbrouck Jonas Mrs., h Bowery n Furnace.
Hasbrouck W., engineer, h Flatbush av n Union av.
Hasbrouck W. L., (Hasbrouck Bros.,) h Union cor Chestnut.
Hasbrouck Mrs., h Pine, (Rondout.)

Cassimeres, No. 5 Wall St., Kingston.

Hase Philip, hats, &c., 35 N Front:
Hasenplaugh Jacob, laborer, h Hasbrouck av n Bridge.
Hassert William, h Abeel W of Wurts.
Hastings Stephen, laborer, h Catherine n Cedar.
Hathaway A. B. Mrs., h Wurts cor Rogers.
Hauck George, (D. Dressel & Co.,) h Holmes n Wurts.
Haulenbeek Tunis, carpenter, h Cedar n Union av.
Haulenbeek W. Scott, clerk, h 28 Wall.
Hauver M., (Kingston Hotel,) Crown bet John and N Front.
Havey Peter H., teamster, h Union av n O'Neil.
Hawkins A., sash and blinds, h Cedar n Union av.
Hawkins Wm. H., painter, h Newkirk av n Chambers.
Hayden Mary, Mrs., saloon, Union av opp Cedar.
Hayden Patrick, teacher, h Chambers n Union.
Hayden Thomas, mason, h Union n Division.
Hayden William, mason, h 4 Union av.
Hayes Augustus, Mrs., h Hone n Holmes.
Hayes A., laborer, h Washington av n N Front.
Hayes George W., clerk, Wall cor N Front.
Hayes John, butcher, Division ab Union, h do.
Hayes M. G., lawyer, h Pierpont n Holmes.
Hayes O., clerk, h Albany av cor Union av.
Hayes Thomas, bds Albany av opp Maiden Lane.
Hayes W. M., (Masten & H.,) h Albany av n Tremper.
Hazzard David, h Cottage Hill, Wilbur.
Hazzard Wm. H., clerk, h Abeel n Wurts.
Healey Emory, carriage maker, h Union av cor St. James.
Healey James, boatman, h Newkirk av n Division.
Heaney James, laborer, h Hanraty n Ravine.
Heaney John, laborer, h Hanraty n Ravine.
Heany Timothy, laborer, h Chambers cor Cross.
Hear Peter A., bar tender, Union Hotel.

Real Estate Agency, Rondout, N. Y.

KINGSTON DIRECTORY. 105

Hearney Mary Mrs., h Meadow n Ann.
Heath E. S., teamster, h Tremper av n Elmendorf.
Heath S. L., physician, Elmendorf n Union av.
Hebert Joseph, h Dederick n Union av.
Hecker F. J., h Hunter n Ravine.
Hecklel Christian, laborer, h Ravine n R. R.
Heerbrandt Adolphus, h Union av n R. R.
Heffern Patrick, laborer, h Prospect n Union.
HEIMER S. J., hair worker, Division cor Union.
Heineman Frederick, butcher, Garden n Ferry, h do.
Heiser J. A., clerk, E Front n John.
Heiser Oliver, carpenter, bds Bowery n Furnace.
Heiz Adam, h Dederick n Union av.
Heitzman S., laborer, h Old Wilbur rd.
Helion John, h Division cor Union.
Hendricks Abram, clerk, h Main n Wall.
Hendricks Isaac P., clerk, 7 Wall.
Hendricks J. E., carpenter, h Fair n St. James.
Hendricks J. P., h Elmendorf n Bruyn.
Hendricks R., laborer, h Pine.
Hendricks Wm. H., boots and shoes, 3 Wall, h Green cor Main.
Henion Frank, laborer, h Second av n R. R.
Henion DeWitt, teamster, h Livingston.
HENKE MARTIN, boots and shoes, Union av cor Cedar, h do.
Hennessy Thomas, laborer, h Cross n Ann.
Henry Frederick, h Spring ab Ravine.
Henry George, h Union n Hone.
Henry James, h Abeel.
Herb Daniel, laborer, h Hasbrouck av ab Garden.
Herbig Edward, hair dresser, Main n Eagle Hotel, h do.
Herdman Eliza Mrs., h Point rd n Livingston.
Herdman Eliza Mrs., h n toll gate.

Blankets, No. 5 Wall St., Kingston.

Losses Equitably Adjusted and Promptly Paid

HERDMAN JAS. Jr., blacksmith, Washington av cor N Front, h Hurley av.
Herdman J. E., clerk, Wall cor N Front.
Herkart F. J., tailor, bds Greenkill av n Union av.
Herkart L., harness maker, Abeel n Ravine h do.
Herley Corn. Mrs., h Hasbrouck av n Garden.
Herman Frederick, h Ravine opp Pine.
Hermance H. L., (H., Newton & Co.,) h Union av n St. James.
Hermance Jacob E., milk, h Adams n Pierpont.
Hermance L. N., Mrs., h Maiden la cor Fair.
HERMANCE, NEWTON & CO., iron founders, St. James cor Prospect.
Hermance O., confectioner,&c., 1 and 2 Music Hall,h do.
Hermance W. W., (H., Newton & Co.,) h Maiden la cor Fair.
Herrick Austin, foreman, h Elmendorf n R. R.
Herrick Daniel, carpenter, h Esther.
Herrick William, laborer, h Point rd.
Herrold Jacob, junk, &c., Garden opp Ferry, h do.
Herrold Max, junk, Dock, h do.
Hesler S., farmer, h Ten Brœck av n O'Neil.
Hess M. J. Mrs., grocer, Ravine n Hasbrouck av, h do.
Hessert E., tabacconist, John cor Fair, h do.
Hessian Michael, laborer, h Union n Wurts.
Hester S. W., (C. M. O'Neil & Co.,) h Green n N Front.
Hetzel John, constable, h German n Ridge.
Hewitt E. S., clerk, Wall, cor N. Front.
HEYBRUCH F., lock and gunsmith, sewing machine repairer, &c., Hasbrouck av n Garden, h do.
Heyser Henry, laborer, h Grand n Esther.
Hibbard G. B., book-keeper, h Spring n Wurts.
Hickey Anna Mrs., h Ann ab Union.

J. O. & G. B. MERRITT, Notions and

At HIRAM ROOSA'S Agency, Rondout, N. Y.

Hickey Thomas, h Abeel W. of Wurts.
Hieber George, laborer, h Cottage n Point rd.
Hiems Hiram, tailor, h 47 Division.
Higgins C. A., Mrs., bds Abcel cor Wurts.
Higgins J., teamster, h Bowery cor Oak.
Higgins James, mason, h Prospect cor Union.
Higgins Michael, h Hone ab Hunter.
Higgins Thomas Mrs., h Ann cor Mill.
Hildron Charles, cooper, h Cottage, cor Point rd.
Hildebrand Conrad, h Hudson.
Hildesheimer Samuel, upholsterer, h Union n Wurts.
Hill D. H., hackman, h 19 N Front.
Hill Gideon, lawyer, Main n E Front, h do.
Hill R. H., h Union av n Elmendorf.
Hill William D., h N Front n Green.
Hill William, agent, h Green cor John.
Hiller Edward, laborer, h Point rd n Livingston.
Hillis Joseph, boatman, h Abeel.
Hillis Margaret, h Ravine cor Pine.
Hillis Samuel, h Pine n Hudson.
HILTBRANT C., boat builder, Abeel n Hudson.
Hillyer James, carpenter, h Cottage n Point rd.
Hines John, barber, Abeel n Hone.
Hinnagan John, laborer, h Union.
Hinsberger N., laborer, h German n Ravine.
Hirsch Isaac, junk, h Hone n Hunter.
Hirschberg M., saloon, Division ab Mansion House, h Lackawanna.
Hoag J. B., police, h Jarrold n Ravine.
Hoar Friend Jr., lawyer, Savings Bank Building, bds Crown cor. John.
Hoar Thomas, laborer, h Newkirk av near DuBois av.
Hoe John, laborer, h Ann cor Union.
Hoes Aaron, grocer, Point rd cor First av.

Trimmings, No. 5 Wall St., Kingston.

HIRAM ROOSA'S Insurance Agency has

Hoes John C. F., Rev. D. D., h Pearl n Fair.
Hoevenburgh Charles, h Union av n St James.
Hoffman Abram Mrs., h N Front cor Green.
Hoffman Charles, brewer, h Mason n Hone.
Hoffman Hiram, farmer, h Green n N. Front.
Hoffman Jacob, h Abeel W of Wurts.
Hoffman John, laborer, h Chambers n Ravine.
Hoffman Luther, salesman, h Mapleton.
Hoffman Peter, carman, h Ravine cor Chambers.
Hoffman Walter, farmer, h N Front cor Green.
Hogan Lawrence, h Division cor Cross.
Hogan P. A., hostler, h Washington av n Depot.
Hogan Patrick, laborer, h Abeel.
Hollahan James Mrs., h Union cor Division.
Holle Casper, barber, Rondout House.
Holley & Shelden, confectioners &c., Lackwanna.
Holly Hanson, barber h Bowery n Furnace.
Hollinger R., bds Albany av opp Maiden la.
Hollingsworth Samuel, h Pine n Hudson.
Holmes Frederick, h Green cor Pearl av.
Holmes Hiram, h Washington av n N Front.
Holmes Jacob, laborer, h Martin's la.
Holmes M. G., clerk, bds Pierpont W of Wurts.
Holmes Wm., dry goods, &c., Washington av. cor Hurley av., h 46 N Front.
Holsapple Henry, h Division opp Rogers.
Holsapple Van Ness, bar-tender, h Smith av n Garden.
Holstein Henry, laborer, h Newkirk av n Hasbrouck av
Holt E. D., clerk, h Henry cor Prospect.
Holt T. M., cabinet maker, h Cedar n Union av.
Holt William T., recording clerk, bds Fair n N Front.
Hommel Egbert, with S. & W. B. Fitch, h Burnett, (Wilbur.)
Hommel Ludwig, h Ravine n R. R.

J. O. & G. B. MERRITT, Dry Goods and

Never had any Disputed Claims.

Hommel M., h Burnett, (Wilbur.)
Hommel P. E., (M., H. & D.,) h Green n N Front.
HOORNBEEK L. D. & CO., commission merchants, wholesale grocers, &c., Ferry.
Hoornbeek L. D., (L. D. Hoornbeek & Co.,) h Abeel bet Division and Wurts.
Hopkins J. D., livery and cigars, Hurley av n Washington av, h do.
Hopper & Romer, grocers, Dock.
Hopper C. R., (H. & R.,) h Union av n City Hall.
Hopper E., gardener, h Wall cor St. James.
Hopper Robert, h Wall cor St. James.
Hopper William, shoemaker, John n Wall, h do.
Horn S., peddler, h Abeel n Hone.
Hornbeck Bonjamin, cigar maker, bds Humphrey's Hotel.
Hornbeck J. J., horse trainer, h E Front n Henry.
Horan C., stable boss, bds Hamilton House.
Horton Charles, laborer, h Tompkins n Columbus av.
Horvers & Cousins, painters, Division cor Lackawanna.
Horvers J., (H. & Cousins,) h Cross n Hasbrouck av.

HOTALING C. M.,

bill poster and expressman, Wynkoop's Store, Wall, h Bruyn n O'Neil.
Hotaling Chauncey, painter, h Livingston n Hasbrouck av.
Houghtaling C. I., carpenter, h Bowery n E Front.
Houghtaling E., butcher, Liberty cor Furnace, h do.
Houghtaling Edward, bar tender, City Hotel.
Houghtaling Edward, printer, Daily Freeman.
Houghtaling H., (Jones & H.,) h Pearl S of Green.
Houghtaling Ira, cigar agent, bds Sutton House.

Carpets, No. 5 Wall St., Kingston.

Your best interest will dictate to Insure with

Houghtaling R. E., carpenter, O'Neil n Union av, h opp do.
Houghtaling Theodore, painter, bds Bowery n E Front.
Houghtaling W. E., supt., h Flatbush av n Prince.
Houghtaling Wesley, laborer, h Henry n Union av.
Houck George, brewer, h Holmes n Adams.
Housen Joseph, clerk, bds Adams.
Howard Mary, h Division cor Cross.
Howard Michael, h Pierpont n School House.
Howard P., hostler, Hamilton House.
Howard Patrick, h Division cor Newkirk av.
Howley Patrick, h Dock.
Hoysradt Francis M., bookkeeper, h Chestnut n Division.
Hubbard R. C., clerk, h Liberty n Union av.
Huber John, saloon, Division ab Union, h do.
Huber J. J., tailor, h Pine n Ravine.
Huber John, clerk, bds German cor Ridge.
Huber N. Mrs., h German cor Ridge.
Huber Peter, clerk, h German cor Ridge.
Hudler Alfred, (M. & H.,) h Cottage Hill, Wilbur.
Hudler Edgar, gas, h Wurts cor Rogers.
Hudler J. H., captain, h Elmendorf n R. R.
Hudler Thomas, boatman, h Ten Brœck av c Elmendorf.
Hudson Henry, h Hone cor Hunter.
Hudson M. Mrs., h Ravine n Hasbrouck av.
Hughes John, saloon, Hunter n Abeel, h do.
Hughes J., h Abeel n Ravine.
Huguenot, saloon, confectionery, &c., Fair n Main.
HUHNE AUG., physician, Abeel opp Wurts, h do.
Hulbert N. R., clerk, Post Office.
Hulbert O. H., h Lucas av.
HULL CONRAD, saloon, Washington av n Hurley av, h do.

J. O. & G. B. MERRITT, Black Silks at

HIRAM ROOSA, Agent at Rondout, N. Y.

Hull John R., butcher, h 108 N Front.
Hull S. T., lawyer, John n Wall, bds Green n John.
Hulse J. E., sewing machines, h Mapleton.
Hultzer John, h Garden n Flatbush av.
HUME R. B. & J W., grocers, &c., 52 N Front.
Hume R. B., (R. B. & J. W. Hume,) h Crown n N Front.
Hume J. W., (R. B. & J. W. Hume,) h 48 N Front.
Humes Catherine, h Washington av n Depot.
Hummal Christian, cooper, h Ravine n Point rd.
Humphrey A., (J. F. Brower & Co.,) h Washington av n Depot.
Humphrey Furry P., tel. oper., bds Hamilton Hotel.
Humphrey H., (pro. Humphrey's Hotel,) Washington av n R. & O. R. R.
Hunt Alonzo, carpenter, h E Front n St. James.
Hunt Lorenzo, carpenter, bds E Front n St. James.
Hunt Orlando, carpenter, h E Front n St. James.
Hurley Jeremiah, laborer, h Mapleton.
Hurley M., laborer, h DeWitt.
Hurvies John, painter, h Newkirk av n Chambers.
HUSSEY JOHN, hats, caps, trunks, &c., Division cor Garden, h Adams n Pierpont.
Hussey John, h Garden n Ferry.
Hutchings E. E., h Abeel W of Wurts.
Hutchingson John, laborer, h Cross n Division.
HUTCHINSON R. W., dentist, 12 Wall.
Hutton Alexander, miner, h Ravine n Point rd.
Hutton Alexander Jr., boatman, h Ravine n Point rd.
Hutton Joseph, capt., h Hasbrouck av n Union.
Hutton James, laborer, h Ravine n Point rd.
Hutton J. Jr., grocer, Columbus av, h Union cor Prospect.
Hutton John, h 45 Division.

Bargains, No. 5 Wall St., Kingston.

If not convenient to call, send your application by

HUTTON WM., lumber, &c., Columbus av N of
  Tompkins, h Chestnut.
HYATT S. M., lime manufacturer, South Rondout.
Hyde Fannie, h 34 Garden.
Hyde Julius, h Pierpont opp School House.
HYLAND JOHN, blacksmith, Wilbur, h do.
Hyland William, saloon, Division opp Rogers.
Hysier John, clerk, h E Front n John.

INGALLS F. W., homeophatic physician, Fair n Main,
  h Union av cor Bowery.
Ingle T., teamster, h Pine n Wilbur Plank rd.
Ingram A. Mrs., h John cor Fair.
Ingraham J. L. S. Mrs., h Wall n St. James.
Irwin Michael, laborer, h Columbus av.
Isaac P., tailor, h Post cor Union.
Israel Adolph, book keeper, bds Hone cor German.

JACOBS JOSEPH, clothier, 38 Garden, h do.
Jacobs Marks, mer. tailor, 22 Garden, h do.
Jacoby C., laborer, h German n Ravine.
Jackson George, h Maiden Lane n Pine.
Jackson J. G., painter, h Main n Wall.
Jackson James H., steward, h Union n Staple.
Jackson M. Mrs., h Chester n Union av.
Jackson Wm. M., painter, h Prospect n Liberty.
Jalley John Mrs., h Cedar n Union av.
James S., hats, &c., Division ab Garden, h Abeel n
  Wurts.
James W. L. Rev., h Wall n St. James.

JANSEN ANDREW E.,
  druggist, E Front cor Albany av, h Crown next
  Kingston Hotel.

J. O. & G. B. MERRITT, Black Alpacas

Mail to HIRAM ROOSA, Insur. Agent, Rondout.

Jansen Harry, clerk, bds Crown next Kingston Hotel.
Jaques E. A., bookkeeper, h Abruyn n Columbus av.
Jarman James B., cigar maker, h St. James n Prospect.
Jarrold Ernest, printer, h Wurts cor Holmes.
Jarrold George, carpenter, &c., h Jarrold n Ravine.
Jaycocks T., harness, &c., 10 N Front, h Hurley av.
Jeager Henry, bds Albany av opp Maiden la.
Jennings J. W., h Maiden la cor Fair.
Jenson L. B. Mrs., h Fair n N Front.
Jockel T., milk, h Meadow n Chambers.
Johns Joseph, laborer, h Ravine n Point rd.
Johnson B., h Wilbur.
Johnson B., (F. & Johnson,) h Washington av n Depot.
Johnson C., boatman, h Hasbrouck av n Newkirk av.
Johnson Charles D., mate, h Fair cor Bowery.
Johnson Dennis, h Pierpont ab Ravine.
Johnson Frank, laborer, h O'Neil cor Bruyn.
Johnson James H., blacksmith, h Prospect n Liberty.
Johnson Mary A. Mrs., h Spring n Hone.
Johnson Michael, laborer, h Ravine n Vine.
Johnson Mrs., h Esther.
Johnson Peter, h Pierpont ab Ravine.
Johnson Thomas, butcher, h St. James opp Green.
Johnson William, h Pierpont ab Ravine.
Johnson William, laborer, h Newkirk av n Division.
Johnston Benjamin, carpenter, h Russell.
Johnston Daniel, harness, &c., 9 Wall, h Wall cor Maiden Lane.
Johnston Daniel, trimmer, h St. James n Union av.
Johnston George, clerk, bds Russell n Spring.
Johnston John, h Russell.
Johnston John J., h Spring n Ravine.

*10

and Brilliantines, 5 Wall St., Kingston.

Insure with no other Agent.

JOHNSTON THERON, liquors, &c., Fair cor N Front,
 h N Front opp Crown.
Johnston T. B., butcher, h St. James hd Green.
JOHNSTON THOMAS L., butcher, John n Wall, h
 St. James hd Green.
Johnston William, h Spring n Ravine.
Jones & Houghtaling, shoemakers, Crown n N Front.
Jones E. Mrs., h Hone n Abeel.
Jones H. H., (J. & H.,) h Green n John.
Jones James, mason, h O'Neil n Union av.
Jones John, cook, h Ann n Meadow.
Jones J. H., supt. W. V. R. Co., h Goshen.
Jones John R., clerk, h Orchard av.
JONES R. & CO., grocer, livery, &c., Ravine n Abeel.
Jones R., (R. Jones & Co.,) h Abeel cor Hudson.
Jones Wm. H., h Division n Spring.
Jordan Andrew, laborer, h Meadow n Ann.
Jordan B. Mrs., h Rogers n Adams.
Jordan Charles, laborer, h Ann n Union.
Joson John, h Pierpont opp Russell.
Joson Michael, h Pierpont opp Russell.
Joy J., baker, &c., Bowery cor Furnrce, h E Front n
 Liberty.
Joy S., foreman, h Washington av n N Front.
Joy Stilwell, Rondout ticket agent, h Elmendorf n
 Union av.
Joy Wm. H., farmer, h Joy's la.

KAFNEY JOHN, h Division n Spring.
Kaley Michael, h Division cor Cross.
Kamp M., h Pierpont cor Russell.
Kane Daniel, laborer, h Garden n Ferry.
Kane James, laborer, h Ann n Union.
Kane P., clerk, bds Ann n Meadow.

J. O. & G. B. MERRITT, Choice Dress

HIRAM ROOSA, Gen'l Ins. Agent, Rondout, N. Y.

Kane S., cooper, h Vine.
Katty Benjamin, h Hunter n Ridge.
Katz William, junk, h St. Mary,
Kavana B., h Wilbur.
Kavanaugh Thomas, laborer, h Chambers n Ravine.
Kealy Richard, laborer, h Meadow n Ann.
Kean Frederick, laborer, h Point rd n R. R.
Keanan Michael, laborer, h Ann n Mill.
Keanan Daniel, laborer, h Ann cor Union.
Kearnan Francis, h Garden and Ferry.
Kearnan James, laborer, h Ann n Union.
Kearnan Owen, laborer, h Ann n Union.
Kearnan Patrick, laborer, h Ann cor Union.
Kearnes James, mason, h Livingston.
Kearnes M., laborer, h Livingston.
Kearney E., book keeper, bds Smith, (Wilbur.)
Kearney John, blacksmith, h Oak n Bowery.
Kearney M., undertaker, h Lucas av.
Kearney John, captain, h Meadow n Chambers.
Keating M. J., clerk, h Cedar n Union.
Keating Wm., laborer, h Second av n R. R.
Keator C., h E Front n John.
KEATOR D. P., grocer, &c., St. James n Prospect, h do.
Keator Edward, h Pierpont ab Ravine.
Keator J. G., clerk, bds John cor Green.
Keble Frederick, tailor, h Dederick n Union av.
Kechner William, h Division ab Union.
Keegan Michael, laborer, h Ann cor Union.
Keeffan Daniel, laborer, h Mill n Prospect.
Keefe A. J., clerk, N Front cor Crown.
Keefe John, foreman, bds Cross n Ann.
Keefe Mary, Mrs., h Cross n Ann.
Keefer Myron, fireman, h Hasbrouck av n Point rd.
KEELAR T., auction and commission, 23 Garden,
    bds Mansion House.

Goods, No. 5 Wall St., Kingston.

HIRAM ROOSA'S Accidental, Life, Fire, Marine

Keeley Peter, laborer, h Ann n Meadow.
Keier Frederick, tailor, h Hunter n Hone.
Keirghry John, cooper, h Abeel.
Kelch Wm., saloon, Abeel n Ravine, h do.
Kelder Brothers, livery, &c., 48 Wall.
Kelder Henry, (Kelder Bros.,) Wall cor St. James.
Kelder Peter, (Kelder Bros.,) h Wall cor St. James.
KELLER K. F., jeweler, Abeel n Division, h Division opp Abeel.
Kelley Wm., clerk, bds Fair cor John.
KELLY & CLOONAN, butchers, Division ab Union.
Kelly B., h Ravine n Hasbrouck av.
Kelly E., watchman, h Greenkill av n Prospect.
Kelly E. H., engineer, h O'Reilly n Union av.
Kelly H., laborer, h St. Mary.
Kelly James, cooper, h Cordts.
Kelly James, teamster, Wall cor N Front.
Kelly John W., h Pierpont ab Ravine.
Kelly John, cooper, Prince n Grand, h Union av bel Grand.
Kelly Michael, mason, h Chambers n Union.
Kelly Michael, laborer, h DeWitt.
Kelly M., boatman, h Meadow n Chambers.
Kelly Philip, (Kelly & C.,) h Division ab Union.
Kelly Patrick H., cooper, h Garden cor Prince.
Kelly Patrick, tailor, h Hasbrouck av n Union.
Kelly Thomas, h Division ab Holmes.
Kelly William, h Chambers n Union.
Kelly William C., cooper, h Union av bel Grand.
Kempt Martin, shoemaker, h Pierpont.
Kennedy D., physician, Garden cor Hasbrouck av, h Pierpont n Wurts.
Kennedy Michael, laborer, h Chambers n Union.
Kennedy Thomas, conductor, h Second av n R. R.

J. O. & G. B. MERRITT, Kid Gloves,

Insurance and Real Estate Agency, Rondout, N. Y.

Kenny Michael, h Abeel.
Kenny K., laborer, h DeWitt.
Kenny Michael, laborer, h Ravine n R. R.
Kenny Philip, seaman, h Cross n Division.
Kent W. J., marble yards, Division n opp Rogers.
Kenyon Patrick, laborer, h Henry n Prospect.
Kenyon W. S., lawyer, Savings Bank Building.
Kenyon W. S. Jr., (Parker & K.,) h Fair n Bowery.
Kenyon Wm., saloon, Washington av n Depot, h do.
Kepar Frietz, carpenter, h O'Reilly n Union av.
Kerley J., dry goods, &c., 4 Mansion House Building, h Hasbrouck av cor Union.
Kermode Edward, mason, h Dederick n Union av.
Kermode Henry, mason, h Union av opp Cedar.
Kernan John, blacksmith, bds Metzger's Hotel.
Kerney M., cabinet maker, h Lucas av.
Kernske Frederick, h Ann ab Union.
Kerr Charles, dept. sheriff, h Court House.
Kerr George A., clerk, h Abeel n Wurts.
KERR JOHN W., sheriff, h Court House.
Kerr R. W., flour, feed, &c., Hasbrouck av ab Garden, h Albany av.
Kerr Wm. F., deputy sheriff, h Green cor John.
Kerr William, Mrs., h N Front cor Green.
Kessler A., saloon, Dock, h do.
Kessel J., h Pierpont n School House.
Ketterer Andrew, harness maker, h Union av c Cedar.
KEYSER DANIEL E., lawyer, John n Wall, h St. James n Pine.
Keyser H. D. W., real estate, John n Wall, h St. James n Pine.
Keyser Jacob, teamster, h Taylor.
Keyser J. D., physician, Fair opp Post Office, h St. James n Pine.

No. 5 Wall Street, Kingston.

HIRAM ROOSA'S Agency represents a Combined

Keyes Theodore, carman, Dederick n Union av.
Kidd John, h Wilbur.
Kieffer N. Mrs., h John n E Front.
Kiere August, laborer, h Hasbrouck av n Point rd.
Kiernan Charles, clerk, bds Union E of Chambers.
Kiernan E., (Cummings & K.,) h Hurley av.
Kierstead Wm. H., clerk, h Union av n R. R.
Kilroy T., butcher, Columbus av n Prospect, h do.
Kimbark George, teamster, h Henry n Sterling.
King C. M. & Bro., ship builders, Kingston Point.
King Chas. M., carpenter, h Abruyn n Chestnut.
King J. N., mate, h Prospect n Union.
King John, laborer, h Pierpont n Holmes.
King William, carpenter, h Ponkhockie n Chestnut.
Kingsburg H., peddler, h Union cor Division.
KINGSBURG W. H. Rev., prin. Hillside Seminary, Greenkill av.
KINGSTON ARGUS, (H. G. Crouch, ed.,) 29 Wall.
KINGSTON HOTEL, (M. Hauver, pro.,) Crown bet John and N Front.
KINGSTON JOURNAL, (Romeyn & Son, eds., &c.,) 33 and 35 Wall.
KINGSTON NATIONAL BANK, Main cor Fair.
KINGSTON PRESS, (D. Bradbury, ed. and pro.,) 30 Wall.
Kipp C. H. Mrs., h Hasbrouck av n Meadow.
Kirchner J. C., clerk, bds Abeel cor Ravine.
Kirchner John, h Hunter n Hone.
Kirchner J. P., h Newkirk av n Hasbrouck av.
KIRCHNER L., groceries, crockery, boots and shoes, Abeel cor Ravine, h do.
Kirchner Peter, teamster, h Post cor Union.
Kirchner W. C., clerk, clerk, bds Abeel cor Ravine.
Kirsch John, tailor, Division opp Rogers.

J. O. & G. B. MERRITT, Gent's

Kirtland H. G., h DeWitt.
Kiser Silas, saloon, Union av n Liberty, h do.
Klauser John, laborer, h Union av cor Cedar.
Klauser Louis, mason, h Union av cor Cedar.
Kleiglein Peter, saloon, Wilbur.
Klein M., veterineary surgeon, h Union n Flatbush.
KLEISNER J., music store, Mill, h do.
Kline John, (pro. Wilbur Hotel,) Wilbur.
Kline J. P., bookkeeper, h Hone n Pierpont.
Klingel P. C., cigar maker, bds Hurley av.
Knab John, h Ravine n Hunter.
KNAPP E. W., druggist, Garden next P. O., h Chestnut cor Wells.
Knapp Jerome, stone cutter, h Bowery n Union av.
Knapp John, carpenter, h Hunter.
Knetch Theodore, h Division ab Union.
Knight John, h Columbus av N of Tompkins.
Knoche John, foreman, h Prince n Union av.
Koanar Henry, upholsterer, h 14 N Front.
Koch Chas., harness manufac., Union av n Cedar, h do.
Kolts Frank, laborer, h Flatbush av n Hasbrouck av.
Kolts Harmon, laborer, h Flatbush av.
Kolts Henry, carriage manufac., Flatbush av cor Hasbrouck av, h opp do.
Koons Anthony, brewer, h Chambers n Ravine.
Kraft J. E., printer, Daily Freeman.
Kraus John, saloon, Point rd cor Livingston.
Krauser Wm., saloon, Union av bel St. James, h do.
Krauser Wm., (Davidson & K.,) bds Union av n St. James.
Krieger Henry, grocer, &c., German cor Ridge, h do.
Kronnick Fred., carpenter and builder, Cedar n Union av, h n do.
Krouse Andrew, laborer, h Point rd n Union av.

Furnishing Goods, 5 Wall St., Kingston.

Krould Peter, laborer, h Third n Elm.
Krum A., stone cutter, h E Front n Cedar.
Krum C. B. Mrs., h Wall n Bowery.
Krum Morgan, carpenter, h Wall n Bowery.
Kuhn F. W., butcher, h Maiden la n Albany av.
Kukuk Henry, mason, h Jerrold n Point rd.
Kumly Jeremiah, salesman, h Garden n Hasbrouck av.

LAFEVER JOSEPH, watchman, h Third av n Elm.
LaFever W., cooper, h Prospect cor Union.
Lafferty John, laborer, h Prospect cor Union.
Laflin & Rand, keg manuf., Jacob's Valley.
LaForge C. Mrs., h Green n Pearl av.
Lahe Morris, captain, h Wilbur.
Lahe Thomas, Mrs., h Wilbur.
Lake John, H., baker, bds 10 Garden.
Lake W. T., physician, Washington av n Depot.
Lamsdorf Andrew, laborer, h Third av n Point rd.
Lamsdorf N., laborer, h Third av n R. R.
Lambertson Charles, mason, h Hasbrouck av n Point rd.
Lanco John, laborer, h Pine n Ravine.
Landing William, bar tender, Western Hotel.
Lane Richard, h Wilbur.
Lane Susan, Miss, bds junc. Green and Crown.
Lang C., blacksmith, Abeel, h Hunter.
Lang Fred., carpenter, bds Newkirk av n Chambers.
Lang Herman, laborer, h Second av R. R.
Lang John, laborer, h Newkirk av n Chambers.
Langan Martin, contractor, h Division ab Union.
LANGAN PATRICK, grocer, Division ab Union.
Langan Thomas, boatman, h Division ab Union.
Langan Thomas, laborer, h Cedar n Union.
Langan Thomas, shoemaker, Meadow n Chambers, h do.
Langendikhoof Otto, laborer, h Esther, cor Grand.

of all kinds. Rondout, N. Y.

Lansing Patrick, h Third n Elm.
Lape Frank, teamster, h Bowery cor Furnace.
Larkin Joseph, boatman, h Ravine n Ann.
Larkin Matthew, boatman, h Ravine n Ann.
LARKIN MATTHEW, Jr., groceries and liquors, 15 Ferry, h Union E of Chambers.
Larkin Michael, laborer, h Union cor Chambers.
Larkin Michael, mason, h Chambers n Union.
Larkin Michael, Jr., clerk, bds Chambers cor Union.
LARKIN M. H., groceries, liquors, &c., Division cor Meadow, h Ann n Meadow.
Larkin Thomas, laborer, h Ann n Union.
Larkin T., mason, h Cross n Chambers.
Larsen C., (G. & Larsen,) h Ann n Mill.
Larter John A., paymaster, h Chestnut n Division.
Lasher George, agent, bds 24 Wall.
Lasher R., butcher, h Washington av n N Front.
Lasher Wm., butcher, h Lucas av.
Lasher Wm. H., butcher, Main n E Front, h Lucas av.
Lasher Mrs., h E Front cor Henry.
Latimer J. H., mason, h Fair n Bowery.
Latin Richard, cooper, h Hone cor Union.
Latting Wm. W., laborer, h Prospect cor Bowery.
Lauber Theodore, clerk, bds Excelsior House.
Laubmeister Wm., cooper, h Ann ab Meadow.
Lauders J. Mrs., h German n Ridge.
Lauson Christian, painter, h Ann n Union.
Lavel Thomas, h Spring ab Ravine.
Lawless Michael, sexton, h Garden ab Prince.
Lawrence Andrew, h Hunter n Hone.
Lawrence E. G., (Crosby, M. & Co.,) bds Maiden la, bet Pine and Fair.
Lawrence H. W., sewing machines, 24 Wall, h do.
LAWTON & STEBBINS, lawyers, Garden cor Division.

Hosiery, No. 5 Wall St., Kingston.

Get an Accidental Policy at

Lawton Wm., (L. & Stebbins,) h Chestnut n Division.
Lay C., butcher, h Hasbrouck av n R. R., h do.
Laycock W., druggist, 43 Division, h Spring n Hone.
Layman A., shoemaker, h Green n Pearl.
Learity Patrick, laborer, h Cedar n Union.
Leavranz Fritz, saloon, 80 Ann, h do.
Ledyard E. D., Rev., h Abeel n Wurts.
Lee Marvin, shoemaker, h Prospect n Liberty.
Lee R. Mrs., h E Front n St. James.
Lee Wm., laborer, h Cedar n Prospect.
Leete D. M., blacksmith, h Cedar n Mill.
LeFever Rufus, book keeper, bds Wilbur rd.
LeFever Silas, h E Front opp John.
LeFever Miss, dress maker, 5 Wall.
LeFevre Abby Miss, h Abeel n Pres. Church.
LeFevre Isaac, carriage maker, h Liberty n Prospect.
Legge William, carpenter, h Point rd.
Lenihan Patrick, laborer, h Livingston.
Lenox T. A., cigar maker, bds Kingston Hotel.
Leonard C. Mrs., h Dock.
Leonard C., laborer, h Hasbrouck av bel Garden.
Leonard Michael, clerk, h Post.
Leonard Thomas J., saloon, Dock n Ravine, h n do.
Levi A., clerk, bds Division ab Mill.
Levi Abram, tailor, h 64 N Front.
Levi B., junk, h Newkirk av n DuBois.
Levi George, junk, h Newkirk av n Hasbrouck av.
Levi H., janitor, Opera House.
Levi Louis, tailor, h Catherine n Hasbrouck av.
Levi Samuel, tailor, h Hunter.
Lewis E., stone yards, Wilbur rd, h Washington av
    cor Linderman av.
Lewis Edward, photographer, John cor Wall, h do.
Licke Frederick, laborer, h Ravine n R. R.

J. O. & G. B. MERRITT, Laces and

HIRAM ROOSA'S Agency, Rondout, N. Y.

Light E., captain, h E Front n Henry.
Linderman J. Mrs., h Green n Pearl.
Lindsley James G., mayor and agent N. L. & C. Mfg. Co., h Hasbrouck av opp Meadow.
Lines A., carpenter, h E Front n Bowery.
Liscomb George G., tobacconist, Garden and Ferry, h Hunter.
Litchfield William B., gen. manager, h Stuyvesant cor Livingston.
Little Samuel, tinsmith, h Cedar n Union av.
Livingston Mrs., h Manor Pl.
Lockwood A. L., stone, &c., h Fair cor Bowery.
Lockwood Philip N. D., stone, &c., Fair c Bowery, h do.
Lockwood Sarah, Mrs., h N Front n Wall.
Logan John, grocer, Wilbur, h do.
Long Anthony, laborer, h St. Mary.
Long Frank, laborer, h Ann n Meadow.
Long Thomas, laborer, h St. Mary n Chambers.
Long William, laborer, h Newkirk av n Chambers.
Longyear & Shultis, livery, &c., Fair N of John.
Longyear G., carpenter, Bruyn n Downs.
Longyear M., (L. & Shultis,) h Main n Fair.
Longyear Nelson, clerk, h Elmendorf n R. R.
Lontus Joseph, laborer, h Livingston.
Loran John B., h Division ab Pierpont.
Lord Charles, clerk, h Union av n Greenkill.
LOUGHRAN B., plumber and gas fitter, 106 N Front, bds 108 do.
Loughran Elbert H., physician, Fair N of John, h do.
LOUGHRAN ROBT., physician, Fair N of John, h do.
LOUNSBURY & DE WITT, lawyers, Savings Bank Building.
Lounsbury Wm., (L. & DeWitt,) h E Front n John.
Low A. M., boots and shoes, 19 Wall, h Maiden Lane n Pine.

Embroideries, No. 5 Wall St., Kingston.

Life Insurance on the Stock, Mutual or Co-

Low G. C., capt., h Ten Broeck av cor Downs.
Low James E., policeman, h Green n Pearl.
Low Wm. H., boatman, h Elmendorf n Ten Broeck av.
Low W. P., carman, h E Front n Henry.
Low Miss, h Green cor John.
Lowe Alonzo, clerk, Union av cor Flatbush av.
Lowe Andrew M., crockery, &c., h Abruyn n cor Chestnut.
Lowe Austin, carpenter, h Cedar n E Front.
Lowe Francis R., saloon, St. James opp Prospect, h St. James n Pine.
Lowe G. T., photographer, h Greenkill av n Prospect.
Lowe J. E. Jr., peddler, h Prospect cor Van Buren.
Lowe R. P. Mrs., h Union av n opp Cedar.
Lowe Wm. G., laborer, h Union av n Henry.
Lowell Frederick, laborer, h Livingston.
Lowerhouse C., barber, Ferry opp Canal, h Spring.
Lowne J. W., hostler, h Prospect n Bowery.
Ludlum J. W., h Hasbrouck cor Cottage.
Ludwig J., harness, &c., Division ab Abeel, h n op do.
Luft George, (R. Jones & Co.,) h Hunter.
Luft H., butcher, Abeel n Hone, h do.
Luft John, h Division cor Stuyvesant.
Lukenbach Jacob, weaver, h Hone cor Hunter.
Lundy Hugh, teamster, h Cedar n Union av.
Lundy Joseph, mason, h Henry n Union av.
Lundy William, mason, h Union av n Greenkill.
Lust John, barber, Division ab Abeel, h n opp do.
Luther H. B., stone cutter, h E Front cor Bowery.
LYDECKER A., fancy goods, &c., 9 Wall, h Bruyn av n Albany av.
Lyden Thomas, laborer, h Ann n Cross.
Lynch D., h Prospect cor Columbus av.
Lynch D., saloon, Dock, h do.

J. O. & G. B. MERRITT, Ladies'

operative Plan at H. ROOSA'S Agency, Rondout.

Lynch Hugh, laborer, h Meadow n Ann.
Lynch Joseph, h Division ab Cross.
Lynch Matthew, laborer, h Wilbur.
LYONS JOHN, harness, trunks, &c., 49 N Front, h Fair n St. James.
Lytle John, police, h Cedar n E Front.

McANDREW MICHAEL, laborer, h Powell Dock.
McAndrew Thomas, captain, h Henry.
McArdle E. clerk, bds Division cor Rogers.
McArthur Sarah, Mrs., h Ravine n Hunter.
McAvoy John, clerk, bds Ann n Meadow.
McBRIDE BARNEY, confectioner, Union av n O'Neil, h do.
McBride Michael, laborer, h Ann cor Union.
McBrien R., teamster, h O'Neil n R. R.
McCabe B., cooper, h Bowery n Pine.
McCabe James, clerk, bds Union n Wurts.
McCabe James, teacher, h Hasbrouck av n R. R.
McCabe L., boatman, h Abeel.
McCabe T., laborer, h Union n Post.
McCall B., h Wilbur.
McCanaan James, teamster, h Hasbrouck av n Flatbush av.
McCann Charles, mer. tailor, 80 N Front, h do.
McCardle James, h Wilbur.
McCarty Bridget, h Hudson.
McCaughy Felix, h Tompkins n Columbus av.
McCausland James, (J. & J. McC.,) h Hunter.
McCausland John, grocer, Division ab Abeel, h Hunter cor Ravine.
McCAUSLAND J. & J., ship builders, Wilbur rd.
McCausland Jefferson, (J. & J. McC.,) h Wilbur rd.
McCausland Jefferson Jr., book keeper, bds Wilbur rd.

*11

Undergarments, 5 Wall St., Kingston.

McCausland J. B., clerk, h Hunter.
McCawley P., h Division cor Meadow.
McCloskey M., shoemaker, Cedar n Catherine, h do.
McCloskey P., laborer, h Tompkins n Union.
McCloskey Patrick, laborer, h Newkirk av n Point rd.
McClung A., h Maiden Lane n Fair.
McClung Richard, painter, h Elmendorf n R. R.
McClure Thomas, laborer, h Pine n Ravine.
McCORMICK P., soap and candles, Division opp St. Mary's school, h do.
McCormick R. Mrs., h Prospect n Union.
McCormick Mrs., h Abeel W of Wurts.
McCreedy William, h Spring n Ravine.
McCue James, teacher, h Second av.
McCullough John, h Hone ab Hunter.
McCullough M. Mrs., h Washington av cor Taylor.
McCullough Robert, h German n Hone.
McCutchen James, laborer, h Union n Division.
McCutchen Patrick, laborer, h Union n Division.
McDermott B., gardener, h Cedar n Mill.
McDermott James, h Division n Spring.
McDermott Harry, laborer, bds Dock.
McDunnough John, laborer, h h Hanratty n Ravine.
McDunnough Michael, h Division ab Cross.
McDunnough, h Division ab Cross.
McElrath James, soap maker, bds Hamilton House.
McELROY WM. H., gun and locksmith, 63 N Front, h Crown n N Front.
McELROY W. H. Jr., saloon, 63 N Front, h Crown n N Front.
McElvare C. & M., clothiers, &c., Lackawanna, h do.
McElvare John, cutter, bds Lackawanna.
McEneaney Owen, basket maker, Division cor Cross.
McENTEE & DILLON, Rondout Iron Works, Garden. on the Dock.

Real Estate Agency, Rondout, N. Y.

McEntee Charles, h Chestnut n Division.
McEntee J., (McE. & Dillon,) h Chestnut.
McEntee James S., farmer, h Chestnut n Division.
McEntee M. W., local ed., h Weinberg.
McEvoy James, mason, h Liberty n Furnace.
McEvoy Joseph, carpenter, h Union n Cedar.
McEvoy Mary Mrs., h Abeel.
McGee F., laborer, h Catherine n Tompkins.
McGeeney James, laborer, h Abeel.
McGeeney John, boatman, h Rogers cor Adams.
McGeough P., clerk, bds Washington av n Depot.
McGerl Thomas, laborer, h Cross n Ann.
McGerrell Michael, laborer, h Union n Ann.
McGill Patrick, grocer, Division ab Holmes.
McGinna James, h Hudson.
McGinnis Patrick, laborer, h Meadow n R. R.
McGivney Patrick, grocer, Division ab Cross, h do.
McGoey B., laborer, h Chambers cor Cross.
McGouan Henry, carpenter, h Cedar n Sterling.
McGovern Frank, carman, h Hasbrouck av bel Garden.
McGovern Peter, laborer, h Van Deusen av.
McGovern Peter, laborer, h Flatbush av n Union av.
McGovern John, saloon, Wilbur.
McGowan James, h Division n Meadow.
McGrane M., laborer, h Columbus av n Prospect.
McGrath Julia Mrs., h Powell Dock.
McGrath M., laborer, h Union n Tompkins.
McGraw Dennis, h Division cor Cross.
McGuinnis William, farmer, h n O'Reilly.
McGuire B. Mrs., h Division ab Meadow.
McGuire Daniel, stone cutter, h Mapleton.
McGuire Patrick, laborer, h Taylor.
McGuire William, bar tender, Humphrey's Hotel.
McHugh Jas., teas, &c., Division opp Mill, h Third av.

Cassimeres, No. 5 Wall St., Kingston.

McIntyre James D., clerk, h Hurley av.
McIntyre S., tinsmith, N Front n Green.
McKee Barney, mason, h Post n Spring.
McKenzie H. E., lawyer, Main n Fair bds Eagle Hotel.
McKiernan James, carman, h Hasbrouck av n Flatbush av.
McKinley J. T., confectionery, h Holmes n Wurts.
McKinley William, mason, h Henry opp Oak.
McKeuen Ann, h Division ab Cross.
McKown C. W., book keeper, bds Union n Hasbrouck av.
McKown Milton, photographer, 12 Wall, h Bowery n Union av.
McKown Patrick, laborer, h Meadow n Ann.
McLoughlan Francis, surveyor, h Mason n Hone.
McLauney James, laborer, h Union cor Prospect.
McLaughlin James, mason, h Cedar n Union av.
McLaughlin James, laborer, h Abeel.
McLaughlin John, h DuBois n Maple av.
McLaughlin Samuel, clerk, h Newkirk av.
McLaughlin Samuel, laborer, h DuBois av n Maple av.
McLawn Lawrence, h Division ab Cross.
McLean Alexander, h Abeel.
McLean James, carpenter, h Ann n Union.
McLean R. J. Mrs., h Hasbrouck av n R. R.
McMahan James, h Pine n Hudson.
McMAHON PETER, grocer, &c., Washington av n Depot, h do.
McMahon P., blacksmith, h Hurley av.
McMannus Patrick, laborer, h Wilbur.
McMillan A., (D. & A. McM.,) h Wurts n Pierpont.
McMILLAN D. & A., ship chandlers, Dock.
McMillan D. (D. & A. McM.,) h Spring n Hone.
McMillan D. C., stenographer, h Chestnut n Division.

J. O. & G. B. MERRITT, Flannels and

At **HIRAM ROOSA'S** Agency, Rondout, N. Y.

McMullen Andrew, h Ravine n German.
McNally Frank, h Spring n Ravine.
McNally James, h DuBois n Newkirk av.
McNally Thomas, laborer, h DuBois av n Maple av.
McNally Thomas, grocer, Division ab Meadow, h do.
McNamara Michael, h Division ab Rogers.
McNaulty Patrick, h Spring ab Ravine.
McNichol Mary, h Catherine n Hasbrouck av.
McNulty James, h Hone cor Hunter.
McReynolds Barney, h 17 Lackawanna.
McShane Jas., grocer, Abeel n Ravine, h do.
McWilliams John Mrs., h Abeel.
Mabie William H., h Pierpont ab Ravine.
Macauley R. F., lawyer, Main n Fair, h John E of Fair.

WM. B. MacMONAGLE,

PRACTICAL

Watchmaker, Jeweler & Engraver

At Winter's News Office, Rondout, N. Y.

American and Imported Watches, Fine Jewelry, Spectacles, Eye Glasses, Pocket Pistols, etc.

Blankets, No. 5 Wall St., Kingston,

HIRAM ROOSA'S Insurance Agency has

KINGSTON DIRECTORY.

Mackey Hugh, h Ravine ab Hunter.
Mackey William, painter, h Pine n Bowery.

MAC MONAGLE WM. B.,
watchmaker and jeweler, Winter's news store Garden, bds Mansion House.

Madden Francis, builder, h Union av n Pine Grove.
Madden James, gardener, h DeWitt.
Madden John, painter, h DeWitt.
Madden M. J., grocer, Division cor Mill, h Chestnut.
Madden Thomas, Wilbur.
Maely Patrick, laborer, h Cedar n E Front.
Maeel Jacob, mason, h Cedar n Union av.
Maeere A., carpenter, h Ravine n R. R.
Magar H., laborer, h Ravine n R. R.
Mahan John, boatman, h Abeel.
Mahan M., h Union cor Division.
Mahan Patrick, laborer, h Cross n Ann.
Mahan Thomas, laborer, h Meadow n Ann.
Mahar A. Mrs., h Taylor.
Mahar John, h Ann ab Meadow.
Mahar John, grocer, &c., Division ab Union.
Mahony John, foreman, h Abruyn n Church.
Maier George, boots and shoes, 78 N Front, h do.
Mains F., laborer, h Greenkill av.
Maines Joseph, stone cutter, h Valley n Prospect.
Maines Solomon, laborer, h Union av n Liberty.
Maisenhelder C., barber, bds Sherer's Hotel.
Malay James, laborer, h Cross n R. R.
Malehy George, laborer, h St. Mary n Chambers.
Maley Austin, laborer, h Hanraty n Point rd.
Mall George, laborer, h r Hasbrouck av n Cross.
Mallon Jennie, dress maker, Division n Mill.

J. O. & G. B. MERRITT, Notions and

Never had any Disputed Claims.

Mallon Patrick, pro Rondout House, Garden and Ferry
Mallon Patrick, Jr., bar-tender, Rondout House.
MALLOY ALBERT, justice peace, Division n Abeel, h Union n Post.
Malloy B., laborer, h Greenkill av n Union av.
Malloy Martin, laborer, h Meadow n Chambers.
Maloney Daniel, blacksmith, h Wilbur Plank rd.
Maloney Michael, laborer, h Hanraty n Ravine.
Malone Thomas, cigars, &c., Cordts, h do.
Managan James, h Ridge cor German.
Manhany Daniel, h Division ab Meadow.
Mann Lucy Miss, h Maiden la n Albany av.
Mansfield John, carpenter, h Hunter n Ridge.
MANSION HOUSE, (W. E. Osterhoudt, pro.,) Division cor Lackawanna.
Manyon M., laborer, h Chestnut n Ponkhockie.
Marcus David, capt., h Union cor Prospect.
Marichol Alonzo, clerk, bds Sutton House.
Maricle W. A., express messenger, h 43 Division.
Markle Charles T., blacksmith, h Wall n Bowery.
Markle L. S., clerk, bds Hasbrouck av n Cross.
Marks Harry, h Russell.
Marony O., laborer, h Point rd n R. R.
Marsh H., carpenter, h junc. Union av and Albany av.
Marsh Samuel, druggist, Union av c St. James, h do.
Marsh W. H., pilot, h Ponkhockie n Union.
Marshall A. D., mason, h Newkirk av n DuBois av.
Marshall Henry, cigar maker, bds Hurley av.
Martin A., laborer, h Prospect n Liberty.
Martin Casper, h Division ab Rogers.
MARTIN HENRY, watchmaker and jeweler, particular attention paid to repairing of watches, 5 Mansion House Building, h Hunter n Hone.
Martin Hugh, h Division ab Rogers.

Trimmings, No. 5 Wall St., Kingston.

Your best interest will dictate to Insure with

Martin R. R., cement manuf., h Fair n Bowery.
Martin Thomas, h Division n Cross.
Martin William, laborer, h Pine.
Marthis & Hudler, flour mill, Wilbur.
Marthis J. S., (M. & Hudler,) h Wilbur.
Marthis R. E., miller, h Cottage Hill.
Marthis W. B., engineer, h Cottage Hill, Wilbur.
Mason A. F., carpenter, h Valley.
Mason W. U., clerk, h Crown n Kingston Hotel.
MASTEN & HAYES, boots and shoes, (wholesale,) 8 Wall.
Masten C. J., druggist, 28 Wall, h do.
Masten E. C. Mrs., h John cor Fair.
Masten H. B., clerk, bds Fair cor John.
Masten Peter, (M. & Hayes,) h Albany av n R. R.
Masten Sarah Mrs., h Crown n N Front.
Matheson Edward W., jeweler, 26 Wall.
Matthews N., grocer, Columbus av n Prospect, h do.
Matthews P., laborer, h Hasbrouck av n Flatbush av.
Mausterstook Levi Mrs., h Hone n Holmes.
MAXON DANIEL, saloon, Division, ab Meadow, h do.
Maxwell John, stone yard, Crane Dock.
Maxwell John, grocer, &c., Dock, h Cedar cor Union.
Maxwell Miles, mason, h Hasbrouck av bel Garden.
Mayer Alexander, book-keeper, bds 6 Garden.
Mayer F. saloon, Hasbrouck av cor Point rd.
Mayer J. M., carriage manufac., Mill, h Hasbrouck av n Union.
Mealey Owen, boatman, h Ann n Union.
Measter John, laborer, h Henry n Sterling.
Meeker E., bds Mansion House.
Meeker Isaac, A., foreman, h Tompkins n Mill.
Meggrath M., laborer, h Cedar n Union.
Meikel A. N., saloon, Hasbrouck av n Ravine.

J. O. & G. B. MERRITT, Dry Goods and

Melburne Henry, laborer, h Ravine n Hasbrouck av.
Melius C., carpenter, h Hunter n Ridge.
Melius II. C., printer, Daily Freeman,
Mellert Joseph, saloon, Cornell's Dock, h do.
MELLERT LOUIS, butcher, Division cor Union, h do.
MELLON ARTHUR J., lawyer, Division cor Mill, h Union cor Wurts.
Mellon Charles, boatman, h Abeel.
Mellon Thomas, laborer, h Catherine cor Tompkins.
Mellor Thos., engineer, h DuBois av n Newkirk av.
Menehen Wm., laborer, h Pine Grove av n Union av.
MENGER FRED., saloon, Hasbrouck n Garden, h do.
Mergendahl A., clerk, h 8 N Front.
Mergendahl Eliza J. Mrs., h Main n Fair.
Mergendahl E., saloon, 8 N Front, h do.
Merkel Stephen, barber, Abeel cor Ravine, h do.
Merricle M. D., painter, h 22 Wall.
MERRIHEW, HOMMEL & DUNWOODY, dry goods, groceries, lumber, &c., 19 and 21 Washington av.
Merrihew E., (M., H. & D.,) h 7 N Front.
Merrihew James E., clerk, 15 Wall.
Merrill Thomas, overseer, bds Wilbur Hotel.
Mersereau Isaac, printer, Daily Freeman.
Merritt A. B., (H. A. M. & Bro.,) h Washington av and Hurley av.
MERRITT C. M. & SON, groceries, &c., 16 Wall.
Merritt C., (C. M. M. & Son,) h E. Front n John.
Merritt C. M., (C. M. M. & Son,) h Fair n John.
Merritt C. O., (Crosby, Merritt & Co.,) h E Front n Liberty.
Merritt George, clerk, h Hasbrouck av n Terrence av.
Merritt G. B., (J. O. & G. B. Merritt,) h Fair bet Bowery & St. James.
Merritt George U., clerk, h Hasbrouck av bel Garden

Carpets, No. 5 Wall St., Kingston.

If not convenient to call, send your application by

Merritt H. A. & Bro., butchers, Washington av and Hurley av.
Merritt I. A., butcher, h Washington av n Depot.

MERRITT J. O & G. B.,
dry goods and carpets, 5 Wall.

Merritt J. O., (J. O. & G. B. Merritt,) h E Front n John.
Merritt J. T., h Fair bet Main and John.
Merritt Peter, clerk, h Elmendorf n R. R.
Merritt W. W., butcher, h Washington av and Hurley.
Messend George, teamster, h Wilbur Plank rd.
Messenger Christian, carpenter, h Third av n R. R.
Messenger George, carpenter, h Third cor Elm.
Messett Robert, laborer, h Cedar n Prospect.
Messing Charles, carpenter, h Ravine n R. R.
Metcalf Asahel, engineer, bds Henry.
Metcalf George, blacksmith, h Henry.
Metcalf H., engineer, h Columbus av N of Tompkins.
Metcalf Levi W., blacksmith, h Grove n Abruyn.
Metz John, laborer, h Ravine n Hasbrouck av.
Metzger A., (Metzger's Hotel,) Division cor Spring.
METZGER'S HOTEL AND LIVERY, (A. Metzger, pro.,) Division cor Spring.
Metzler Adam, painter, h Second av n R. R.
Meyer (Isaac) Bros. (Julius,) clothing, 55 N Front, h do.
Meyers Christopher, wagon maker, h Union av n Dederick.
Meyers William, capt., h Union av n Chester.
MICK H. & CO., butchers, Wall cor St. James.
Mick H., butcher, h Green n Lucas av.
Mickens William, carpenter, h Pine n Maiden Lane.

J. O. & G. B. MERRITT, Black Silks at

Mail to **HIRAM ROOSA,** Insur. Agent, Rondout.

Middagh Alexander, foreman, h Pearl av n Green.
Middagh J. H., laborer, h St. James n Wall.
Miles Cornelius, h Pierpont opp Holmes.
Millard James, pro. Kingston and Rondout Machine Works, Union av cor Grand, h do.
Millegan E. E., ins. agt., h Wall n St. James.
Miller John, tailor, h Hasbrouck av n Point rd.
Miller A. S., (M. & Bro.,) h Summer cor Susan.
Miller Bros., small beer brewers, Jacob s Valley
Miller C. D., tinman, h Love Lane.
Miller C., laborer, h Wilbur Plank rd.
Miller E., shoemaker, Hasbrouck av n Cross.
Miller Frederick, carpenter, Union n Wurts, h do.
Miller G. J., clerk, h 58 N Front.
Miller H. S., (Seaman & M.,) bds Mill.
Miller Henry, painter, h Union av cor Elmendorf.
Miller J. B., (M. & Bro.,) h Rondout.
Miller J. B., cooper, h Livingston n Point rd.
Miller John, segar maker, bds Union av n Albany av.
Miller Louis, laborer, h Livingston.
Miller William, painter, h Wilbur Plank rd.
Miller, cooper, h Wilbur.
Miller Mrs., h Ann ab Union.
Mills E., saloon, h Ann ab Union.
Mills Henry, stone cutter, h Henry n Furnace.
MILLS J. & BRO., stone sawing, planing, &c., Wilbur.
Mills J., stone cutter, h Henry n Fair.
Mills S. D., carpenter, h Grand n Esther.
Mills M. S., stair builder, h Flatbush n Prince.
Mink Charles, laborer, h Chambers cor Newkirk av.
Mink William, clerk, Garden and Ferry.
Miner A. G., teacher, h Prospect n Liberty.
Miner S. V. K., blacksmith, Maiden Lane n E Front.
Miner Norris, watchmaker, bds Pine n Maiden Lane.

Bargains, No. 5 Wall St., Kingston.

Insure with no other Agent.

Miner Owen, foreman, h Union av n Flatbush av.
Miner Charles, sash, blinds, Union av ab Chestnut h do
Milligan Scott, clerk, h Pierpont n Wurts.
Mitchell Arthur, carpenter, h Ponkhockie c Chestnut.
Mitchell John, laborer, h Chambers n Ravine.
Mitchell Lawrence, mason, h St. Mary n Chambers.
Mitchell L., laborer, h Division cor Union.
Mitchell S., laborer, h Hasbrouck av cor Newkirk av.
Mitchell Thomas, carpenter, h Cross n Hasbrouck av.
Moda Isaac, toys, &c., Division opp Mill, h Union.
Moe J. F., shoemaker, h 23 Washington av.
Molynaux Peter, shoemaker, h Abeel.
Mondschine S., tobacconist, Division n Ferry, bds Mansion House.
Monk Thomas, boatman, h St. Mary n Chambers.
Monks Edward, h Ann ab Meadow.
Montanye I. D. L., supt. of alms, h Bowery cor Prospect.

MONTANYE W. D. L.,
homoeopathic physician, 17 Garden, h Holmes opp Wurts.

Montgomery James, laborer, h DeWitt.
Monvine Patrick, laborer, h Ravine cor Chambers.
Mooney Dennis, laborer, h Ravine n Vine.
Mooney Patrick, mason, h Wilbur rd n Hudson.
Mooney Patrick, blacksmith, h Abeel n Hone.
Mooney, blacksmith, h Orchard av.
Moore Horace, butcher, Union av cor O'Neil, h do.
Moore Wm. H., fireman, h Newkirk av cor Point rd.
Moran C., laborer, h DeWitt.
Moran Ellen Mrs., h Dock.
Moran E. T., book keeper, h Wilbur.

J. O. & G. B. MERRITT, Black Alpacas

HIRAM ROOSA, Gen'l Ins. Agent, Rondout, N. Y.

Moran Hugh, h Wilbur.
Moran John, laborer, h Chambers cor Cross.
More B. L., clerk, bds Pierpont n of Wurts.
More Byron, teamster, bds Pierpont n Wurts.
More Charles E., clerk, h 45 Division.
More William C. Mrs., h Point rd n Hasbrouck av.
Morgan William, Maiden la n Albany av.
Morris S. P., blacksmith, h Russell.
Morse G. W., tailor, h Washington av n Pearl av.
Morse Jane, Miss, h Fair n St. James.
Morshead Henry, laborer, h Ravine n Point rd.
Morss B. G., consulting engineer N. Y. K. & S. R. R., office Rondout Depot.
Morton Joseph, tailor, bds John n Crown.
Morwood Samuel, Mrs., h Maiden la n E Front.
Moser Joseph, saloon, Washington av ab Hurley av, h do.
Mothre Philip, laborer, h Ann n Meadow.
Mower Joseph, carman, h Ridge.
Mower Nicholas, h Ridge cor German.
Mower Peter, h Ridge cor German.
Mowle George, teamster, h Oak n Bowery.
Mowle Ira, clerk, h Oak n Bowery.
Muldoon John, boatman, h ft. Chambers.
Muldoon John, clerk, Division cor Meadow.
Muldoon Martin, laborer, h Meadow n Chambers.
Mulford E. D., h Prospect n St. James.
Mulhair Wm., laborer, h Abeel.
Mulhall P., h Division n Spring.
Mulherren Patrick, h Garden n Ferry.
Mulherin Wm., carpenter, h Union av cor Henry.
Mulks George B., h Hunter n Ravine.
Mulks Moses, h E Front n John.
Mull Alonzo, carriage trimmer, h Wurts n Pierpont.
Mullen A., tobacconist, Lackawanna, h German n Ravine. *12

and Brilliantines, 5 Wall St., Kingston.

Mullen E., tobacco, 4 N Front, h Hurley av.
Mullen John, captain, h Jarrold n Point rd.
Mullen Samuel, blacksmith, bds Western Hotel.
Muller C. D., tinsmith, h Love la.
Mulligan John, saloon, Washington av n Depot.
Mulvehill Mary, dress maker, h Division ab Union.
Mulvene Patrick, laborer, h Ravine n Ann.
Mulvey Thomas, h Division ab Rogers.
Murphy Andrew, h Division cor Meadow.
Murphy Andrew, laborer, h Meadow n Chambers.
Murphy Charles, stone cutter, h Cedar cor Prospect.
Murphy Daniel, engineer, h Ann cor Meadow.
MURPHY EDWARD, shoemaker, Main n E Front, bds Wall cor Pearl.
MURPHY FRANK, livery, Mansion House stables, Division, h Garden n Sherman House.
Murphy James, cooper, h Tompkins n Union.
MURPHY JAS., hardware, stoves, &c., 2 Division, h Chambers cor Stuyvesant.
Murphy John, foreman, h Hasbrouck av n Newkirk av.
Murphy John, machinist, h Union n Wurts.
Murphy John P., clerk, h Stuyvesant cor Chambers.
Murphy Martin, laborer, h Hanraty n Point rd.
Murphy M. Mrs., h Union cor Tompkins.
Murphy M & B., milliners, Garden n Hasbrouck av.
Murphy Mrs., h Division opp Rogers.
Murphy N., stoves, &c., 70 N. Front.
Murphy Nicholas Mrs., h Meadow cor Ann.
Murphy P., h Catherine n Hasbrouck av.
Murphy Robt. M., engineer, h Meadow cor Ann.
Murphy Wm., grocer, Washington av n bridge.
Murran B., clerk, h Union av n Flatbush av.
Murran E., saloon, Union av n Flatbush av.
Murran Patrick, laborer, h Abeel.

Murray Bernard, laborer, h Meadow n R R.
Murray James, laborer, h Ann cor Union.
Murray James, laborer, h Cedar n E. Front.
Murray John, laborer, h Cedar n Union.
Murray John Mrs., h Division n Cross.
Murray J. B., Rev., h Wurts cor Spring.
MURRAY J. J., grocer, Division n Cross, h do.
Murray L. M., captain, h Albany av n Smith av.
Murray M., cooper, h Abeel.
Murray Michael, laborer, h Meadow n Chambers.
Murray Owen, laborer, Flatbush av cor Hasbrouck av.
Murray Patrick, laborer, h Cross n Division.
Murray Peter, laborer, h Hanraty n Point rd.
MURRAY WM., grocer, Abeel bet Hone and Ravine, h do.
Musson T. H., (Donaldson & M.,) h Hone n Spring.
Myer B. S., (Fries & M.,) h John cor E Front.
Myer George, h Hudson.
Myer Jesse, physician, John cor E Front, h do.
Myer L., clothing, Lackawanna, h do.
Myer Martin, teamster, h r Hasbrouck av n Cross.
Myers Frederick, boatman, h Abeel cor Ravine.
Myers Hiram, police, h E Front n Liberty.
Myers John, confectioner, St. James n Union, h do.
Myers J. C., saloon, 78 N Front, h 76 do.

NADLE W. Mrs., h Abeel n Hunter.
Nalion Michael, h Division ab Union.
Nash Nancy, h Dock n Ravine.
Nathan Henry, mer. tailor, Division n Spring.
NATIONAL BANK OF RONDOUT, Ferry.
NATIONAL ULSTER CO. BANK, Wall cor John.
Naughton John, h Division ab Cross.
Nealon M., h Summer.

Nealon Patrick, laborer, h Cross n n R. R.
Near Andrew, h Green n Lucas av.
Near A. L., cigar maker, h Liberty n Union av.
Neat Peter, laborer, h Mason n Wurts.
Neff Frank, mason, h E Front opp Cedar.
Neher C. Mrs., h Pearl av cor Green.
Neice J. B., carpenter, h E Front n Henry.
Neice J. H., foreman, h E Front cor Henry.
Neidlinger, Schmidt & Co., malsters, South Rondout.
Neil Wm., peddler, h E Front n Henry.
Nelson Patrick, laborer, h Hanraty n Ravine.
Nelting A. Mrs., h Hudson.
Nes John, repairer, h Division ab Rogers.
NESTELL FRANK M., gas fitter, Fair opp Music Hall, h E Front n Bowery.
Netherwood D. W., tailor, h Cedar, n Prospect.
Neuman Henry, hotel, Wilbur.
NEWARK LIME AND CEMENT MANUFAC. CO., Garden and Union.
Newark Lime and Cement Mfg. Co.'s Store, Columbus av cor Tompkins.
Newbanks A., (Cloonan & Co.,) h Division cor Spring.
Newcomb A., student, h E Front n opp John.
Newcomb S. H., h E Front n John.
Newkirk B., h E Front cor Henry.
NEWKIRK BEAUMAN, butcher, Washington av opp Hurley av h do.
Newkirk D., clerk, bds E Front cor Henry.
Newkirk E. D., cashier, h Division cor Stuyvesant.
Newkirk Jane, Miss, h Liberty n E Front.
Newkirk J., undertaker, &c., 39 N Front, h Lucas av.
Newkirk M. T., clerk, bds St. James n E Front.
Newland S., grocer, Garden opp Ferry, h do.
Newman Michael, Rev., h Division opp St. Mary's Church.

J. O. & G. B. MERRITT, Kid Gloves,

Newnan Patrick, h Ann ab Union.
NEWWITTER M., dry goods, &c., Divison nearly opp Mansion House, h do.
Nichols A. G., harness, &c., 37 N Front, h E Front n John.
Nichols Charles E., printer, Argus office.
Nichols E. J., harness maker, h E Front n John.
Niese B. F., bookkeeper, bds Abeel cor Wurts.
Nietsckie G., tailor, h Ann n Cross.
Niffin Wm. H., (Staples & N.,) h Point rd n Cottage.
Nifle Henry, h German cor Ridge.
Noble James, cigar maker, h Hurley av.
Noble John, laborer, h Union n Cedar.
Nofgar Carl, laborer, h Ravine n R. R.
Nolan Mary, h Division ab Cross.
Nolen Patrick, carpenter, h Catherine cor Tompkins.
Nolen Thos., stone cutter, h Henry n Prospect.
Noney J. H., expressman, h Division opp Abeel.
Noonen Patrick, hostler, Hamilton House.
Norris Geo. A., saloon, Ferry n Division, h Rogers n Adams.
Norris Judson, vegetables, h 44 N Front.
Norris J. H. Mrs., h 45 N Front.
North David A., engineer, h Orchard n Union av.
North George, bds Mansion House.
NORTH GEO. Jr., insurance, Newkirk building, Division, h Wurts.
North I. M., agt., h Rogers n Adams.
North Z. M., freighting, h Wurts n opp Rogers.
Northrop B., expressman, h Union av n Elmendorf.
Northrop Mary, h Catherine n Hasbrouck av.
Northrup C. H., printer, h Washington av n Depot.
Northrup C. P., clerk, h Washington av n Depot.
Norton James, clerk, bds City Hotel.

No. 5 Wall Street, Kingston.

HIRAM ROOSA Insures Vessels and Cargoes

NORTON J. C., dentist, 15 Wall, h do.
Norton Thomas, laborer, h Hanraty n Point rd.
Nowlan Wm., h Liberty n Union av.
Noyes, Mrs., h Fair n Bowery.
Nugent C. Mrs., h Cedar n Catherine.
Nugent James, boatman, h Cedar n Catherine.

O'BRIEN ANN, groceries, Ponkhockie cor Chestnut.
O'Brien A. Mrs., h Division ab Meadow.
O'Brien C. Mrs., h Taylor.
O'Brien Edward, carpenter, h Meadow n Chambers.
O'Brien James, laborer, h Cedar n Union.
O'Brien James, saloon, Wilbur.
O'Brien John, laborer, h Cross n Division.
O'Brien M., shoemaker, h Abeel.
O'Brien Michael, blacksmith, Abeel cor Ravine.
O'Brien P., hostler, h Mill n Hasbrouck av.
O'Brien T., h Division ab Holmes.
O'Brien Thomas, boatman, h Cross n Division.
O'Connor John, grocer, Division ab Union, h do.
O'Donnell & Featherly, carriage manufac., E Front n City Hotel.
O'Donnell Roger, (O'D. & Featherly,) h Henry cor. Sterling.
O'Donnall T., shoemaker, Ferry n Division, h Hasbrouck av n Union.
O'FARRELL MICHAEL CARTHAGE, Rev., h Division opp St. Mary's Church.
O'Hara Thomas, chair maker, h Pine n Greenkill av.
O'Harren Cornelius, h Ann ab Meadow.
Ohraus Gotlieb, laborer, h Newkirk av n Division.
O'Keefe, John, clerk, bds Holmes n Hone.
O'Leary J. P., physician, bds Dock.
Olibet Alonzo, engineer, h Cedar n Union av.

J. O. & G. B. MERRITT, Gent's

of all kinds. Rondout, N. Y.

KINGSTON DIRECTORY. 143

Oliver G. N., (Payntar, Burhans & Oliver,) bds N Front cor E Front.
Oliver James, book keeper, bds Elmendorf n R. R.
Olwell James, h Catherine n Hasbrouck av.
O'Neil Charles, saloon, Ann n Meadow.
O'NEIL C. M. & CO., dry goods, groceries, lumber, lime, cement and fertilizing compost, 16 and 18 N Front.
O'Neil C. M., (C. M. O'Neil & Co.,) h 20 N Front.
O'Neil Jas., watchman, h Hasbrouck av n Newkirk av.
O'Neil John, laborer, h Cross n Division.
O'Neil Michael, h Garden n Ferry.
O'Neil Michael, laborer, h Pine Grove av n Union av.
O'Neil Neal, laborer, h Union n Post.
O'Neil Thomas, laborer, h Cedar n Union.
O'Pray P. J., (pro. City Hotel,) Canal cor Ferry.
O'Reilly Andrew, clothing, Lackawanna, h do.
O'Reilly Andrew, mason, h Meadow n R. R.
O'Reilly B. Mrs., saloon, Columbus av cor Cedar.
O'REILLY CHAS., groceries and liquors, Dock and Abeel, h do.
O'Reilly E., grocer, 19 Lackawanna, h do.
O'Reilly E., h Division ab Union.
O'Reilly John, real estate agent, h Union av opp City Hall.
O'Reilly M. J., student, bds Union av bet St. James and Elmendorf.
O'Reilly P., blacksmith, h Hasbrouck av n Garden.
O'Reilly P., blacksmith, Division cor Union, h opp do.
O'Reilly Philip, carpenter, h Ann n Union.
O'Reilly T. Mrs., h Mill.
O'Roark John, bar tender, Opera House.
Ormerod A., clerk, bds Sherer's Hotel.
Orr John, carpenter, h Hunter n Ridge.

Furnishing Goods, 5 Wall St., Kingston.

Get an **Accidental Policy** at

Osgood George, engineer, bds Mansion House.
Osterhoudt A., bookkeeper, h St. James n Fair.
Osterhoudt Albert, carpenter, h Henry.
Osterhoudt Alexander C., carpenter, h Mapleton.
Osterhoudt E. Mrs., h Henry n Oak.
OSTERHOUDT H., coal and lumber, Main opp Eagle Hotel, h E Front bet Pearl and Maiden la.
Osterhoudt H. & Bro., coal, &c., Wilbur.
Osterhoudt Jane Mrs., h John E of Fair.

OSTERHOUDT JULIUS,

coal, h E. Front bet Pearl and Maiden la.
Osterhoudt J. J., fireman, h St James n Union.
Osterhoudt P. L., (pro American Hotel,) Union av cor St. James.
Osterhoudt Robert, coachmen, h O'Neil cor R R.
Osterhoudt S. M. Mrs., h St. James n Fair.
Osterhoudt W. E., (pro. Mansion House,) Division cor Lackawanna.
Ostrander Eliza Miss, bds junc. Green and Crown.
Ostrander James, engineer, h Ravine n Chambers.
Ostrander John, butcher, h Union av cor Orchard.
Ostrander J. E., treas. S. B., h Main bet Green and Wall.
Ostrander J. T., photographer, h n hd Staple.
Ostrander L., Rev., h Fair cor Pearl.
OSTRANDER T. P., dentist, Garden over Winter's News Store, bds Mill.
Ostrander Wm., butcher, Ulster Market, h Union av.
Ostrander W. B., h Wilbur.
Ostrander Wm., Jr., butcher, h Chester cor Bond.
O'Sullivan M. L., clothing, &c., Dock, h do.
Otis E. T., mason, h Tremper av cor O'Neil.

J. O. & G. B. MERRITT, Gloves and

HIRAM ROOSA'S Agency, Rondout, N. Y.

Otis H. W., mason and builder, Hasbrouck av n R. R., h Union av n Bowery.
Otis James, mason, h Elmendorf n Tremper av.
Otis R. L., mason, h Hone cor Spring.
Ougheltree L., carpenter, h Abruyn n Grove.
Overbaugh Benjamin F., coal, h Flatbush av.
OVERBAUGH D. C., coal, lumber, &c., Union av opp Cedar, h Smith av n Grand.
Overbaugh E., harness maker, bds Fair n N Front.
Owen Jacob, laborer, h Second av n R. R.
Owens S. J., carpenter, h n hd Staple.
Owl Henry, hostler, h E Front n Cedar.

PAINE E., peddler, h Flatbush n R. R.
Palen Eli, clerk, h 17 N Front.
Palen Henry W., carpenter, Wall n Bowery, h do.
Palmer Emma R., h Union av n O'Neil.
Palmer Herbert, candy maker, bds Union av n O'Neil.
Palmel John, mason, h Cedar cor Prospect.
Pardee Charles A., coal, h Abruyn n Union.
Pardee E. F., engineer, h Flatbush av cor Prince.
Pardee Isaac, Mrs., h E Front n St. James.
PARKER & KENYON, lawyers, John cor Wall.
Parker A. B., (P. & Kenyon,) h E Front n John.
Parker C., h Ravine opp Pine.
Parker C. Mrs., h Hone n Hunter.
Parker Nelson, saloon, Dock, h do.
Parker W. H., stoves, Dock.
Parish M. C., cooper, h Tompkins opp Catherine.
Parnell Wm., painter, h O'Reilly n Union av.
Parnham W. F. Jr., sail maker, 15 Ferry, h Pierpont cor Hone.
Parsell David Jr., carpenter, h Holmes n Wurts.
Parsell Edward, tailor, bds City Hotel.

Hosiery, No. 5 Wall St., Kingston.

Life Insurance on the Stock, Mutual or Co-

Parsell J. S., h Pearl n Fair.
Parslow James, h Van Deusen av.
Parslow J., shoemaker, h Washington av n Depot.
Partlan T., blacksmith, Meadow n Division, h Division cor Pierpont.
PATCHEN L. I., livery, &c., Mill, bds Mansion House.
Patterson Abel, carpenter, h Post n Spring.
Patterson A. E. Mrs., h E Front n Bowery.
Patterson C. M. Mrs., h Hasbrouck av n Cross.
Patterson George, laborer, h Prospect.
Paulding Samuel D., h Greenkill av opp Prospect.

PAYNTAR, BURHANS & OLIVER,
hardware, iron, &c., N Front cor Crown.

Payntar A. B., (Payntar, Burhans & Oliver,) h Fair n Maiden Lane.
Pelham Henry, carpenter, h hd Staple.
Pelham Sherman, laborer, h German n Ravine.
Pells G. E., boatman, h Henry.
Pendergast William, saloon, Lackawanna, h do.
Penniman Samuel, Mrs., h Spring n Hone.
Penny Henry, caulker, h Abruyn cor Union.
Penny James, caulker, h Hunter n Hone.
Penny James, Jr., caulker, h Hunter n Hone.
Penny J. A., clerk, 15 Wall.
Penny Thomas, h Hunter n Hone.
Penny Thomas F., clerk, bds Hunter.
PEREZ ALEXANDER, hairdresser, Lackawanna, h Holmes.
Perkins E. K., physician, Abeel opp Post, h do.
Perkins M. Mrs., h Chester n Union av.
Permann Frederick, saloon, Main n Eagle Hotel, h Rosendale rd.
Perrine A. J., carriage maker, Washington av n Depot, h n opp do.

J. O. & G. B. MERRITT, Laces and

operative Plan at H. ROOSA'S Agency, Rondout.

Perrine I. D., h Wurts cor Spring.
Perrine L. W., dentist, bds Wurts cor Spring.
Perrine M. D., (pro. City Hotel,) E Front opp Main.
Perrine Nelson, clerk, h Hasbrouck av n Cross.
Perry Lon., clerk, Kingston Hotel.
Pertsche William, h Spring cor Hone.
Peters Edward, hostler, Hamilton House.
PETERS F. F., stoves, tinware, &c., 76 N Front, h E Front bet John and N Front.
PETERS HENRY, supt., h South Rondout.
Peters Rogers, blacksmith, h Hunter.
PETERS WM., carriage manufac., Washington av ab Hurley av, h n do.
Peterson C., carpenter, h Chester n R. R.
Peterson C. E., turner, h Furnace n Cedar.
Pettit John, supt., h E Front cor Bowery.
Pettit Richard, laborer, h Old Wilbur rd.
Pettit William, laborer, h Old Wilbur rd.
Pfrommer John, baker, Division ab Union h do.
Phelan Alexander, carman, h Wilbur.
Phelan M., groceries and liquors, Union av n Henry.
Phelps B. H., clerk, bds 104 N Front.
Phillips A., clerk, St. James cor E Front.
Phillips David, laborer, h Mapleton.
Phillips Isaac, tailor, h Hurley av.
Phillips Owen, foreman, h Catherine n Cedar.
PHILLIPS PETER, boot inspector, D. & H. Canal Co. h Chestnut.
Phillips Wm., gardener, h Elmendorf n Tremper av.
Philips Wm., ship carpenter, h Hunter n Hone.
Pierce A. F., segar maker, Garden opp Ferry.
Pierson Jane Mrs., h Prospect n Liberty.
Pierson James M., carpenter, h Staple n Union av.
Pillsworth Patrick, laborer, h Post n Union.

Embroideries, No. 5 Wall St., Kingston.

HIRAM ROOSA'S Insurance and

KINGSTON DIRECTORY.

Pine Eliza Mrs., h Main N. Wall.
Pine James S., (Brodhead & P.,) h Wall cor Main.
Pine Olive Mrs., h Main n Green.
PINNER LOUIS, hats, caps, boots and shoes, 82 and 84 N Front, h do.
PITTS C. V. L., crockery and glassware, 14 Wall h do.
Pitts George E., ship carpenter, h 7 Wall.
Pitts H. H., gen. merchandise, Wilbur.
Plass Abram H., butcher, h Union av n Albany av.
Platner Charles, saloon, Hasbrouck av cor Cross.
Plato A., tailor, h 12 N Front.
Plopp Gotleib, laborer, h Chambers n Newkirk av.
Plough Jacob, blacksmith, Wall n Linderman av, h Linderman n Wall.
Plough John, restaurant, St. James n E Front.
Plough Peter, trimmer, h Elmendorf n R. R.
Plunkett John, laborer, h Catherine n Cedar.
Plunkett Luke, laborer, h Columbus av cor Cedar.
Plunkett Luke, saloon, Columbus av cor Cedar.
Polock Mrs., h Ann cor Cross.
Poole & Luther, marble works, Wall n Pearl.
Poole F. W., (P. & Luther,) h Wall n Maiden la.
Porter Benjamin, laborer, h Ann n Meadow.
Portugee Wm., baker, h Flatbush av opp Prince.
Post Aaron, boatman, h E Front cor Bowery.
Post C., foreman, h Cedar n Prospect.
Post Wm., coachman, h Wilbur.
Post Wm., carpenter, h Second av n R R.
Powell C. H., clerk, bds Wurts cor Abeel.
Powell P. M., engineer, h Hasbrouck av n Union.
Powers James, h Division ab Meadow.
Powers Michael, laborer, bds Dock.
Powers Wm., h Division ab Cross.
Powley Francis, h Abeel n Wurts.

J. O. & G. B. MERRITT, Ladies'

Real Estate Agency, Rondout, N. Y.

Powley J. L., builder, h Ponkhockie n Union.
Powley S. W., supt., h Rogers n Adams.
Pratt C. R., stone measurer, h Hasbrouck av cor Newkirk av.
Pratt Wm. H., machinist, h Hasbrouck av n Union.
Preston C. M., lawyer, Garden, over Market.
Preston G. C., (L. D. Hoornbeek & Co.,) h Union av n City Hall.
Preston T. J., fish &c., Ulster Market, h Meadow opp gas house.
Proper C. G., teamster, h Newkirk av cor Maple av.
Proper George Mrs., h Summer cor S Sterling.
Prout G. E. Mrs., h Meadow n Hasbrouck av.
Prout Lewis H., engineer, h Hudson cor Wilbur rd.
Prull Wm., tailor, 9 Wall.
Prull W. F., tailor, h E Front cor Maiden la.
Pulver Frank, segar maker, Garden opp Ferry.
Purcell J., surveyor, h Smith av cor Elmendorf.
Purroy F. M., physician, Holmes opp Wurts, h do.
Purvis Richard, laborer, h Wilbur.
Purvis William, h Wilbur.

QUACKENBOSS F. H., h Garden cor Smith av.
QUENTEL JULIUS, physician, Hone n Abeel, h do.
Quentel Oscar, physician, Hone n Abeel, h do.
Quigley John, saloon, Hone ab Hunter, h do.
Quigg J., h Cedar n Catherine.
Quigley James, h Spring ab Ravine.
Quigley John, ice dealer, Wilbur.
Quigley Martin, h Spring n Ravine.
Quigley Owen, boatman, h Union n Post.
Quigley Patrick, boatman, h Abeel cor Hunter.
Quigley Thomas, caulker, h German n Ridge.
Quigley Thomas, clerk, h Hone.

*13
Undergarments, 5 Wall St., Kingston.

Losses Equitably Adjusted and Promptly Paid

KINGSTON DIRECTORY.

Quillard C. V., architect, Garden, h Hone cor Lord.
Quinlin John, laborer, h Chestnut n Ponkhockie.
Quinn John, h Division ab Rogers.
Quinn O., clerk, bds Washington av n Depot.
Quinn Thomas, laborer, h Meadow n Ann.
Quimby Stephen, butcher, h Wall n St. James.
Quirk Thomas, laborer, h Meadow n Ann.
Quitman E. Miss, bds N Front cor E Front.
Qumeskey J., blacksmith, h Washington av n Depot.

RADCLIFF HIRAM, farmer, bds Kingston Hotel.
Radcliff P. F., (Decker & R.,) h Washington av n Pearl av.
Radel Charles, barber, bds Freileweh Hotel.
Radel W., h Ann ab Meadow.
Radikin John, laborer, h Newkirk av n Maple av.
Raeling John, gardener, h Post n Union.
Raenhart F. A., (Tilson & R.,) h Oak n Bowery.
Rafferty Ellen Mrs., h St. Mary n Chambers.
Rafferty George, laborer, h Catherine n Cedar.
Rafferty John, laborer, h Catherine cor Tompkins.
Rafferty Owen, cooper, h Cedar n Union.
Rafferty Patrick, h Cedar n Catherine.
Rafferty Thomas, laborer, h Tompkins n Union.
Ragan Dennis, laborer, h Hunter n Ravine.
Ragan James, blacksmith, h Point rd.
Ragan Julia, Mrs., h Abeel.
Rahmer G., jeweler, Ferry n Division, h do.
RANDEL JOHN, carman, h Union b Wurts and Hone
Randolph R. H., clerk, bds Union cor Tompkins.
Randolph S., carpenter, h Ponkhockie cor Chestnut.
Rardenberg C. W., cigar manuf., Newkirk av n Division, h do.
Rarey Adam, carpenter, h German n Ravine.

J. O. & G. B. MERRITT, Cloths and

At **HIRAM ROOSA'S** Agency, Rondout, N. Y.

Raschke Theodore, tobacconist, Abeel n Division, h do
Ratican Lawrence, laborer, h Point rd n Hasbrouck av
RAUFEASEN JOHN, Rev., h Wurts n Pierpont.
Rawson M. L., agent A. E. Co., h Lucas av n Green.
Reader, John, laborer, h Flatbush av n Union av.
READING JOHN P., cracker baker, Hasbrouck av ab Mill, h Ponkhockie n Union.
Readon H. S., machinist, h Hasbrouck av n Newkirk.
Rearden C. Mrs., h Abeel.
Recktenwald Andrew, laborer, h Newkirk n Chambers
Recktenwald Francis, teamster, h Ravine n German.
Recktenwald Jacob, clerk, bds Hone n Hunter.
Recktenwald John, h Ravine n German.
Reddick Charles, machinist, h Union av n St. James.
Reddin Jeremiah, laborer, h Dock.
Redman Thomas, laborer, h Catherine n Cedar.
Reed Charles, h Prospect n St. James.
Regndhal Wm., farmer, h Voorhees la.
Reid Albert, laborer, h Cedar n Union av.
Reid D. C., boots, shoes, and agt. A. E. Co., 34 Garden, h Pierpont cor Adams.
Reid Wm. H., book-keeper, bds Mansion House.
Reickle A., boatman, h Pine n Ravine.
Reily John, pattern maker, bds Pearl cor Wall.
Reily Philip, h Catherine n Hasbrouck.
Reinmoth Adam, cooper, h Holmes n Wurts.
Reis Frederick, laborer, h Pine n Ravine.
Reise Louis, butcher, bds St. James, hd Green.
Reis Michael, boatman, h Main n Wurts.
Relyea Charles, laborer, h Love Lane.
Rettenman Andrew, stone cutter, h Newkirk av n Chambers.
Reynier E., carpenter, h Oak n Henry.
Reynolds C., freight agent, h Maiden Lane.

Cassimeres, No. 5 Wall St., Kingston.

Reynolds C. Mrs., h Maiden Lane n E Front.
Reynolds Chas., (Sahler, Reynolds & DuBois,) h Green opp Maiden Lane.
Reynolds Elisha, machinist, bds Ravine n Vine.
Reynolds H. H. Mrs., h Albany av E of Union av.
Reynolds J. S., sash, h St. James n Wall.
Reynolds J. W., confectionery, 11 Wall, h do.
Reynolds Michael, grocer, &c., Dock n Ravine.
Reynolds Reuben, stoves, &c., 30 Wall, bds Wall cor Pearl.
Reynolds Samuel, clerk, bds Wall cor Pearl.
Rhodes John W., h Hudson.
RICE A., musical instruments, watches and jewelry, Division ab Mill, h do.
Rice John B., h Pierpont ab Ravine,
RICE M., baker, Division ab Union, h do.
Rice Margaret, h Pierpont ab Ravine.
Rice Philip, repairer, Abeel ab Division, h Abeel n Wurts.
Rice R., boatman, h Pierpont n School House.
Rice Thomas, painter, h Cedar n Union av.
Ricely C., cooper, h Elmendorf n R. R.
Ricely Henry, cooper, h Elmendorf n R. R.
Rich John, carman, h Pine n Bowery.
Richardson E., h Pierpont n School House.
Rickly B., h Wilbur rd cor Hudson.
Rickey William H., h John cor Crown.
RIDENOUR & SLEIGHT, furniture, undertakers, &c, 21 Wall.
Ridenour C. P., (Ridenour & Sleight,) h Maiden Lane n Fair.
Ridger Charles, carpenter, h Ravine n Point rd.
Rider Jacob, h Crown n Green.
Riel James, painter, h Flatbush cor Gage.

Never had any Disputed Claims.

KINGSTON DIRECTORY. 153

Rieser Adolph, tailor, h Abeel n Hone.
Rieser A. & Co., dry goods, &c., Hone cor Abeel.
Rieser Wm. & Bro. (A.,) mer. tailors, Abeel n Hone.
Rifenbary J. H., baker, h Ponkhockie n Union.
Rifenbary Samuel, carpenter, h Bowery n Union av.
Rigney Dennis, laborer, h Flatbush n Prince.
Rigney Thomas, saloon, Garden n Ferry, bds do.
Rigney Wm., laborer, h Cross n Division.
Riker V. O., carpenter, h E Front cor Henry.
Rilley John J., cooper, h Bowery n Prospect.
Rinehart R., mason, bds Pearl n Wall.
Rippe George, saloon, Columbus av cor Cedar, h do.
Ritter Henry, watchmaker, bds Hamilton Hotel.
Rivers Elizabeth, Mrs., h Hurley av.
Roark K., laborer, h Abeel.
Robb John, laborer, h Hanraty n Point rd.
Roberson Alexander, mason, h Pine n Henry.
Robertson John, ship rigger, h Chambers n Union.
Robertson Wm., boatman, bds Dock.
Robinson & Gilmore, fancy goods, &c., 47 Division.
Robinson Blandina Mrs., h Hunter n Ridge.
Robinson G., h Pierpont ab Ravine.
Robinson J. H., mason, h Pine n Henry.
Robison James, boarding, h Abeel n Pres. Church.
ROBSON WILLIAM, boat builder, South Rondout.
Rockefeller H. Mrs., h Union n Hone.
Rackgaver Andrew, laborer, h Hasbrouck av n R R.
ROCKWELL C. A., boarding house, Washington av cor Lucas av.
Rodie James, foreman, h Abruyn opp Grove.
Rodie William, clerk, h Abruyn.
Roe A. Mrs., h Prospect n Liberty.
Roe James, teamster, h Smith cor Cedar.
Roe John B., carman, h Ford.

Blankets, No. 5 Wall St., Kingston.

Your best interest will dictate to Insure with

Roe John H., teamster, h 106 N Front.
Roe R., teamster, h Washington av n Hurley av.
ROE THOS., engineer, h Ten Broeck av n Flatbush av.
Rogers F. L., clerk, bds Smith cor Dunn, (Wilbur.)
Romer & Tremper, forwarders, &c., Ferry.
Romer Charles, (H. & R.,) h Dock.
Romer J. H. Rev., h Pearl av n Washington av.
Romer Wm. F., (R. & Tremper,) h Fair cor Maiden la.
Romeyn & Son, eds, &c. Kingston Journal, 33 and 35 Wall.
Romeyn Theo. M., (Romeyn & Son,) h St. James n Fair.
Romeyn W. H. & J. C., eds. &c., h Rogers n Adams.
Romeyn Wm. H., (Romeyn & Son,) h St. James n Fair.
RONDOUT & KINGSTON GAS WORKS, Meadow cor Chambers.
RONDOUT HOUSE, (P. Mallon, pro.,) Garden and Ferry.
Rondout Savings Bank, Garden cor Division.
Ronk John, Mrs., h Green n Pearl.
Roof F., machinist, h Tompkins n Union.
Rooney D., h Division ab Union.
Rooney Patrick, Mrs., h Meadow n Ann.
Rooney T., h Division cor Meadow.
Roosa A. P., h St. James n Prospect.
ROOSA C. D., painter, Fair n St. James, h St. James n Fair.
Roosa D. W., carpenter, h St. James opp Prospect.
Roosa H. Mrs., h Fair n St. James.

ROOSA HIRAM,
general insurance and real estate, 7 Division, Mansion House Building, h Post bet Abeel and Union.

J. O. & G. B. MERRITT, Notions and

HIRAM ROOSA, Agent at Rondout, N. Y.

Roosa Isaac, laborer, h Union av n O'Neil.
ROOSA ISAAC I.,
   livery stables, E Front cor Main, h O'Neil n Union av.
Roosa Levi, laborer, h Prospect n Valley.
Roosa Lewis, hostler, bds O'Neil n Union av.
Roosa Peter, shoemaker, h 7 Wall.
ROOSA SAMUEL, painter, O'Neil bet Bruyn av and Ten Broeck av, h do.
Roosa Thomas, porter, h Ten Broeck av n O'Neil.
Roosa Z., clerk, Romer & Tremper's.
Rosa H., (Frisselle & R.,) h Union av n St. James.
Rose Charles A., clerk, Division cor Garden.
Rose D. B., cigar maker, h E. Front n St. James.
Rose Henry, h Division ab Holmes.
Rose John, carpenter, h Wall n St. James.
Rose Truman, bds Albany av opp Maiden la.
ROSEKRANSE H. C., hair-dresser, John n Wall, h do
Rosenblatt B., hats, &c., h E Front cor Cedar.
Rosendale, dry goods, h Union n Wurts.
Rosenstine D., tailor, h Mill cor Ann.
Rosenthal B., mer. tailor, Division n Garden, h Union n Abeel.
Ross Thomas Mrs., h Hasbrouck av cor Garden.
Rourk James, laborer, h Flatbush av n Union.
Rourke M. Miss, h Cross n R. R.
Rourke Patrick, boatman, h Abeel.
ROUSE HENRY & CO., grocers, Hasbrouck av cor Garden and Division cor Mill.
Rouse Henry, (H. Rouse & Co.,) h Pierpont n Wurts.
Rouse Mrs., h Spring n Hone.
Rowe Augustus, h Ann ab Meadow.
Rowe E. Miss, music teacher, h Abeel ab Post.

Trimmings, No. 5 Wall St., Kingston.

Rowe H. W., teamster, h Union opp Cedar.
Rowland Thomas, h Spring cor Ravine.
Rudnitske M. Mrs., h Washington av n N Front.
Ruhl Augusta Mrs., h Cedar n Union av.
Rundell H. E., (Wakelle & R.,) bds N Front n Green.
Rundell John, teamster, h Union n Wurts.
Rupp Gotleib, butcher, Garden cor Smith av.
Rurakas Peter, carpenter, h Point rd.
Rush Mary Mrs., grocer, Wilbur.
Russell James, h Washington av n Hurley av.
Russell John, h Hurley av.
Russell John F., stone cutter, h Hurley av.
Russell P., laborer, h Union cor Tompkins.
Rutzer M. Mrs., h Fair n Bowery.
Ryan B. Mrs., h Cedar n Columbus av.
Ryan Catherine, h Division ab Meadow.
Ryan Daniel, h Catherine n Hasbrouck av.
Ryan James, h Division n Rogers.
Ryan James, captain, h Point rd.
Ryan James, laborer, h Wilbur.
Ryan John, h Catherine, n Hasbrouck av.
Ryan John, laborer, h Ravine n Point rd.
Ryan John, laborer, h Prospect n Union.
RYAN JOSEPH, undertaker, Division opp St. Mary's Church.
Ryan Mrs., h Division cor Cross.
Ryan Martin, machinist, h Cross n Chambers.
Ryan Patrick, laborer, h Chambers n Union.
Ryan P., laborer, h Division cor Cross.
Ryan P. J., h Division cor Union.
Ryan Thomas, h Catherine n Hasbrouck av.
Ryan Thomas, laborer, h Union n Cedar.
Ryerson A. L. Mrs., h Elmendorf n R. R.
Ryon C. M., teacher, h Union n Wurts.

J. O. & G. B. MERRITT, Dry Goods and

Mail to HIRAM ROOSA, Insur. Agent, Rondout.

SAFFORD & CARTER, watchmakers and jewelers, 26 Wall.

SAFFORD & CARTER,
Manufacturing Jewelers,
AND DEALERS IN
DIAMONDS, WATCHES, CLOCKS & JEWELRY,
SOLID SILVER AND PLATED WARE,
No. 26 WALL STREET, KINGSTON, N. Y.

☞ Fine Watches of all kinds Repaired in the best manner and warranted to give satisfaction.

Safford C. B., (S. & Carter,) h 26 Wall.
SAHLER, REYNOLDS & DU BOIS, hardware, steel, iron, &c., Wall cor N Front.
Sahler Artemus, (Sahler, Reynolds & DuBois,) Fair cor Maiden Lane.
Sahler Eliza Mrs., h Pearl n E Front.
Sahler E. Miss, music teacher, h Abeel ab Post.
Sahloff Henry, laborer, h Newkirk av n Division.
Saloff Joseph, boatman, h Newkirk av n Chambers.
Salzmann J. W., baker, Cedar n Columbus av, h do.
SALZMANN LOUIS, baker, Abeel opp Washington Hall, h do.
Sampson E. & Co., clothing, Division and Canal.
Sampson E., shoe store, Division cor Lackawanna.
Sampson J., (E. S. & Co.,) h Division and Canal.
SAMPSON LOUIS, merchant tailor and clothing, 64 N Front, h do.
Sampson Philip, clerk, Division cor Lackawanna.

Carpets, No. 5 Wall St., Kingston.

Insure with no other Agent.

SAMTER ALEX., tobacconist, Division n Garden, bds Mansion House.
Samter B. L., toys, &c., 12 N Front, h do.
Samter L., dry goods, &c., 60 N Front, h do.
Samter M., tobacconist, 53 N Front, h do.
SAMTER MORRIS, tobacconist, 21 Garden, h Garden n Excelsior Hotel.
Samuels Charles, merchant, bds Eagle Hotel.
Sanders C. M., foreman, h E Front cor Maiden la.
Sandford, boatman, h Vine.
Sapp Matthew, fruits, &c., Ulster Market, h Russell.
Sassidy John, h Division cor Meadow.
Saulpaugh G. W., pilot, h Chester n R. R.
Sauvestre J., cutter, bds N Front cor E Front.
Savoy H. M. Mrs., h Henry n Prospect.
Sawyer George, agent, bds 24 Wall.
Sawyer John, h Prospect cor Liberty.
Sayles M. A., waiter, h Henry n Prospect.
Saylor H. Mrs., meat market, Bowery n Oak, h opp do.
Schackley Joseph, h Wilbur.
Schaffer George, blacksmith, h Hone n Holmes.
Schaffer Jacob, weis bier, South Rondout.
Scanlan Michael, foreman, h ft Chambers.
Scanlan P., h Division ab Meadow.
Scharschu Charles, h Hudson.
Schaller John, stone cutter, Greenkill av n Union av.
Schattle Christian, baker, German cor Ridge, h do.
Schdel John, clerk, h Ravine cor Abeel.
Schenck Joseph, saloon, Dock, h do.
Schepmoes A., justice peace, John n Fair, h Pearl n Washington av.
Schepmoes A. E., ins. agt., h Pearl av n Green.
Schepmoes C. C., clerk, 29 Wall.
Schepmoes, John, laborer, h Ann n Meadow.

J. O. & G. B. MERRITT, Black Silks at

HIRAM ROOSA, Gen'l Ins. Agent, Rondout, N. Y.

Schepmoes M. W., (Ellsworth & S.,) h E Front cor Liberty.
Schepmoes T. H., laborer, h Liberty n Union av.
Schepmoes U., blacksmith, h Liberty n Union av.
Schepmoes W. T., cabinet maker, h Pearl av n Green.
Scherger Frank, saloon, Ravine n Chambers, h do.
Schermerhorn C. A., (English & S.,) bds Pearl n Wall.
Schermerhorn G. D., book keeper, h Newkirk av ab Hasbrouck av.
Schetzle O., laborer, h Ravine n German.
Schick C., butcher, Abeel W of Wurts, h do.
Schick Casper, saloon, h Wilbur.
Schick Geo. R., bone dust, h Cottage Hill, Wilbur.
Schleyer Wm., watchmaker, bds Metzgar's Hotel.
Schlotterer J., tailor, h Mill.
Schmidt George, weaver, h Hunter.
Schmidt John, laborer, h Union av bel Grand.
Schnitzler John, saloon, Mill n Division, h do.
Schook, boatman, h Abeel n Hone.

Schoonmaker & Van Wagenen,
furniture, Pearl n Green.
Schoonmaker Anthony, millwright, h Orchard av.
Schoonmaker Augustus, h 36 N Front.
SCHOONMAKER A. Jr., lawyer, John n Wall, h Crown cor John.
Schoonmaker A. S., agent, h E Front n Cedar.
Schoonmaker C. M., h Wall n Henry.
Schoonmaker C. L., boots and shoes, 88 N Front.
Schoonmaker Edward, h Garden ab Smith av.
Schoonmaker G. N., laborer, h Newkirk av u DuBois av.
Schoonmaker G. M., carpenter, h E Front n Bowery.
SCHOONMAKER H., flour, feed, commission merchant, &c., ft Division, h Adams cor Rogers.

Bargains, No. 5 Wall St., Kingston.

HIRAM ROOSA'S Accidental, Life, Fire, Marine

Schoonmaker H. Mrs., h E Front n Maiden la.
Schoonmaker H. M., (S. & Van Wagenen,) h Pearl av n Green.
Schoonmaker J., teamster, h Washington av n Bridge.
Schoonmaker John N., h Prospect n Liberty.
Schoonmaker Julius, h Wall n Henry.
Schoonmaker J. W., constable, h St. James cor Pine.
SCHOONMAKER MARIUS, lawyer, 30 Wall, h Wall cor Love la.
Schoonmaker Peter, book keeper, h Crown n John.
Schoonmaker P. E., book keeper, bds Adams, cor Rogers.
Schoonmaker Richard, h Division ab Rogers.
Schoonmaker Stephen, pilot, h Union av cor Prince.
Schoonmaker Wm. I., h Tremper av n Elmendorf.
Schoonoven Charles, carpenter, h Flatbush av n Prince.
Schreiber C. H., cabinet maker, h Pine.
Schreiber John, farmer, h Stuyvesant n Hasbrouck av.
SCHREIBER JOHN H., grocer, liquors, crockery, &c., Garden and Ferry, h Hasbrouck av c Stuyvesant.
Schreiber P., clerk, bds Hasbrouck av cor Stuyvesant.
Schrivner Charles, laborer, h Cross n Hasbrouck av.
Schryver J. A., blacksmith, h Spring n Hone.
Schryver John H., h Fair n Bowery.
Schryver H., carpenter, h E Front n St. James.
Schryver Oliver, sewing machine agt., h St. James n Wall.
Schultz J., carriage manufac., Mill cor Hasbrouck av, h Union n Post.
Schultzel S., h German n Ridge.
Schumann F. C., saloon, Dock, h do.
Schwalbach B., (pro. Grand Central Hotel,) h Union av cor Pine Grove av.
Schwartz P., clothing, Canal cor Lackawanna, h do.

J. O. & G. B. MERRITT, Black Alpacas

Insurance and Real Estate Agency, Rondout, N. Y.

Schwenk Jacob, laborer, h Hone cor Union.
Scott Rachel, washing, h O'Neil n Bruyn av.
Scott Thomas, h Fair n Henry.
Scott Walter, hostler, Hamilton House.
Scott Wm. B., (S. & Weber,) h Abeel n Hone.
Schuler Philip, laborer, h Pine n Ravine.
Scrreider John, mason, h Third av n Point rd.
Scubar Louis, laborer, Point rd n Union av.
SCULLEY & CONROY, grocers, 23 Washington av.
Sculley T. H., (S. & Conroy,) h 13 N Front.
Sculley William, farmer, h 35 N Front.
Seabert C., laborer, h Columbus av.
SEAMAN & MILLER, wholesale and commission merchants, &c., Ferry.
Seaman A., marble cutter, h Union av cor Greenkill.
Seaman George, laborer, h Bowery n Pine.
Seaman L. S., (S. & Miller,) h Union av n toll gate.
Sebastic John, h Pine, (Rondout.)
SECORE GEO. S., hats, caps, furs, &c., 26 Garden, h Sleightburg.
Secor H. E., baggage master, h Garden opp Ferry.
Seeley Karner, carpenter, h St. James n Prospect.
Seeley, teacher, h Hurley av.
Sefrin Daniel, milk, h Ann cor Union.
Seitz C., h Union n cement works.
Seitz Robert, clerk, Division cor Garden.
Sellemer O., h Pierpont n School House.
Setton John, boatman, h Cross n Ann.
Shader Catherine, h St. James n Union av.
Shader C. T., painter, h Union av bel St. James.
Shader DeWitt, beer, &c., h 25 Washington av.
Shader Henry V. B., cigar maker, h St. James n Union av.
Shader Herman R., wagon maker, h St. James n Union av. *14

and Brilliantines, 5 Wall St., Kingston.

HIRAM ROOSA'S Agency represents a Combined

Shader S., harness, Washington av n Depot, h Hurley av.
Shader William, carriage manuf., St. James n Union, av h do.
Shafer F. A., h John n Main.
SHAFER LEVI, physician, Maiden la n Pine, h do. OFFICE HOURS, 7 to 9 A. M., 12 to 2 and 6 to 8 P. M.
Shannon Alexander, boatman, h Division opp Abeel.
Sharkey Edward, stone cutter, h Cedar cor Sterling.
Sharkey John, stone cutter, h O'Neil n Tremper.
Sharpe George H., General, h Albany av cor E Front.
Shatsle Andrew, laborer, h Flatbush av n Hasbrouck av.
Shaw Charles H., clerk, bds Fair cor John.
Shaw G. W. & Co., harness and trunks, 77 N Front.
Shaw G. W., (G. W. Shaw & Co.,) h St. James n Fair.
Shaw H. F., clerk, bds Excelsior House.
Shaw H. W., clerk, bds Columbus av cor Tompkins.
Shaw S. H., (G. W. Shaw & Co,) h St. James n Fair.
Shaw William, h Fair n Maiden la.
Shay Martin, laborer, h Cedar n Mill.
Shay Simon, laborer, h Cordts.
Sheahan Peter, laborer, h Meadow n Ann.
Shearns John, h Ann cor Meadow.
Shears S., h Crown n Green.
Shelightner J., (DuBois & S.,) h Wall n Bowery.
Shellton James, barber, h Hasbrouck av n R. R.
Sheppard Wm., blacksmith, Columbus av, h Prospect.
Sherer Edwin, hotel, Division cor Ferry.
Sheridan P., grocer and liquors, Dock, h do.
Sherman A., mason, h Furnace n Henry.
Sherwood John, h Hasbrouck av n Newkirk.

SHERWOOD V.,
dentist, Newkirk's building, Division, h Hasbrouck av ab Newkirk av.

J. O. & G. B. MERRITT, Choice Dress

Shetcle O., h Point rd cor Third av.
Shinners Richard, teamster, h Cedar cor Prospect.
Short David, h Wilbur rd cor Hudson.
SHORT LORENZO, photographer, Division opp Mill, h Newkirk av.
Short L. M., printer, h Holmes n Hone.
SHORT M. E., baker and confectioner, Pierpont cor Russell.
Short Peter, h Spring ab Ravine.
Short W., brakeman, h Hasbrouck av n Newkirk av.
Short William H., confectioner, h Pierpont c Russell.
Shortall Michael, mason, h ft Chambers.
Shovling Patrick, h Columbus av n Prospect.
Shwedes Wm., hostler, h Ravine n Hasbrouck av.
Shutes John, wire maker, h Henry n Prospect.
Shultis J. A., carriage maker, h Prospect n St. James.
Shultis L., pilot, h Henry n Oak.
Shultis Philip, (Longyear & S.,) h E Front n Henry.
Shultis William H., carpenter, h E Front n Liberty.
Sherer A., h Spring ab Ravine.
Sherer J. L., carpenter, h Chester, n School House.
Sherwood R. A., clerk, Mansion House.
Sickler C., clerk, h Point rd n Third av.
Sickler John, h Ann cor Meadow.
Sickler S., laborer, h Cedar n Sterling.
Sickler Solomon, carman, h ft Chambers.
Sickler Silas, laborer, h Union n Hone.
Sickler William, teamster, h ft Chambers.
Sickles Ann, Mrs., Maiden la n Fair.
Sickley M. A., Mrs., h Chambers n Stuyvesant.
Siefrec I., carman, h Ravine n R. R.
Sigler William, cabinet maker, h Union n Wurts.
Silverstein Abram, tailor, h Division cor Pierpont.
Silverstein H., tailor, h Division ab Union.

Simmons B. W., ship carpenter,h Hudson cor Wilbur rd.
Simons James, boatman, h Ann n Union.
Simon S., confectioner, Abeel W of Wurts, h do.
SIMS WM., insurance agent and variety store, Mill, h do.
Sirrine L. E., conductor, h Orchard av.
Sission F. A., clerk, bds Kingston Hotel.
Sissons F. H., restaurant, Main n E Front, bds Kingston Hotel.
Sishop George, h Hunter n Hone.
Skane Ellen, h Union opp Cedar.
Skeihn Martin, laborer, h Ravine n Ann.
Skeihn Patrick, laborer, h Cedar cor Prospect.
Skelton J. R., barber, Ferry n Hasbrouck av, h Hasbrouck av ab Mill.
Skelton T. S., shoemaker, Division n Spring, bds Metzgar's Hotel.
Slater C. Mrs., h Division ab Holmes.
Slater Israel, mason, h Bowery n Union av.
Slater O., teamster, h Pearl av n Green.
Slater Silas, miller, h Cedar n Union av.
Slattery John, clerk, h Ann.
Slattery Mary, Mrs., h Ann ab Cross.
Slawson George, fireman, h Newkirk av n Chambers.
Sleight John, laborer, h Cordts.
SLEIGHT GEORGE S. & CO., general merchandise, Sleightburg.
Sleight J. D., (Ridenour & Sleight,) h Fair bel St. James.
Smedes James, h Division ab Rogers.
Smedes N. B., baker, h Prospect n Cedar.
Smedes Washington, clerk, h 21 Washington av.
Smeeder Jacob, laborer, h St. Mary n Hasbrouck av.
Smith Abram, mason, h 5 Washington av.

of all kinds. **Rondout, N. Y.**

KINGSTON DIRECTORY. 165

Smith A., real estate, Greenkill av cor Union av, h do.
Smith Adam, boatman, h St. Mary n Chambers.
Smith Andrew, hostler, bds Freileweh Hotel.
Smith A. C., gen. ticket and freight agent, bds City Hotel.
Smith Charles, h Division cor Stuyvesant.
Smith Charles, laborer, h Greenkill av.
Smith Clark, farmer, h Mapleton.
Smith C., laborer, h Cottage cor Point rd.
Smith Cortland, laborer, h Cedar n Union av.
Smith C. B., h John cor Crown.
Smith Cordelia Mrs., h Pierpont ab Ravine.
Smith D., laborer, h Flatbush av.
Smith Edward, h Hunter n Ravine.
Smith Frederick, carman, h Third av n Point rd.
Smith F. A., painter, h Hasbrouck av n Garden.
Smith F. W., carpenter, h Pine n Ravine.
Smith George, cooper, h Hasbrouck av n Bridge.
Smith George, weaver, h Hunter n Ravine.
Smith George Mrs., h 58 N Front.
Smith G. A., livery, h Wall n Maiden Lane.
Smith G. A. & R. F., livery, Wall n Pearl.
Smith George B., miner, h Union n Hasbrouck.
Smith George C., (Crispell & Smith,) bds Chestnut.
Smith G. J. Mrs., tobacconist, 45 N Front, h n opp do.
Smith G. W. Mrs., h Second n R. R.
Smith Gotleib, cooper, h Hasbrouck av n Bridge.
Smith Hiram, h Green n Lucas av.
Smith H. J. Mrs., h Fair n St. James.
Smith James, captain, h Liberty n Furnace.
Smith James, laborer, h Maiden la.
Smith John, boatman, h Pine n Ravine.
Smith John, laborer, h St. Mary.
Smith John, laborer, h Union n Hone.

No. 5 Wall Street, Kingston.

Get an Accidental Policy at

KINGSTON DIRECTORY.

Smith John, Mrs., h Albany av E of Union av.
Smith John B., h Abeel ab Post.
Smith John C., h Cottage Hill, Wilbur.
Smith J. Mrs., h Pearl cor Wall.
Smith J. S., General, h Albany av opp Ten Brœck av.
Smith J. W., blacksmith, h Flatbush av n R. R.
Smith Jerome, h Flatbush av opp Garden.
Smith L., stone cutter, h Bowery n Prospect.
Smith L. B., clerk, bds Wall cor Pearl.
Smith Mary, h Spring ab Ravine.
Smith M., agent, h Henry cor Prospect.
Smith M. A. Mrs., boarding, h Albany av opp Maiden Lane.
Smith M. R., carpenter, h Cedar n E Front.
Smith N. Mrs., h St. James n Prospect.
Smith O., carpenter, h Henry n Union av.
Smith P., laborer, h Cedar n Catherine.
Smith Robert F., livery, h Wall n Pearl.
Smith Theodore, carpenter, h Abruyn cor Union.
Smith Theodore, tailor, h Hasbrouck av n Bridge.
Smith Thomas, h German n Hone.
Smith William, h Ravine opp Pine.
Smith William, bookkeeper, bds E Front n John.
Smith William, clerk, bds Hasbrouck av n Cross.
Smith William, sash, h Henry n Sterling.
Smith W. E., h Columbus av N of Tompkins.
Smith W. H., civil engineer, Wall cor John, bds Fair ab St. James.
Smith Wm. O., bookkeeper, bds E Front n John.
Snelling J. B., capt., h Hasbrouck av n Union.
Snyder B., nursery, Linderman av, h do.
Snyder C., grocer, Washington av cor Hurley av, h N Front.
Snyder C. A., farmer, h Mapleton.

J. O. & G. B. MERRITT, Gent's

HIRAM ROOSA'S Agency, Rondout, N. Y.

Snyder C. H. Miss, dress maker, 19 Garden.
Snyder Charles M., clerk, bds Hone cor Pierpont.
Snyder Clement, saloon, Chambers n Ravine.
Snyder E., engineer, h Greenkill av.
Snyder E., carriage manufac., h Prospect n Liberty.
Snyder Frederick, boatman, h Ridge.
Snyder H. B., clerk, h Hone cor Pierpont.
Snyder Levi, horse farrier, h Prospect n Liberty.
SNYDER M. B., flour, fish, &c., Ulster Market building, Ferry, h Hone cor Pierpont.
Snyder T., laborer, h Cedar n E Front.
Soilberger Gus., (D. & S.,) h Meadow.
Soll Otto, painter, h Ravine n opp R. R.
Solomon M., hats, Lackawanna, h Union n Wurts.
Solomon S., clothing, Lackawanna, h Union.
Sooler Morris, rags, &c., h Newkirk av n Chambers.
Souers Anna M., saloon, h Abeel n Hone.
Soule S. D., lawyer, John n Fair, h Linderman av.
Sours Charles, brewer, h Mason n Hone.
Souser John, butcher, E Front cor Henry.
Southard G., carpenter, h Bruyn n O'Neil.
Southard T. G., carpenter, h Bruyn av n O'Neil.
Southwick Thomas, L., leather, &c., 85 N Front, bds Green opp Main.
Spangenberger Lawrence, peddler, h Adams n Holmes.
Sparday Michael, h Hudson.
SPARLING D. W., lawyer, John n Wall, h Liberty n Union av.
Sparling George, laborer, h Cedar n Sterling.
SPARTY ROMAN, saloon, Division ab Mansion House, h do.
Spatz G. Mrs., h Union n Wurts.
Spatz Peter, engineer, h Division ab Union.
Spelt Charles, boatman, h St. Mary n Chambers.

Furnishing Goods, 5 Wall St., Kingston.

Spencer Alvin D., carman, h Hurley av.
Spencer Charles, agent, h Henry n Union av.
Spencer E. E., carpenter, h Washington av n N Front.
Spencer Luther, cabinet maker, h Elmendorf.
Spielman C. L., cooper, h Union av n Elmendorf.
Spoilt John, laborer, h Ravine n R. R.

SPORE THEODORE,

stoves, furnaces, tinware, &c., 62 N Front, h Maiden Lane n Fair.

Springsteen S. M. H. Mrs., h Union av cor Point rd.
Stack C., laborer, h Hasbrouck av n Point rd.
Stafford C., h Ravine opp Spring.
Stafford James, laborer, h Post n Spring.
Stafford John, clerk, bds Post n Spring.
Stahle Joseph, laborer, h Chambers n Stuyvesant.
Stale Mary Mrs., h Hunter.
Stanley James, ship carpenter, h Spring cor Ravine.
Stanley Wm., carpenter, h Hunter n Abeel.
STAPLES A. S., flour, feed, &c., Hasbrouck av, Garden and Ferry, h Abeel n Pres. Church.
Staples Charles, carpenter, h Grove n Abruyn.
Staples Sherwood, grocer, Hone cor Union, h Chestnut.
Staples Stephen, h Union av n Toll Gate.
Staples S. Jr., bookkeeper, bds Union av n Toll Gate.
Staples William, clerk, bds Union n Toll Gate.
Starr N. W., teacher, h Green n opp Main.
STATE OF NEW YORK NATIONAL BANK, Wall cor John.
STAUBACHER CHARLES, lager beer brewer, Hone cor German.
Stearn Charles, peddler, h Mason n Hone.
Stearns W. H., bar tender, Union Hotel.

operative Plan at H. ROOSA'S Agency, Rondout.

Stebbins J. N., dry goods, h Ponkhockie n Union.
STEBBINS JOHN R. & CO., dry goods and carpets, Garden and Ferry.
Stebbins John R., (John R. Stebbins & Co.,) h Columbus av cor Prospect.
Stebbins S. L., (Lawton & S.,) h Abeel opp Wurts.
Steeger S. Mrs., h Wall n St. James.
Steele John, bookkeeper, bds Abeel n Hone.
Steele William, laborer, h Mason n Hone.
Steiger Conrad, barber, Washington av n Depot, h do.
Steiner J. M., Rev., h Hunter cor Ravine.
Steltz Andrew, h Pierpont cor Russell.
Stemant August, saloon, Point rd cor Jarrold.
Stengline Joseph, blacksmith, bds Metzger's Hotel.
Stephan Charles, marble yard, Union n R. R.

STEPHAN F. & CO.,

brewers, Abeel n Ravine.
Stephan Frederick, (F. Stephan & Co.,) h Union av, opp Point rd.
Stephan George, milliner, h Abeel W of Wurts.
Stephan George F., book keeper, h Abeel n Washington Hall.
Stephens Michael, laborer, h Meadow n Ann.
Stephens Peter, carpet weaver, Greenkill av n Union av, h do.
Stevens Charles, marble works, &c., Union av n Dederick, h do.
Stevens George, bar tender, h Greenkill av.
Stevens Henry, pilot, h Hone n Spring.
Stewart Charles, baker, h Smith av n Garden.
Stewart Henry, milkman, h O'Neil n R. R.
Stewart Henry, laborer, h Cedar n Union av.

Hosiery, No. 5 Wall St., Kingston.

Stewart John H., tel. operator, bds 14 Cedar.
Stewart John, cooper, h Catherine n Tompkins.
Stiles C. H., painter, h Henry n Union av.
Stilson Geo., carpenter, h Cedar n E Front.
Stitsal Frederick, h Hudson.
Stitt Chas. H., Rev. D. D., h Fair cor Pearl.
Stilwell C. S., sewing machines, 104 N Front, h do.
Stock M., furniture, &c., Division ab Union, h do.
Stoddard G. N., grocer, Garden and Ferry, h Adams.
Stoddard H. E., clerk, bds Adams.
STOKES JAMES Jr., groceries, crockery, &c., Union av cor St James, h do.
Stokes R., Jr., clerk, h Union av cor St. James.
Stone D. C., Mrs., h Prospect n Liberty.
Stone Moses, (F. & S.,) h Elmendorf n Smith av.
Stoneman M. G., sail maker, 15 Ferry.
Stoll J., cabinet maker, h N Front n Green.
Stortz Matthew, h Hone ab Hunter.
Story A. J., h St. James n E Front.
Story Charles H., grocer, h E Front cor Bowery.
Stott T., stone cutter, h Prospect.
Stoutenburgh D., laborer, h Bowery opp Oak.
STOW & BENSON, insurance and real estate, Garden cor Division.
Stow D. B., (Stow & Benson,) h Union av n toll gate.
Strahley Fred., h Hunter n Ridge.
Stratford J., grocer, E Front cor Greenkill av.
Strafford Wm., stone cutter, h Prospect n Greenkill av.
Straub Mary, h Ann ab Meadow.
Stribling N., h Pine n Ravine.
Strips Peter, h Spring n Ravine.
Strong L. B., carpenter, &c., Elm cor Third av, h do.
Strong S. M. Mrs., h Tremper av cor Downs.
Strump & Gerber, hair-dressers, John n Wall.

Real Estate Agency, Rondout, N. Y.

Strump Charles, (S. & Gerber,) h N Front n Green.
Sturtz F. Rev., h Livingston n Stuyvesant.
Styles A. L., clerk, h Pearl n Green.
Styles E. H., foreman, h Liberty n Union av.
Styles E. W., h Lucas av n Green.
Styles George B., jeweler, 27 Wall h Green c Lucas av
Styles George, painter, h Bowery n Prospect.
Styles H., builder, h Union av cor O'Neil.
Styles J. E., carpenter, Pearl av n Green, h Green cor Pearl av.
Styles J. J., plane maker, St. James n Pine, h n do.
Styles J. R., carpenter, h E Front n Center.
Styles Palmer C., teamster, h Union av cor Dederick.
Styles Wm. H., painter, h Prospect n Liberty.
Sudam Harison, lawyer, h Main cor Wall.
Sullivan Daniel, laborer, h Cross n Division.
Sullivan Dennis, laborer, h Cedar n Mill.
Sullivan David, laborer, h Prospect n Union.
Sullivan D., bds Mansion House.
Sullivan James, laborer, h Newkirk av n Point rd.
Sullivan James, laborer, h Meadow n Ann.
Sullivan J., laborer, h Cross n R. R.
Sullivan John, laborer, h Point rd n R. R.
Sullivan Michael, seaman, h Ravine n Point rd.
Sullivan Michael, laborer, h DeWitt.
Sullivan William, h Mason n Wurts.
Suppies Augus., shoemaker, Union av n Liberty, h do.
Suppies H., shoemaker, Abeel W of Wurts.
SUTTON C. B., (pro. Sutton House,) Hurley av n Washington av.
Sutton Charles G., laborer, h Livingston.
Sutton D., laborer, h Washington av n N Front.
Sutton Lawrence, captain, h Hanraty n Point rd.
Sutton Samuel, h Wilbur Gate.

Embroideries, No. 5 Wall St., Kingston.

Losses Equitably Adjusted and Promptly Paid

Swab Jacob, Mrs., h Pierpont n School House.
Swab John, h German n Hone.
Swart A. L., clerk, bds Wall n Pearl.
Swart C. Mrs., h Holmes n Wurts.
SWART J. O., grocer, &c., 51 Wall cor Pearl, h Wall
 n Pearl.
Swart Peter, Mrs., h Wall n Pearl.
Swart William, painter, h St. James n Fair.
Swart Wm. T., h Main next Eagle Hotel.
Swart William, bds Kingston Hotel.
Swartz Jacob, h German n Ravine.
SWEENEY JAMES, North River blue stone, Wilbur.
Sweeney James, laborer, h Hanraty n Point rd.
Sweeney Owen, laborer, h Hanraty n Point rd.
Sweeney Peter, laborer, h Hanraty n Ravine.
Sweeney Wm. A., salesman, h Wilbur.
Swink Benjamin, Mrs., h Mill.
Swint Ann, saloon, h Chambers n Ravine.

TAMMANY J. R., cooper, bds Chestnut n Abruyn.
TAMMANY R. G., U. S. guager, h Chestnut n
 Abruyn.
Tammany W. G., cooper, bds Chestnut n Abruyn.
Tanner Alfred, carpenter, h St. James n Wall.

Tappen, Burhans & Webster,
 dry goods, Wall cor John.
Tappen J. R., (T., Burhans & Webster,) h Green n
 John.
Tappen Kiersted Mrs., h St. James n R. R.
Tappen M. Mrs., h Maiden Lane n E Front.
Tappen Mary Mrs., h E Front n Henry.
Tappen S. C. Mrs., h Green n John.

J. O. & G. B. MERRITT, Ladies'

At HIRAM ROOSA'S Agency, Rondout, N. Y.

KINGSTON DIRECTORY. 173

Tarpp Thomas, laborer, h Abeel.
Taylor Alexander, teamster, h Taylor.
Taylor Charles, farmer, h Chester cor Hasbrouck av.
Taylor Maria Mrs., h Union av n Chester.
Taylor Martin A., clerk, bds Chambers cor Union.
Taylor T. O., clerk, bds Union av n City Hall.
Tebow Edward, clerk, bds Lucas av.
Tebow Peter, h Hurley av
Ten Broeck A. D., farmer, h Ten Broeck av c Downs.
Ten Broeck C. C., clerk, h Elmendorf n R R.
Ten Broeck Cornelius, h E Front cor Bowery.
Ten Broeck James, laborer, h Hasbrouck av n Bridge.
Ten Broeck M. Miss, h Green cor Main.
Ten Broeck P. N., coal, h Elmendorf, c Ten Brœck av.
Ten Broeck W. W. & P. N., coal, St. James n Wall.
Ten Broeck Westley, farmer, h Albany av n Ten Broeck av.
TELLER WM. S. & Sons, (George & Myron,) tannery, 2 N Front, h Maiden la cor Pine.
Teller Wm. S., tannery, h Maiden la cor Pine.
Terpening Peter, boatman, h Henry n Union av.
Terwilliger Aaron B., car driver, h Orchard av.
Terwilliger Charles L., captain, h Union av n Chester.
Terwilliger H., laborer, h E Front opp Cedar.
Terwilliger H. S., clerk, bds Excelsior Hotel.
Terwilliger J. H., boatman, Hasbrouck av n Bridge.
Terwilliger W. B. Mrs., h Ponkhockie n Union.
Terzenlae August, laborer, h Second av n R. R.
Thacker James A., shoe maker, h Wall n Bowery.
The Courier, (W. H. & J. C. Romeyn, ed., &c.,) 17 Garden.
THIELE V., saloon, Division opp Abeel, h do.
Thiele Jerome, fish, &c., Ulster Market.
Thomas Charles M., printer, h Hurley av.

*15

Undergarments, 5 Wall St., Kingston.

HIRAM ROOSA'S Insurance Agency has

Thomas Henry, laborer, h Third av n Elm.
Thomas Henry, h Pierpont ab Ravine.
Thomas William, laborer, h Chambers cor Newkirk av.
Thomas Wm., miner, h Hasbrouck av n Stuyvesant.
Thompson Austin S., smoker, h Pierpont n Hone.
THOMPSON GEO. & SONS, provisions, &c., Hunter.
Thompson Hugh, h Ravine ab Hunter.
Thompson J. R. G., teamster, h Union av n St. James.
Thompson John, h Hunter n Ravine.
Thompson M. Mrs., h Love la.
Thompson Peter, boatman, h Post cor Union.
Thompson Reuben, boot and shoemaker, Henry cor Prospect, h do.
Thompson Robert, caulker, h German n Ravine.
Thompson Robert, butcher, h Maiden la n Pine.
Thompson Robert, h E Front n Henry.
Thompson W., slater, h Russell.
Thompson William, h Ann cor Meadow.
Tibbals H. W., bookkeeper, h Wall n St. James.
Tibbitts Daniel, printer, h Abeel n Ravine.
Tice Samuel, moulder, Liberty n Furnace.
Tice William, moulder, h O'Neil n R. R.
Ticehurst R. L., carpenter, h Pine cor St. James.
Tiegen William H., boarding, h Livingston.
TIENCKEN SEBA, boarding, Wall n Bowery, h do.
Tiencken R., currier, Green n Pearl.
Tierney Thomas, h Hasbrouck av n Flatbush av.
Tietjen W. H. & Co., brick manufac., hd Livingston.
Tillou C. W., fish, 37 N Front, h Fair n N Front.
Tillford Thos., coachman, h Albany av n Maiden la.
TILLSON & BRINK, sash, blinds, doors, &c., Union av n Elmendorf.
Tillson J. D., (T. & Brink,) h Union av n Elmendorf.
Tilson & Raenhart, carpenters and builders, Henry n Sterling.

J. O. & G. B. MERRITT, Cloths and

Never had any Disputed Claims.

Tilson Geo., (T. & Raenhart,) h Cedar.
Tilson Isaac, carpenter, h Elmendorf n R. R.
Timm Adolph, harness, Washington av n Depot h do.
Timmons John, segar maker, bds City Hotel.
Tobin William, mechanic, h Prospect n Union.
Tolley Juliette N. Mrs., copyist, h Green n Pearl.
Tolley William F., cashier, bds Green n Pearl.
Tomberger Charles, h Spring ab Ravine.
Tomost August, h Hunter n Hone.
Tompkins Edward, quarry supt., h hd Grove.
Tompkins S. Mrs., h Hunter n Ridge.
Tongue James, Sr., contractor, h Ravine n Vine.
Tongue James, Jr., clerk, h Hasbrouck av n Meadow.
Tongue William, laborer, h Ravine n Point rd.
Tootill R., mer. tailor, 18 Wall, h 34 N Front.
Totter F., bowling alley, John n Wall, h Wilbur rd.
Town Peter, cooper, h Cedar n Union av.
Townsend C. J., millinery, &c., 13 Wall, h do.
Townsend George, carpenter, h Bowery n Pine.
Townsend R. G., h Hunter n Ravine.
Townsend W. H., clerk, h Hunter.
Townsend William, h N Front cor E Front.
Tracy John, laborer, h Cedar cor Union.
Trainor Sarah, h Garden n Ferry.
Traphagen M. Mrs., h Prospect cor Bowery.
Traver C. L., station agent, h Pine n St. James.
Traver David, carpenter, h Smith av n Garden.
Traver Jared, grocer, Garden cor Smith av.
Traver John H., machinist, h Prince junc. Smith av.
Traver J. H., engineer, h Pine n St. James.
Traver L., cooper, h Columbus av n Prospect.
Traver Theo. A., restaurant, Ferry House, h opp do.
Treadwell J. C., (E. & T.,) bds Washington av.
Treat A. A., clerk, h Newkirk av.

Cassimeres, No. 5 Wall St., Kingston.

Your best interest will dictate to Insure with

Treat David, cooper, h Second av n R. R.
Trelease Richard Mrs., h Tompkins cor Union.
Trelease Thomas H., clerk, h Tompkins n Union.
Trelease Wm., foreman, h Hasbrouck av cor Meadow.
Trembly Mary, h Newkirk av cor Point rd.
Tremper J. H., (Romer & T.,) h Albany av cor Esther.
Tremper J. H. Jr., (T. H. Tremper & Bro.,) h Albany av n R. R.
Tremper T. H. & Bro., flour, feed, &c., Ferry.
Tremper T. H., (T. H. Tremper & Bro.,) h Albany av n R. R.
Trenkle Joseph, saloon, Chambers cor Cross, h do.
Trice William, laborer, h Chambers n Ravine.
Tripp A. J., engineer, h Hone cor Lord.
Tripp Francis, laborer, h Hasbrouck av n Stuyvesant.
Tripp J. H., clerk, h Hasbrouck av ab Stuyvesant.
Tripp Joshua, h Union av cor Point rd.
Tripp Richard, miner, h 87 Hasbrouck av.
Tronson I., carpenter, h Henry opp Oak.
Thorp M. V., clerk, bds Abeel n Wurts.
Trowbridge Charles, clerk, bds Plank rd.
Trumpbour Mary, Miss, h Green opp Main.
Trumpbour M. T., asst. treasurer, Savings Bank, h Fair cor St. James.
Tubby J. G., gravel roofing, h Pierpont n Russell.
Tubby John, h Pierpont n Russell.
TUBBY JOSEPH, paints, oils, &c., 21 Garden, h Spring cor Hone.
Tuny P., h Division ab Cross.
TURCK & BURHANS, lumber and builders, Garden opp Ferry.
Turck Marius, h Newkirk av n DuBois av.
Turck W. J., (T. & Burhans,) h Spring n Wurts.
Turner Francis, painter, h Union av cor Flatbush av.

J. O. & G. B. MERRITT, Flannels and

HIRAM ROOSA, Agent at Rondout, N. Y.

Turner Samuel, machinist, h Hasbrouck av n Newkirk av.
Turner W. H., Supt. R. & K. Gas Works, h E Front cor St. James.

UHLE HENRY, butcher, h Abeel cor Post.
Uhle Martin, saloon, Abeel cor Post, h do.
Ulrich Frederick, cigar, h Russell.
ULSTER COUNTY SAVINGS INSTITUTION, Wall opp Court House.
Underwood Daniel, laborer, h Hasbrouck av n Union.
UNION HOTEL, (S. A. Webster, pro.,) Wall cor John.
Uppermann Louis, butcher, h Garden n Ferry.
U. S. Express Co., 9 Wall and Mansion House.
Utt A., h Ridge cor German.

VAIL E. P., grocer, h 25 Garden, h do.
Valkenburgh A. L., h Crown n Green.
Valentine Casper, mason, h Union av cor O'Neil.
Vallett George A., photographer, Division ab Mansion House, h Spring n Hone.
VanAken & Crook, lumber, &c., St. James cor Pine.
VanAken A. M. Mrs., h Union av n opp Cedar.
VanAken Abram, h Abeel n Wurts.
VanAken A., mason, h Cedar n Union av.
VanAken B. I., lumber, h Union av n St. James.
VanAken E. peddler, h E Front n Bowery.
VanAken H. C., laborer, h Chambers n Stuyvesant.
VanAken Jonas, bds Albany av opp Maiden Lane.
VanAken Wm., farmer, h Washington av n Pearl av.
VanAken Wm. P., dockbuilder, h Prince ab Union av.
VanAnden Chas., gen. merchandise, 15 N Front, h Main ab Green.

Blankets, No. 5 Wall St., Kingston.

If not convenient to call, send your application by

178   KINGSTON DIRECTORY.

VanAnden George, clerk, h Green n Lucas av.
VanBramer A., h Union av cor O'Neil.
VanBrayman Peter, laborer, h Cedar n Union.
VanBrayman Wm., cigar maker, h Mason n Wurts.
VanBuren A. H., bds Main n E Front.
VanBuren A. L., local editor, Kingston Press, h E Front.
VanBnren A. P., grocer, Division cor Abeel, h do.
VanBuren Anna, Mrs., h St. James, h Union av.
VanBuren C. Jr., butcher, bds Wall cor Maiden la.
VanBuren Charles, copyist, h Maiden la n Albany av.
VanBuren C. Mrs., h Prospect n Liberty.
VanBuren D. T., surveyor, Main n Eagle Hotel, h Fair cor Maiden la.
VanBuren Eliza, Mrs., h Green junc. Crown.
VAN BUREN HENRY, butcher, Wall n Maiden la., h Wall.
VanBuren H., teacher, h E Front n St. James.
VanBuren I. Mrs., h Green cor Maiden la.
VanBuren James, hides and leather, Ferry, h Fair n St. James.
VanBuren John, blacksmith, h Henry cor Sterling.
VanBuren M. T., carpenter, h Wall cor Maiden la.
VanBuren M., h Crown n N Front.
VanBuren Peter, mer. tailor, 14 N Front, h Green opp John.
VanBuren Peter Jr., butcher, bds Green opp John.
VanBuren R. A. Miss, teacher, bds Main n E Front.
VanBuren T. Mrs., h Green n St. James.
VanBuren William, moulder, h E Front n Liberty.
VanBuskirk H. W., ship carpenter, h Hone n Abeel.
VanDamark John, caulker, h Abeel.
VanDemark J. C., foreman, h Newkirk av n DuBois av
VanDemark James, h Washington n Bridge.

J. O. & G. B. MERRITT, Notions and

Mail to **HIRAM ROOSA**, Insur. Agent, Rondout.

VanDemark Wm., wagon maker, h Hasbrouck av n Flatbush av.
VanDemark William H., clerk, h Pearl n Fair.
VanDerburgh George W., chair maker, h 44 N Front.
VanderLyn J. Jr., artist, 72 N Front, bds Fair n N Front.
Vanderveer D. N. Rev., h Main n Wall.
VanDerzee Thomas, captain, h Summer n Susan.
VAN DEUSEN BROTHERS, druggists, 6 Wall, N Front cor Crown, Garden and Ferry.
VanDeusen Columbus, (VanDeusen Bros.,) h Hasbrouck av n Meadow.
VanDeusen Cornelia, Mrs., h Fair n N Front.
VanDeusen G. N., (VanD. Bros.,) h Fair bet Main and John.
VanDeusen J. B., (VanD. Bros.,) h John bet Fair and E Front.
VanDeusen J. C., clerk, bds Kingston Hotel.
VanDeusen J. L., (VanD. Bros.,) h Chestnut.
VanDevoort James O., agent, bds Mansion House.
Vandling A. H., supt., h Abruyn n Columbus av.
VanDyke Peter, h Garden ab Smith av.
VANETTEN & CLEARWATER, lawyers, John n Wall.
VanEtten A., mason, h St. James n E Front.
VanEtten E. A. Mrs., h St. James n Union av.
VanEtten Edward, h Spring n Hone.
VanEtten George, surveyor, John n Wall, h Wall opp Bowery.
VanEtten Gilbert, bds Wall n St. James.
VanEtten J. A., h Wall n Bowery.
VanEtten John E., (VanE. & C.,) Fair n Henry.
VanEtten S. E., teamster, h Hurley av.
VanEtten William G., laborer, h Wall n St. James.

Trimmings, No. 5 Wall St., Kingston.

Insure with no other Agent.

VanEtten W. Gehi, sprinkler, h Hurley av.
VanGaasbeek & Wolven, carpenters, Maiden Lane n Albany av.
VanGaasbeek A. A., toll collector, Wilbur gate.
VAN GAASBEEK A. E., carpenter, builder, sash, blinds, &c., Union av n City Hall, h n do.
VanGaasbeek C. Mrs., h St. James n Union av.
VanGaasbeek C. H., pres., Fair cor Main.
VanGaasbeek C. H. Jr., book keeper, h Fair cor Main.
VAN GAASBEEK EDGAR, butcher, St. James n Union av, h do.
VanGaasbeek H. H., h Garden ab Smith av.
VanGaasbeek H. L., clerk, 72 N Front.
VanGaasbeek Henry Mrs., h Point rd n Livingston.
VanGaasbeek J., carpenter, h TenBroeck av n Downs.
VanGaasbeek J. B., hats, caps, &c., 72 N Front, h St. James n Union av.
VanGaasbeek Jacob, carpenter, h Liberty n E Front.
VanGaasbeek John, gardener, h Chester n R. R.
VanGaasbeek L. B., teller, h Fair cor Main.
VanGaasbeek L., butcher, h Furnace opp Van Buren.
VanGaasbeek Peter, garden, h Union av n Toll Gate.
VanGaasbeek Rachel, h Union av n Toll Gate.
VanGaasbeek R. M., toll collector, Union av.
VanGaasbeek S. Mrs., h Liberty n Prospect.
VanGaasbeek T., laborer, h Prospect.
VanGaasbeek W., blacksmith, h Prospect n Greenkill av.
VanGaasbeek W., h Liberty n Prospect.
VanGaasbeek Wm., engineer, h Union av n R. R.
VanGaasbeek Wm. H., carpenter, h Esther.
VanGraven Lewis, engineer, h DuBois av n Maple av.
VanGraven Wm., h Hasbrouck n Stuyvesant.
VanHoesen Francis, h Hone cor Holmes.

J. O. & G. B. MERRITT, Dry Goods and

HIRAM ROOSA, Gen'l Ins. Agent, Rondout, N. Y.

VanHoesen Perry, printer, h Holmes cor Hone.
VanHoesen Teunis, foreman, h Abruyn n Chestnut.
VanHœvenberg J. D., h Wall n St. James.
VAN HŒVENBERG J. O. & H., physicians, Green junc. Crown, h Crown bet John and N Front.
VanKeuren Abram, mer. tailor, 33 Wall, h John n Crown.
VanKeuren B., mason, h E Front n Henry.
VanKeuren Cyrus, Mrs., h Liberty n Prospect.
VanKeuren Charles T., clerk, bds John n Crown.
VanKeuren Henry R., clerk, bds Mansion House.
VanKeuren James G., clerk, 5 Wall.
VanKeuren J., painter, h E Front n Henry.
VanKeuren John, mason, h Union av n Henry.
VanKeuren Mary E. Mrs., h Union av n St. James.
VanKeuren R., mason, h Greenkill av.
VanKeuren S. A. Mrs., h St. James n E Front.
VanKeuren W. H., blacksmith, Cedar n E Front.
VanLeuvan C. Mrs., h Prospect n Liberty.
VanLoon George A., h Russell cor Spring.
VanNamee S., h 12 Wall.
VanNostrand A., bookkeeper, h Wall cor Maiden la.
VanNostrand C., mason, h Fair n St. James.
VAN NOSTRAND E. T., builder, St. James cor Fair, h do.
VanNostrard M., clerk, h Bowery n Pine.
VanSantvoord C., Rev. D. D., E Front n N Front.
Wood William, oil dealer, h Henry.
Woods James, boatman, h Hunter.
VanSteenburgh J. F., h Catherine n Hasbrouck av.
VanSteenburgh M. Mrs., h Hasbrouck av cor Cross.
VanSteenburgh Simon, car driver, h Mapleton.
VanSteenburgh A. Jr., sash and blind maker, h Wall opp Bowery.

Carpets, No. 5 Wall St., Kingston.

HIRAM ROOSA'S Accidental, Life, Fire, Marine

VanSteenburgh Hiram, carpenter, h Albany av.
VanSteenburgh H., laborer, h Union av n Liberty.
VanSteenburgh J. D., tinman, h 76 N Front.
VAN RENSSELAER W. A., physician, Union av bet St. James and Elmendorf, h do.
VanValkenburg Isaac, engineer, h Abeel n Wurts.
VanValkenburg Wm., grocer, Hone cor Pierpont.
VanVliet Moses, boatman, h Point rd n Livingston.
VanVooris & Knapp, stone, Fair n Henry.
VanVooris William F., h Downs cor Tremper av.
VAN WAGENEN E. D., manager, Columbus av cor Tompkins.
VanWagenen E., clerk, h Henry.
VanWagenen Frederick, h Pierpont ab Ravine.
VanWagenen H., grocer, Abeel W of Wurts.
VanWagenen L. B., (J. R. Stebbins & Co.,) h Abeel n Wurts.
VanWagenen L. B., builder, Fair cor Bowery.
VanWagenen R. C., carpenter, h Henry n E Front.
VanWagnen I. B., barrel heads, h Maiden Lane n Albany av.
VanWagner Robert S., boatman h Wurts n Pierpont.
VAN WAGONEN & DURHAM, lawyers, John bet Crown and Wall.
VanWagonen H. D., teamster, h Union av cor Elmendorf.
VanWagonen J. M., (VanW. & D.,) bds Kingston Hotel.
VanWagoner L., carpenter, h Fair n St. James.
VAN WAGONER McD., lawyer and local ed., John n Wall.
VanWoert C. H., bookkeeper, h Flatbush av n Garden.
VanWoert A., boatman, h Pierpont n Hone.
Vedder William O., clerk, bds N Front n Green.

J. O. & G. B. MERRITT, Black Silks at

Vignes J., jeweler, 93 N Front, h Fair S of St. James.
Villey William, h Union n Hone.
VOGEL & REINHEIMER, sale and exchange stables, Abeel W of Wurts.
Vogel Charles, mason, h Henry n Sterling.
Vogle S., (Vogel & R.,) h Abeel W of Wurts.
Vohringer August, laborer, h Union n Post.
Volk Joseph, saloon, Point rd cor S Second.
Volle C., saloon, Abeel W of Wurts.
Von Beck G. F., bds City Hotel.
Voone Luke, stone, h Washington av n Depot.
Voorhees A. M., Mrs., h E Front n N Front.
Voorhees Peter S., farmer, h E Front n N Front.
Voss F., laborer, h Abeel cor Ravine.
Voots Henry, baker, h Union av n Henry.
Vredenburgh R. H., clerk, bds Main n Wall.
Vredenburgh Wm., insurance, h Green cor Pearl.
Vreeland Lydia, Mrs., h Hasbrouck av n Point rd.

WACHMEYER GEORGE, h Abeel n Hone.
Wachmeyer G. L., furniture, Abeel n Hone, h Hone opp Union.
Wackerhagen C. Mrs., Green opp St. James.
Wadsworth T. W., books, bookbinder, &c., Mill, h Hunter.
Wager Augustus, h Abeel W of Wurts.
Wagner George, saloon, Union av n R. R.
Wagner Henry, cigar maker, bds Kingston Hotel.
WAKELEE & RUNDELL, furniture and undertakers, 102 N Front.
Wakelee N., (W. & Rundell,) h Bowery cor Furnace.
Waid James, laborer, h Ann cor Union.
Walch Patrick, laborer, h Meadow n Ann.
Walden William, laborer, h Abeel.

Waldron C. Mrs., h Abeel.
Walker Benjamin, carriage maker, h Elmendorf n R. R.
Walker E. B., clerk, h Prospect n Liberty.
Walker George E., stone cutter, h Bowery n Prospect.
Walker H., carriage maker, h St. James n E Front.
Walker Joseph, millinery, &c., 21 Wall, h do.
Walkill Valley Railway Co., Division cor Mill.
Wallace Isaac, bds Albany av opp Maiden Lane.
Wallace John, boatman, h Abeel.
Walsh Mary Mrs., h Cross n Chambers.
Walsh M., blacksmith, Wilbur Plank rd.
Walsh Thomas, h Division cor Pierpont.
Walter Anthony, carpenter, h Hunter n Abeel.
Walter Edward, painter, h Spring n Hone.
Walter Jacob, carpenter, h German n Ridge.
Walters E., painter, h Bowery cor Oak.
Walters Henry, miner, h Ravine n Point rd.
Walton Thomas, laborer, h Meadow n Chambers.
Wands John B., bookkeeper, h Prince ab Union av.
Ward L., shoemaker, h Cedar n Mill.
Ward Patrick, h Ann ab Union.
Ward Peter, laborer, h Hasbrouck av n Newkirk av.
Ward Wm., boatman, h Prospect n Union.
Ward William, laborer, h Ann ab Cross.
Wardell S. R., mason, h Henry n Columbus av.
Warner Adam, h Division ab Union.
Warner D. S., ship carpenter, h Hone n Hunter.
Warner P. B., harness, Abeel ab Division, bds n do.
Warner S. P., sewing machines, h Pearl av n Green.
Warner William, carman, h Elm n Third av.
Warren H. Mrs., h Maiden la n Green.
Warren J. G., clerk, bds 5 Washington av.
Washburn L. W., pro. Opera House, Lackawanna.
Washington George, coachman, h Liberty n E Front.

Capital of $50,000,000. Rondout, N. Y.

WASHINGTON HALL, (Scott & Weber, pros.,) Abeel n Hone.
Waters F. A., teller, h Green n Maiden Lane.
Waters George Rev., Green n Maiden Lane.
Watson Ann, h German n Ridge.
Watson William, h Ravine cor German.
Watts George, carpenter, h Grand n Union av.
Weaver Adam, h Pierpont opp Spring.
Weaver A. G., book keeper, Excelsior House.
Weaver Frederick, h Hunter n Hone.
Weaver Frederick, butcher, h Ann n Meadow.
Weaver George, painter, h Prince cor Grand.
Weaver Peter, (pro. Excelsior House,) Garden cor Hasbrouck av.
Weaver William, painter, h Cedar n Prospect.
Weaderman August, laborer, h Point rd n Livingston.
Webber Walter, h Catherine n Hasbrouck av.
Weber F. & Son, butchers, Ulster Market.
Weber Frederick, h Union av cor Chester.
Weber Frank, (A. Rieser & Co.,) h Hone cor Abeel.
Weber George, (Scott & W.,) Abeel n Hone.
Weber John & Co., butchers, Division cor Abeel.
Weber Jacob, butcher, Hasbrouck opp Pond, h do.
Weber Jacob H., butcher, h Mill.
Weber John A., teacher, h Hone cor Hunter.
Weber John, (J. Weber & Co.,) Division cor Abeel.
Weber J. Jr., (F. Weber & Son,) h Holmes.
Webster Grove, teller, F. N. B., h Abeel n Wurts.
Webster O. C., (Tappen, B. & W.,) h Maiden la n Pine.
Webster S. A., pro. Union Hotel, Wall cor John.
Weed Thomas N., captain, h Abeel n Wurts.
Weekly H., h Union cor Division.
Weeks Henry, carpenter, h E Front cor Henry.

*16

and Brilliantines, 5 Wall St., Kingston.

HIRAM ROOSA Insures Vessels and Cargoes

Weeks Jesse B., watchman, h Smith av n Garden.
Weeks S., sash maker, h O'Neil n R. R.
Weeks Whiting, mason, h Greenkill av.
Weeks William, carpenter, h E Front n Liberty.
Weidman Frederick, h Ravine opp Pine.
Weil Mayer, dry goods, &c., 6 Garden, h do.
Weimer J., shoemaker, h Division n Meadow.
WEINER SAM'L, wholesale liquors, 8 Garden, h do.
Weireter Casper, machinist, h Mill n Tompkins.
Weiss Alonzo, engineer, h Cedar n Prospect.
Welch Edward, foreman, h Union n Cedar.
WELCH WM., merchant tailor, Masonic Hall Building, 4 Garden, h Adams n Rogers.
Welder A., shoemaker, Ravine cor Abeel, h German cor Ravine.
Weldon A., h Ravine cor German.
Wellman H., shoe maker, h Chambers n Ravine.
Wells Ellison, boatman, h Hone ab Pierpont.
Wells G. & S., carriage manuf. St. James n Fair.
Wells George, (G. & S. Wells,) h St. James n Fair.
Wells L. P., clerk, bds Fair n N Front.
Wells Solomon, (G. & S. Wells,) h St. James n Fair.
Welsh J., laborer, h Chambers n Union.
Welsh William, mason, h Hasbrouck av bel Garden.
Wescott Charles, operator, bds N. Y. K. & S. R. R. Depot.
West Samuel, boatman, h Greenkill av.
Westbrook Charles B., clerk, bds Fair ab St. James.

WESTBROOK C. D.,

general insurance agent and civil engineer, Wall cor John, h Fair ab St. James.

Westbrook DuBois, agent, 16 Wall.

J. O. & G. B. MERRITT, Choice Dress

of all kinds. Rondout, N. Y.

Westbrook F. L., (T. R. & F. L. Westbrook,) h E Front opp John.
Westbrook G. D., clerk, bds Wurts cor Spring.
Westbrook H. & M. A., milliners, Fair n Main.
WESTBROOK S. S., auction and commission, 32 Wall, h Fair n Bowery.
Westbrook T. B., lawyer, Wall cor John, bds Fair n Bowery.
WESTBROOK T. R. & F. L., lawyers, Wall c John.
Westbrook T. R., (T. R. & F. L. Westbrook,) h Fair n Bowery.
WESTERN HOTEL, (Geo. Cook, pro.,) Washington av n Depot.
WESTERN UNION TELEGRAPH CO., Mansion House and 4 Music Hall.
Westfall C. A. Mrs., h Point rd cor Hanraty.
Westley Mary Mrs., h Cedar n Union av.
Westveer Adrian Rev., h Prince bel Garden.
Wetterhahn M., grocer, Abeel W of Wurts, h do.
Weyl William, laborer, h Cross n Chambers.
Whalen James, laborer, h Meadow n Ann.
Whalen John, laborer, h DeWitt.
Whalen John, blacksmith, h Division opp Mansion House.
Wheeler E., h Union av n Elmendorf.
Wheeler George, carpenter, h Henry cor Furnace.
Welan J. H., grocer, Meadow cor Chambers, h do.
Wheeler J. W., carpenter, h Cedar n Prospect.
Whitaker D. E., foreman, h Main next Eagle Hotel.
Whitaker Jas. F., carpenter, h DuBois av n Maple av.
Whitaker John W., carpenter, h Albany av cor Union av.
Whitaker Louis, laborer, h Cedar n Prospect.
Whitaker Wm. H., sash, &c., Bowery n Furnace, h do.
Whitbeck Frank, h Pine n Bowery.

Goods, No. 5 Wall St., Kingston.

Get an Accidental Policy at

Whitbock Moses, clerk, h Green cor John.
White John, laborer, h Ravine n Point rd.
White John, h Division cor Cross.
White Lawrence, Mrs., h Chambers cor Meadow.
White M., milk peddler, h Cedar n Union av.
White P., laborer, h Division cor Cross.
White Stephen, h Division ab Pierpont.
Wieber E. Mrs., h Adams n Holmes.
Wiegel Charles, shoemaker, h Ten Brœck av n O'Neil.
Wier James, laborer, h Ravine n Hunter.
Wiest Isaac, mason, h Henry n Union av.
Williams J. C., crockery, &c., Division opp Abeel, h Post n Abeel.
Williams J., kindling wood, Linderman av n Wall, h do.
Williams Jerome, segar maker, bds Post n Abeel.
Williams Joseph, coachman, h Post n Union.
Williams Maria, washing, h O'Neil n Bruyn av.
Williams M. Mrs., h O'Neil n Ten Broeck.
Williams M. Mrs., h Valley.
Williams S. F. Mrs., drossmaker, h Wall n St. James.
Williams Willam, h Greenkill av.
Willis C., h N Front n Wall.
Willis E. E., book keeper, Wall cor N Front.
Willis J. S., h Pearl n Wall.
WILLMOTT EDW'D, butcher, Abeel opp Hone, h do.
Willmott Henry, h Hunter n Ravine.
Willmott James, h Hunter n Hone.
Willmott John, h Hunter n Hone.
Willmott L. Mrs., h Hunter n Ravine.
Wilson Andrew, boatman, h Post n Spring.
Wilson Benjamin, h Division ab Union.
Wilson Camilla D., Miss, h St. James n R. R.
Wilson H. S., (Best & W.,) h Main cor Crown.

J. O. & G. B. MERRITT, Kid Gloves,

Wilson John, captain, h Hasbrouck av n Union.
Wilson R., bookkeeper, bds Green opp St. James.
Winans Henry, plumber, h Downs.
Winans Nelson, h Downs n Ten Brœck av.
Winchel Henry, saloon, Wilbur.
Winchel M., bookkeeper, h Wilbur Plank rd.
Winchell Simon, clerk, Division cor Garden.
Winfield J., carriage maker, Cedar n E Front, h St. James.
Winfield Stephen, clerk, h Adams cor Rogers.
Winger Louis, carpenter, h Point rd cor Jarrold.
Winglan Andrew, laborer, h Jarrold n Point rd.
Winne Thomas H., h Mapleton.
Winne William, farmer, h Hurley av.
Winnie H. W., (pro. Eagle Hotel,) Main bet E Front and Fair.
Winnie I. D., clerk, bds E Front n John.
Winnie L. S., clerk, Wall cor N Front.
Winslow Fred., upholsterer, bds Metzgar's Hotel.
Winter A., (Winter Bro.,) h Staple n Union av.
Winter B. K. O., clerk, bds Hone bet Holmes and Pierpont.
WINTER EDW'D, books, music, &c., 4 Music Hall, h Pearl n Fair.
WINTER WM., books, news, &c., Garden n Division, h Hone n Pierpont.
Wirter Stephen C., sash, &c., h Spring cor Ravine.
Wise Daniel, bar tender, h Prospect n Liberty.
Wise Philip, h Pierpont opp School House.
Wiseline Michael, weaver, Chester cor Bond.
Woerner C., saloon, Hasbrouck av n St. Mary.
Wolf Jacob Mrs., h Newkirk av n Hasbrouck av.
Wolf Moses, carman, h Union n Wurts.
Wolfer John A., ice, &c., h Chestnut n Division.

Life Insurance on the Stock, Mutual or Co-

KINGSTON DIRECTORY.

Wolferstig Henry, h Ridge n German.
Wolff David, Rev., h Union n Wurts.
Wolsey John, carpenter, h Henry n Fair.
Wolsey Richard, boatman, h Abeel.
Wolven John G. Mrs., h Main n Wall.
WOLVEN WILLIAM R., boot and shoemaker, Centre n E Front, h do.
WOOD A., mineral water, Union av cor Chester, h do.
Wood B. B., agent, bds Wall n St. James.
Wood Charles, carpenter, h Union av cor Chester.
Wood E. S., lawyer, Garden cor Division, bds Abee n Division.
Wood J. W. Jr., h Hone cor German.
Wood L. W., agent, bds Wall n St. James.
Wood Orlando, soda water, h Division cor Chester.
Wood Peter, h Pine, (Rondout.)
Wood Silas, clerk, h Wall n St. James.
Wood Silas, Jr., artist, h Pine n St. James.
Wood S. H., ship carpenter, h Abeel ab Post.
WOOD S., dry goods, &c., Garden, n Hasbrouck av.
WOOD WM., portable gas lamps, &c., Sleightburg Ferry House, h Columbus av.
Woods James, laborer, h Post n Spring.
Woods John, laborer, h Post n Spring.
Woods W. J., carpenter, h Hone cor Union.
Woodward George, h Orchard av.
Woolsey C., teamster, h Division opp Abeel.
Woolsey G. C., lawyer, Abeel cor Post, h n do.
Woolsey James, h Hudson.
Woolven Abram, carpenter, h Main cor E Front.
Worden Joseph, foreman, bds Mansion House.
Wright Amos, contractor, bds City Hotel.
Wright E., cooper, h Greenkill av.
Wurts Charles, laborer, h Van Buren n Sterling.
Wygant Sebastian, laborer, h Wilbur.

J. O. & G. B. MERRITT, Gent's

operative Plan at H. ROOSA'S Agency, Rondout.

Wynkoop Derrick C., teamster, h Green n Crown.
WYNKOOP F. S. Jr., books, stationery, wall paper, &c., 29 Wall, h Elmendorf n Tremper av.
Wynkoop Henrietta, h Albany av E of Union av.
Wynkoop Mary, h Cedar n Union av.
Wynkoop Wm., laborer, h Albany av n Union av.
Wylant John, h 64 N Front.
Wynne D., grocer, Division cor Union.
Wynne Martin, Mrs, dress maker, h Ann cor Union.
Wynne P., laborer, h Division cor Union.

YAGAR LOUIS, h Newkirk av n Hasbrouck av.
Yellig Matthew, shoemaker, Wilbur.
York Ida, bds 45 N Front.
York W. E., tailor, h Fair n St. James.
Yost E. Mrs., h Newkirk av n Hasbrouck av.
Yost Henry, stoves, &c., Abeel n Ravine, h Newkirk av
Yost Jacob, agent, h Flatbush av n R R.
Yost William, carpenter, h Ravine n Point rd.
Young F. W., tailor, h Washington av n Hurley av.
Young Peter, h Wilbur.
Younger Samuel, segar maker, bds Excelsior House.
Youngman M. D., clerk, bds Rogers n Adams.
Youngman Thomas, book-keeper, h Rogers n Adams.
Youngs Addison, pilot, h Henry n Sterling.
Youngs Hiram, bds Fair n North Front.
Yous John, tailor, h Ann n Mill.
Yous Paul, boatman, h Abeel n Ravine.
Yuayluelsyke John, laborer, h Third av n Elm.
Yurrvorske Johanas, laborer, h Third av n Elm.
Yurrvorske Jacob, laborer, h Third av n Elm.

ZANG ERNIST, drover, h Ravine n Point rd.
Zeail Lawrence, h Hunter n Ridge.

Furnishing Goods, 5 Wall St., Kingston.

HIRAM ROOSA'S Insurance and KINGSTON DIRECTORY.

Zeeh Jacob, h German.
Zimmer Catherine, saloon, 36 Garden, h do.
Zimmermann Bruno, cigar maker, Greenkill av, n Union av, h do.
Zimmermann Frederick, junk, h Union n Ann.
Zoller Daniel, gen. merchandise, Wilbur.
Zoller George, carman, h Wilbur.

WM. B. MacMONAGLE,

PRACTICAL
Watchmaker, Jeweler & Engraver

At Winter's News Office, Rondout, N. Y.

American and Imported Watches, Fine Jewelry, Spectacles Eye Glasses, Pocket Pistols, etc.

J. O. & G. B. MERRITT, Gloves and

Real Estate Agency, Rondout, N. Y.

BUSINESS DIRECTORY.

ACADEMIES.
Kingsburg W. H., Greenkill av.

AGENTS EXPRESS.
American Express Co., 83 N Front and 34 Garden.
Hotaling C. M., Wynkoop's store, Wall.
U. S. Express Co., 9 Wall and Mansion House, Division.

AGENTS INSURANCE AND REAL ESTATE.
Chipp J. Deyo, Eagle Hotel, Main.
Clay C. S., 28 Wall.
Finch Wm. B. & Son, Fair n John.
Fredenburgh Wm. H., Main n Fair.
North George Jr., Newkirk Building, Division.
Roosa Hiram, 7 Division, Mansion House Building.
Sims William, Mill.
Stow & Benson, Garden cor Division.
Westbrook C. D., Wall cor John.

AGENTS, SEWING MACHINES.
Bolles J. E., Garden n Hasbrouck av.
Chapman C. E., 68 N Front.
Lawrence H. W., 24 Wall.
Stilwell C. S., 104 N Front.

ARCHITECTS.
Brink Edward, E Front n St. James.

Hosiery, No. 5 Wall St., Kingston.

Losses Equitably Adjusted and Promptly Paid

Chatfield, Garden over Market.
Quillard C. V., Murray's Building.

BAKERS AND CONFECTIONERS.

Allen George E., Pierpont n Hone.
Ballard D. M., 5, 7 and 9 Washington av.
Barth Ambrose, Abeel cor Hone.
Breitenbucher Edward, Abeel opp Hone.
DuBois Lorenzo, Prince cor Hasbrouck av.
Edmonds C. L., 10 Garden.
Elley J. Mrs., Union n Greenkill av.
Ellsworth & Schepmoes, E Front cor Liberty.
Gronbach Frederick, Abeel W of Hone.
Hermance O., 1 and 2 Music Hall.
Holley & Shelden, Lackawanna.
Huguenot, saloon, Fair n Main.
McBride Barney, Union av n O'Neil.
Myers John, St. James n Union av.
Pfrommer John, Division ab Union.
Reading J. P., Hasbrouck av ab Mill.
Reynolds J. W., 11 Wall.
Rice M., Division ab Mill.
Salzmann J. W., Cedar n Columbus av.
Salzmann Louis, Abeel opp Washington Hall.
Short M. E., Pierpont cor Russell.
Simon S., Abeel W of Wurts.

BANKS.

First National Bank of Rondout, Garden cor Division.
Kingston National Bank, Main cor Fair.
National Ulster County Bank, Wall cor John.
Rondout Savings Bank, Garden cor Division.
State of New York National Bank, Wall cor John.
The National Bank of Rondout, Ferry.
Ulster County Savings Institution, opp Court House.

J. O. & G. B. MERRITT, Laces and

At **HIRAM ROOSA'S** Agency, Rondout, N. Y.

KINGSTON BUSINESS DIRECTORY.

BILL POSTER.

Hotaling C. M., Wynkoop's store, Wall.

BLACKSMITHS.

Atkinson Thomas, Hurley av c Taylor.
Brown John A., Dock.
Cobbold & Epps, Van Buren n Prospect.
Conway John, Wilbur.
Hyland John, Wilbur.
Decker D. L., Columbus av n Cedar.
DuBois & Shelightner, Henry cor Fair.
Elmendorf Geo., Washington av ab Hurley av.
Herdman J. Jr., Washington av cor N Front.
Lang C., Abeel n Spring.
Miner L. V. K., Maiden Lane n E Front.
O'Brien Michael, Abeel cor Ravine.
O'Reilly P., Division cor Union.
Portlan T., Meadow n Ann.
Sheppard William, Columbus av.
Van Keuran W. H., Cedar n E Front.
Walsh M., Wilbur Plank rd.

BOAT AND SHIP BUILDERS.

Allen Bros., Columbus av ft Abruyn.
Delaware & Hudson Canal Co., Light Boat Dock.
Dunn John, Dock.
Everson Morgan, Sleightburg.
Gokey William, Columbus av ft Prospect.
Hiltbrant C., Abeel.
King C. M. & Co., Kingston Point.
McCausland J. & J., Wilbur rd.
Robson William, South Rondout.
Warner Daniel S., Abeel.

Embroideries, No. 5 Wall St., Kingston.

HIRAM ROOSA'S Insurance Agency has

KINGSTON BUSINESS DIRECTORY.

BOOK BINDERS.

Ager C., Savings Bank building, Wall.
Wadsworth T. W., Mill.

BOOK SELLERS AND STATIONERS.

Agar C., Savings Bank building opp Court House.
Daly P., Division n Ferry.
Wadsworth T. W., Mill.
Winter Edward, 4 Music Hall.
Winter William, Garden n Division.
Wynkoop F. S. Jr., 29 Wall.

BOOT AND SHOE DEALERS.

Burger I., Ferry n Division.
Burke Thomas, Division n Garden.
Davis & DeGraff, Savings Bank Building.
Davis L. L. H., 21 Garden.
DeVeau S., Division ab Garden.
Dippold M., Division opp Abeel.
Green E., Wall n Pearl.
Grimes James, Lackawanna.
Hendricks William H., 3 Wall.
Henke Martin, Union av cor Cedar.
Kirchner L., Abeel cor Ravine.
Low A. M., 19 Wall.
Maier George, 78 N Front.
Masten & Hayes, (wholesale,) 8 Wall.
Murphy Edward, Main n E Front.
Pinner Louis, 82 and 84 N Front.
Reid D. C., 34 Garden.
Sampson E., Division cor Lackawanna.
Schoonmaker C. L., 88 N Front.
Wolven William R., Center n E Front.

J. O. & G. B. MERRITT, Ladies'

Never had any Disputed Claims.

KINGSTON BUSINESS DIRECTORY.

BREWERS.

Cummings & Kiernan, Hurley av cor Washington av.
Dressel G. & Co., Holmes cor Wurts.
Drake J., (small beer,) Pine cor Wilbur Plank rd.
Hargraves James, Wilbur Plank rd.
Miller Bros., (small beer,) Jacob's Valley.
Schaffer Jacob, South Rondout.
Schwalbach B., Valley.
Staubacher Charles, Hone cor German.
Stephan F. & Co., Abeel n Ravine.

BUTCHERS.

Boyce James M., Columbus av n Cedar.
Breitenbucher Jacob, Abeel cor Hone.
Dayton & Co., Hasbrouck av n Cross.
Freileweh G. J., 19 N Front.
Haenamrnn Fred., Division ab Meadow.
Hayes John, Division ab Union.
Heinman Fred., Garden n Ferry.
Houghtaling J. E., Liberty cor Furnace.
Johnston Thomas L., John n Wall.
Kelly & Cloonan, Division ab Union.
Kilroy T., Columbus av n Prospect.
Lasher Wm. H., Main n E Front.
Luft H., Abeel n Hone.
Mellert Louis, Division cor Union.
Merritt H. A. & Bro., Washington av n Hurley av.
Mick H. & Co., Wall cor St. James.
Moore Horace, Union av cor O'Neil.
Newkirk Beauman, Washington av opp Hurley av.
Ostrander Wm., Ulster Market.
Rupp Gotleib, Garden cor Smith av.
Saylor H. Mrs., Bowery n Oak.
Schick C., Abeel W of Wurts.

*17

Undergarments, 5 Wall St., Kingston.

Your best interest will dictate to Insure with

Van Buren Henry, Wall n Maiden Lane.
Van Gaasbeek Edgar, St. James n Union av.
Weber F. & Son, Ulster Market.
Weber John & Co., Division cor Abeel.
Willmott Edward, Abeel opp Hone.

CARRIAGE MANUFACTURERS.

Conroy James, Wilbur Plank rd.
Curtis J. P., Union av n O'Neil.
DuBois & Freer, St. James n Prospect.
Klots H., Flatbush av cor Hasbrouck av.
Mayer J. M., Mill.
O'Donnell & Featherly, E Front n City Hotel.
Perrine A. J., Washington av n Depot.
Peters Wm., Washington av ab Hurley av.
Schultz J., Mill cor Hasbrouck av.
Shader Wm., St. James n Union av.
Snyder Edward, Union av n St. James.
Wells G. & S., St. James n Fair.
Winfield J., Cedar n E Front.

CARPENTERS AND BUILDERS.

Burhans Albert, Hoffman n Union av.
Fisk L. L. & Bro., Hasbrouck av n Cross.
Gill John, Chestnut n Union av.
Houghtaling R. E., O'Neil n Union av.
Konnick Frederick, Cedar n Union av.
Mickens W. B., E Front n Liberty.
Otis H. W., Hasbrouck av n Mill.
Palen H. W., Wall n Bowery.
Strong L. B., Elm cor Third av.
Styles J. E., Pearl av n Green.
Tilson & Raenhart, Henry n Sterling.
Turck & Burhans, Garden opp Ferry.

J. O. & G. B. MERRITT, Cloths and

HIRAM ROOSA, Agent at Rondout, N. Y.

Van Gaasbeek & Wolven, Maiden la n Albany av.
Van Gaasbeek A. E., Union av n City Hall.
Van Nostrand E. T., St. James cor Fair.
Van Wagenen L. B., Fair cor Bowery.

CHINA, CROCKERY AND GLASSWARE.

Pitts C. V. L., 14 Wall.
Williams J. C., Division opp Abeel.
Wood William, Sleightburg Ferry House.

COAL AND LUMBER DEALERS.

Burhans & Felton, E Front cor Main.
Davis E. D., Furnace n Liberty.
Folant & Budington, Union av cor Henry.
Hale W. L., Union cor Chester.
Hutton Wm., Columbus av N of Tompkins.
Merrihew, Hommel & Dunwoody, 19 and 21 Washington av.
O'Neil C. M. & Co., 16 and 18 N Front.
Osterhoudt H., Main opp Eagle Hotel.
Osterhoudt H. & Bro., Wilbur.
Overbaugh D. C., Union av opp Cedar.
Ten Broeck W. W. & P. N., St. James cor Wall.
Van Aken & Crook, St. James cor Pine.

COMMISSION MERCHANTS.

Hoornbeek L. D. & Co., Ferry.
Keelar T., 23 Garden.
Schoonmaker H., ft Division.
Seaman & Miller, Ferry.
Westbrook S. S., 32 Wall.

DENTISTS.

Colburn E., 9 Wall.
Frisselle & Rosa, John c Wall and Garden n Division.

Cassimeres, No. 5 Wall St., Kingston.

If not convenient to call, send your application by

KINGSTON BUSINESS DIRECTORY.

Hutchinson R. W., 12 Wall.
Norton J. C., 15 Wall.
Ostrander T. P., Garden over news depot.
Sherwood V., Newkirk's Building, Division.

DRUGGISTS.

Curtis N. & J. A., 3 Music Hall.
Eltinge J. H., Washington av cor Hurley av.
Jansen A. E., E Front n Albany av.
Knapp E. W., Garden next P. O.
Laycock W., 43 Division.
Marsh Samuel, Union av cor St. James.
Masten C. J., 28 Wall.
Van Deusen Bros., N Front cor Crown, 6 Wall, and Garden and Ferry.

DRY GOODS AND GROCERS.

Aaron Samuel, South Rondout.
Abbey D. J., Flatbush av n Prince.
Ackert J. S., St. James cor E Front.
Allen J. H., Pierpont n Hone.
Ballard D. M., 5, 7 and 9 Washington av.
Bash C., Hasbrouck cor St. Mary.
Benson & Hart, 10 Wall.
Block Henrietta, Division ab Union.
Brannan Mary, Division ab Union.
Brodhead & Pine, Wall cor Main.
Bronder Peter, Ulster Market.
Browor J. F. & Co., Washington av n Depot.
Burger & Wells, St. James n Pine.
Burger Israel, Ferry n Division.
Burhans J. S., E Front cor Pearl.
Carey Patrick, Abeel n Wilbur.
Carle David, Division and Canal.
Carpenter O. P., Union av cor O'Neil.

J. O. & G. B. MERRITT, Flannels and

Mail to **HIRAM ROOSA**, Insur. Agent, Rondout.

KINGSTON BUSINESS DIRECTORY. 201

Casey Patrick, Washington av n Depot.
Cashin E., Garden cor Hasbrouck av.
Cloonan Thomas, Division cor Union.
Colloten B., Prospect cor Union.
Colvill R., Hunter cor Hone.
Conwell M., Abeel cor Hone.
Corbin J. G., Hasbrouck av cor Meadow.
Crosby, Merritt & Co., 7 Wall.
Cullen James, Ann cor Meadow.
Davis Isaac F., Union av n O'Neil.
Decker & Radcliff, Wall.
Delanoy E. & Son, Cedar n Prospect.
Denike Isaac, Wilbur.
Derrenbacher J. & J. P., Dock cor Ravine.
DeWitt & Gillespie, 12 Wall.
Deyo John H., 17 Garden.
Deyo Richard, Garden & Ferry.
Diamond J., 27 Garden.
Dingee John, St. James, n Union av.
Disbrow D. A., Union av cor St. James.
Dodge D. G., 9 N Front.
Duffy Bernard, Cedar n Union.
Ennist Alonzo, Washington av opp Hurley av.
Everett & Treadwell, 3, 5 and 7 N Front.
Ewen G. W., Main cor E Front.
Fitzgerald & Johnson, Washington av n Depot.
Flannigan James, Dock n Ravine.
Fletcher George, Union av n Greenkill.
Flynn P. J., Division cor Meadow.
Forst Isidore, Abeel opp Hone.
Frame S., Crown n N Front.
Fries & Myer, 79 N Front.
Gage George A., Prince cor Grand.
Gassen & Ellsworth, Union av cor Flatbush av.

Blankets, No. 5 Wall St., Kingston.

Insure with no other Agent.

Geil Lazarus, Abeel W of Wurts.
Glennon James, Dock n Ravine.
Golden William, Union n Division.
Goldstein B. & Bro., Division ab Union.
Hale Wilber L., Union av cor Chester.
Hanratty F., Division n Mill.
Hasbrouck Bros., Columbus av ab Tompkins.
Holmes William, Washington av cor Hurley av.
Hopper & Romer, Dock.
Hopper C. R., Union av n toll gate.
Hulme R. B. & J. W., 52 N Front.
Hutton J. Jr., Columbus av.
Jones R. & Co., Ravine n Abeel.
Joy James, Bowery cor Furnace.
Keater D. P., St. James n Prospect.
Kerley J., 4 Mansion House Block.
Kirchner L., Abeel cor Ravine.
Krieger Henry, German cor Ridge.
Langan Patrick, Division ab Union.
Larkin Matthew, Jr., 15 Ferry.
Larkin M. H., Division cor Meadow.
Logan John, Wilbur.
McCauseland John, Division ab Abeel.
McGill Patrick, Division ab Holmes.
McGivney Patrick, Division ab Cross.
McMahon Peter, Washington av n Depot.
McNally Thomas, Division ab Meadow.
McShane James, Abeel n Ravine.
Madden M. J., Division cor Mill.
Mahar John, Division ab Union.
Maxwell John, Dock.
Merrihew, Hommel & Dunwoody, 19 and 21 Washington av.
Merritt C. M. & Son, 16 Wall.

J. O. & G. B. MERRITT, Notions and

HIRAM ROOSA, Gen'l Ins, Agent, Rondout, N. Y.

Merritt J. O. & G. B., 5 Wall.
Murphy William, Washington av n Bridge.
Murray J. J., Division n Cross.
Murray William, Abeel bet Hone and Ravine.
Newark Lime and Cement Manuf'g Co., Columbus av cor Tompkins.
Newland S., Garden opp Ferry.
Newwitter M., Division n opp Mansion House.
O'Connor John, Division ab Union.
O'Neil C. M. & Co., 16 and 18 N Front.
O'Reilly Charles, Dock and Abeel.
O'Reilly E., 19 Lackawanna.
Phelan N., Union av n Henry.
Pitts H. H., Wilbur.
Reynolds Michael, Dock n Ravine.
Rieser A. & Co., Hone cor Abeel.
Rouse Henry & Co., Hasbrouck av cor Garden.
Samter L., 60 N Front.
Schreiber John H., Garden and Ferry.
Sculley & Conroy, 23 Washington av.
Sheridan P., Dock.
Sleight George S. & Co., Sleightburg.
Snyder C., Washington av cor Hurley av.
Staples Sherwood, Hone cor Union.
Stebbins John R., Garden and Ferry.
Stoddard George N., Garden and Ferry.
Stokes James, Jr., Union cor St. James.
Stratford J., E Front cor Greenkill av.
Swart James O., Wall cor Pearl.
Tappen, Burhans & Webster, Wall cor John.
Thompson G. & Sons, Hunter.
Traver Jared, Garden cor Smith av.
Van Anden Charles, 15 N Front.
Van Buren A. P., Division cor Abeel.

Trimmings, No. 5 Wall St., Kingston.

HIRAM ROOSA'S Accidental, Life, Fire, Marine

Van Valkenburg Wm., Hone cor Pierpont.
Van Wagenen H., Abeel W of Wurts.
Vail E. P., 25 Garden.
Weil Mayer, 6 Garden.
Wetterhahn M., Abeel W of Wurts.
Whelan J. H., Meadow cor Chambers.
Wood S., Garden n Hasbrouck av.
Wynne D., Division cor Union.
Zoller Daniel, Wilbur.

DYER AND SCOURER.

Baylor A. H., Wilbur Plank rd.

FANCY GOODS.

Lydecker A., 9 Wall.
Sims William, Mill.

FISH DEALERS.

Boss John G., Sleightburg Ferry.
Decatur R. W., John n Wall.
Tillou C. W., 37 N Front.

FLORISTS.

Burgevine C., Lucas av.
Burgevine V., hd Pearl av.
Snyder B., Linderman.

FURNITURE AND UNDERTAKERS.

Decker B. P. & Bro., 39 and 41 Division.
Newkirk John, 39 N Front.
Ridenour & Sleight, 21 Wall.
Ryan Joseph, Division opp St. Mary's Church.
Schoonmaker & Van Wagenen, Pearl av n Green.
Stock M., Division ab Union.
Wachmeyer G. L., Abeel n Hone.
Wakelee & Rundell, 102 N Front.

J. O. & G. B. MERRITT, Dry Goods and

Insurance and Real Estate Agency, Rondout, N. Y.

GLUE MANUFACTURERS.

Hall John & Son, Greenkill av.

GRAIN, FLOUR AND FEED.

Abby S. & Son, Ferry.
Derrenbacher John, Abeel n Ravine.
Kerr R. W., Hasbrouck av ab Garden.
Marthis & Hudler, Wilbur.
Schoonmaker H., ft Division.
Snyder M. B., Ferry.
Staples A. S., Hasbrouck av Garden and Ferry.
Tremper T. H. & Bro., Ferry.

HAIRDRESSERS.

Arold J. J., Savings Bank Building.
Bower Fred., Abeel opp Hone.
Burger A., E Front opp Main.
Crosby A. A. & Co., Division cor Garden.
Dangler Simon, Union av bel St. James.
Detis John, Hone cor Union.
Frickel Peter, Union av cor Cedar.
Harley W. H. G., Fair n John.
Heimer S. J., Division cor Union.
Herbig Edward, Main n Eagle Hotel.
Holle C., Rondout House.
Lowerhouse C., Ferry opp Canal.
Lust John, Division ab Abeel.
Merkel Stephen, Abeel cor Ravine.
Perez Alexander, Lackawanna.
Rosekranse H. C., John n Wall.
Skelton J. R., Ferry.
Steiger Conrad, Washington av n Depot.
Strump & Gerber, John n Wall.

Carpets, No. 5 Wall St., Kingston.

HIRAM ROOSA'S Agency represents a Combined

HARDWARE, STOVES AND TINWARE.

Canfield P. A., Garden and Ferry.
Dodge A., Garden and Ferry.
Donnelly & Soilberger, Ferry cor Division.
Drautz George, Hone n Abeel.
Flintoff William, Union av n Elmendorf.
Gallagher Peter, 109 N Front.
Halloran D., Hasbrouck av n Garden.
Murphy James, 2 Division.
Murphy N., 70 N Front.
Parker W. H., Dock.
Payntar, Burhans & Oliver, N Front cor Crown.
Peters F. F., 76 N Front.
Reynolds Reuben, 30 Wall.
Sahler, Reynolds & DuBois, Wall cor N Front.
Spore Theodore, 62 N Front.
Yost Henry, Abeel n Ravine.

HARNESS, SADDLES AND TRUNKS.

Coons H. H., Main n E Front.
Herkart L., Abeel n Ravine.
Jaycocks T., 10 N Front.
Johnston Daniel, 9 Wall.
Ludwig J., Division ab Abeel.
Lyons John, 49 N Front.
Nichols A. G., 37 N Front.
Shader S., Washington av n Depot.
Shaw G. W. & Co., 77 N Front.
Timm Adolph, Washington av n Depot.

HATS, CAPS AND FURS.

Best & Wilson, 74 N Front.
Hase Philip, 35 N Front.
Hussey John, Division cor Garden.

J. O. & G. B. MERRITT, Black Silks at

Capital of $50,000,000. Rondout, N. Y.

James S., Division ab Garden.
Pinner Louis, 82 and 84 N Front.
Salomon M., Lackawanna cor Canal.
Secore George S., 26 Garden.
Van Gaasbeek J. B., 72 N Front.

HOTELS.

American Hotel, Union av cor St. James.
Central House, Hasbrouck av n Point rd.
City Hotel, Canal cor Ferry.
City Hotel, E Front opp Main.
Eagle Hotel, Main bet E Front and Fair.
Excelsior House, Garden Hasbrouck av and Ferry.
Freileweh Hotel, 5, 7 and 9 Green.
Grand Central Hotel, Union av cor Pine Grove av.
Hamilton House, Division opp Abeel.
Humphrey's Hotel, Washington av n Depot.
Kingston Hotel, Crown bet John & N Front.
Mansion House, Division cor Lackawanna.
Metzgar Hotel, Union cor Spring.
Neuman Henry, Wilbur.
Rondout House, Garden and Ferry.
Sherer Edwin, Division cor Ferry.
Sutton House, Hurley av n Washington av.
Union Hotel, Wall cor John.
Washington Hall, Abeel n Hone.
Western Hotel, Washington av n Depot.
Wilbur Hotel, Wilbur.

HORSE DEALERS.

Colligan Henry, Abeel n Ravine.
Dreyfus Charles, Abeel W of Wurts.
Forst Henry, Abeel opp Hone.
Vogel & Reinheimer, Abeel W of Wurts.

Bargains, No. 5 Wall St., Kingston.

HIRAM ROOSA Insures Vessels and Cargoes

KINGSTON BUSINESS DIRECTORY.

IRON FOUNDERS AND MACHINISTS.

Blackwell, Gross & Co., Albany av cor Union av.
Hermance, Newton & Co., St. James cor Prospect.
McEntee & Dillon, Garden on the Dock.
Millard James, Union av cor Grand.

JUNK DEALERS.

Bacharch L., Garden.
Frank Myer, Abeel W of Wurts.
Gile L., Dock.
Herrold Max, Dock.
Hirsch I., Garden.

KINDLING WOOD.

Williams J., Linderman av n Wall.

LOCK AND GUNSMITHS.

Berry Gilbert, 81 N Front.
Hoybruch F., Hasbrouck av n Garden.
McElroy William H., 63 N Front.

LAWYERS.

Adams G. R., Garden over Market.
Bernard & Fiero, Main n Fair.
Brandow E. D., 17 Garden.
Carpenter & Fowler, Fair n Main.
Champlin C. R. V., Murray's Building, Garden.
Chipp Howard, 30 Wall.
Chipp Howard, Jr., 30 Wall.
Cockburn Howard, Savings Bank Building.
Cooper James M., Savings Bank Building.
DuBois J. H., John cor Wall.
Hayes M. G., Pierpont opp Holmes.
Hill Gideon, Main n E Front.
Hoar Friend, Jr., Savings Bank Building.

J. O. & G. B. MERRITT, Black Alpacas

of all kinds. Rondout, N. Y.

KINGSTON BUSINESS DIRECTORY. 209

Hull S. T., John n Wall.
Keyser Daniel E., John n Wall.
Kenyon W. S., Savings Bank Building.
Lawton & Stebbins, Garden cor Division.
Lounsbury & DeWitt, Savings Bank Building.
McKenzie H. E., Main n Fair.
Macauley R. F., Main n Fair.
Mellon Arthur J., Division cor Mill.
Parker & Kenyon, John cor Wall.
Preston C. M., Garden over Market.
Schoonmaker A. Jr., John n Wall.
Schoonmaker Marius, 30 Wall.
Sparling D. W., John n Wall.
Soule S. D., John n Fair.
Van Etten & Clearwater, John n Wall.
Van Wagonen & Durham, John bet Crown and Wall.
Van Wagoner McD., John n Wall.
Wood E. S., Garden cor Division.
Woolsley George C., Abeel cor Post.
Westbrook T. B., Wall cor John.
Westbrook T. R. & F. L., Wall cor John.

LEATHER AND FINDINGS.

Southwick Thomas L., 85 N Front.
Van Buren James, Ferry.

LIME AND CEMENT.

Briggs A. R., Wilbur.
Gross F. W., Hasbrouck av cor Ravine.
Hyatt S. M., South Rondout.
Newark Lime & Cement Co., Garden and Union.

LIVERY STABLES.

Rostwick A., St. James cor Pine.
Hopkins J. D., Hurley av.

*18

and Brilliantines, 5 Wall St., Kingston,

Get an Accidental Policy at

KINGSTON BUSINESS DIRECTORY.

Jones R. & Co., Ravine n Abeel.
Kelder Brothers, 48 Wall.
Longyear & Shultis, Fair N of John.
Metzgar A., Division cor Spring.
Murphy Frank, Mansion House Stables, Division.
Patchen L. I., Mill.
Roosa Isaac I., E Front cor Main.
Smith G. A. & R. F., Wall n Pearl.

MALSTERS.
Neidlinger, Schmidt & Co., South Rondout.

MARBLE WORKS.
Kent William J., Division n opp Rogers.
Poole & Luther, Wall n Pearl.
Stevens Charles, Union av n Dederick.

MERCHANT TAILORS AND CLOTHIERS.
Aaron L., Lackawanna.
Appleton Louis, 15 Garden.
Bernstein Isaac, Wall cor N Front.
Cohen A. & Corn, 47 and 94 N Front.
Davis P. J., 5 Music Hall.
Dreyfus Edward, 19 Garden.
Elting Jacob, 50 N Front.
Elting Louis, 96 and 98 N Front.
English & Schermerhorn, Savings Bank Building opp Court House.
Fisher & Stone, 35 Wall.
Giere Ernst, Prospect n Bowery.
Jacobs Joseph, 38 Garden.
Jacobs Marks, 22 Garden.
McCann Charles, 80 N Front.
McElvare C. & M., Lackawanna.
Meyer Bros., 55 N Front.

J. O. & G. B. MERRITT, Choice Dress

Meyer L., Lackawanna.
Nathan Henry, Division n Spring.
O'Reilly Andrew, Lackawanna.
O'Sullivan M. L., Dock.
Resenthal B., Division n Garden.
Rieser Wm. & Bro., Abeel n Hone.
Sampson E. & Co., Canal and Division.
Sampson Louis, 64 N Front.
Schwartz P., Canal cor Lackawanna.
Solomon S., Lackawanna.
Tootill R., 18 Wall.
Van Buren P., 14 N Front.
Van Keuren Abram, 33 Wall.
Welch William, 4 Garden.

MILLINERS.

Atkins & DeGraff, Fair cor John.
Atkinson Sisters, 5 Mansion House Block.
Deudney A. L., 26 Garden.
Douglass Eliza, Division ab Union.
Fassett E. H., 22 Wall.
Haley Martin, Division n Holmes.
Murphy M. & B., Garden n Hasbrouck av.
Robinson & Gilmore, 47 Division.
Stephan George, Abeel W of Wurts.
Townsend C. J., 13 Wall.
Walker Joseph, 21 Wall.
Westbrook H. & M. A., Fair n Main.

MUSIC STORES.

Kleisner J., Mill.
Rice A., Division ab Mill.

NEWSPAPERS.

Daily & Weekly Freeman, Mill.

Goods, No. 5 Wall St., Kingston.

Life Insurance on the Stock, Mutual or Co-

Kingston Argus, 29 Wall.
The Courier, 17 Garden.
Kingston Journal, 33 and 35 Wall.
Kingston Press, 30 Wall.

NORTH RIVER BLUE STONE.

Booth Nathaniel, Wilbur.
Donovan D. E., Wilbur.
Fitch S. & W. B., Wilbur.
Hallahan Michael, Wilbur.
Lewis E., Wilbur rd.
Mills J. & Bro., Wilbur.
Sweeney James, Wilbur.

PAINTERS.

Ballard J., Van Buren cor Furnace.
Belfe & Becker, Cedar n Union.
Dolson Peter J., Union av n Elmendorf.
Goetcheus & Larsen, Garden n Division.
Horvers & Cousins, Division cor Lackawanna.
Kiser Silas, Union av n Liberty.
Roosa S., O'Neil bet Bruyn av and Ten Broeck av.
Tubby Joseph, 21 Garden.

PHOTOGRAPHERS.

Auchmoody D. J., Garden and Ferry.
Lewis E., John cor Wall.
McKown Milton, 12 Wall.

Short Lorenzo, Division opp Mill.
Vallett George A., Division ab Mansion House.

PHYSICIANS.

Basten George, Garden.
Brown J. P., Union av n St. James.

J. O. & G. B. MERRITT, Kid Gloves,

operative Plan at H. ROOSA'S Agency, Rondout.

Chalker A. P., Division cor Mill.
Crispell & Smith, Lackawanna next Mansion House.
Crispell G. D., Fair cor Pearl.
Covel C. C., Union av n Pine Grove av.
Davis W. B., St. James cor E Front.
Douglas A. T., Garden.
Gippert A., Abeel W of Wurts.
Heath S. L., Elmendorf n Union av.
Huhne Augustus, Abeel opp Wurts.
Ingalls F. W., Fair n Main.
Kennedy D., Garden cor Hasbrouck av.
Keyser J. D., Fair opp Post Office.
Lake W. T., Washington av n Depot.
Loughran Elbert H., Fair N of John.
Loughran Robert, Fair N of John.
Montanye W. D. L., 17 Garden.
Myer Jesse, John cor E Front.
O'Leary J. P., Dock.
Perkins E. K., Abeel opp Post.
Purroy F. M., Holmes opp Wurts.
Quentel Julius, Hone n Abeel.
Quentel Oscar, Hone n Abeel.
Shafer Levi, Maiden Lane n Pine.
Van Hoevenberg J. O. & H., Green junc. Crown.
Van Rensselaer W. A., Union av bet St. James and Elmendorf.

PLUMBERS AND GAS FITTERS.

Loughran B., 106 N Front.
Nestell Frank M., Fair opp Music Hall.

PRINTERS.

Hageman & Fisher, Division cor Mill.

PUMPS.

Farrell John, E Front next City Hotel.

No. 5 Wall Street, Kingston.

RESTAURANTS AND SALOONS.

Bishop Charles E., Dock.
Bragaw John A., Main n E Front.
Brauchle V., Division cor Newkirk av.
Broas R. H., Wall opp Court House.
Brocker Peter, Pierpont cor Russell.
Brunner J. M., Union av n Cedar.
Bug George, Garden.
Cogswell James, Sleightburg.
Colligan Henry, Abeel n Ravine.
Conlan Wm., Columbus av cor Prospect.
Castor J. Mrs., Canal.
Costello John H., Garden.
Costello M., Division ab Union.
Crossman N., Garden cor Ferry.
Decker J., Taylor, Fair S of Main.
Dertenbacher John P. Jr., Ravine n Abeel.
Desmond D. J., Division ab Union.
Diehl Charles, Garden opp Ferry.
Dittus L., Abeel W of Wurts.
DuBois C. D., Washington av cor Hurley av.
Dunn Catherine, Wilbur.
Eisenla Christian, Union av bel Grand.
Englert John, Division ab Abeel.
Ertelt Frank, Ravine cor Vine.
Finch Jeremiah, 49 Wall.
Fisher Ida, Garden n Ferry.
Flannery K., Wilbur rd n Hudson.
Flick Lawrence, Ravine ab Abeel.
Flick Michael, Division opp Holmes.
Foley Thomas, Garden n Ferry.
Forrest James, Division opp Holmes.
Fox B. Mrs., Division ab Holmes.
Fox Jacob, Garden n Division.

Real Estate Agency, Rondout, N. Y.

Fox Jacob, South Rondout.
Frickel Peter, Union av n Cedar.
Gassen Joseph, Union av cor Flatbush av.
Geisler John, Division n Abeel.
Glass Jacob, 27 Washington av.
Hayden Mary, Union av opp Cedar.
Hirschberg M., Division ab Mansion House.
Huber John, Division ab Union.
Hull Conrad, Washington av n Hurley av.
Hyland Wm., Division opp Rogers.
Kleiglein Peter, Wilbur.
Kelch William, Abeel n Ravine.
Kenyon William, Washington av n Depot.
Kessler A., Dock.
Kraus John, Point rd cor Livingston.
Krauser Wm., Union av bel St. James.
Leavranz Fritz, 80 Ann.
Leonard Thomas J., Dock.
Lowe F. R., St. James opp Prospect.
Lynch D., Dock.
McElroy W. H. Jr., 63 N Front.
McGovern John, Wilbur.
Mayer F., Hasbrouck cor Point rd.
Maxon Daniel, Division ab Meadow.
Mellert Joseph, Cornell's Dock.
Menger Frederick, Hasbrouck av n Garden.
Mergendahl E., 8 N Front.
Moser Joseph, Washington av ab Hurley av.
Mulligan John, Washington av n Depot.
Murrin E., Union av n Flatbush av.
Myers J. C., 78 N Front.
Norris G. A., Ferry n Division.
O'Brien James, Wilbur.
O'Reilly B. Mrs., Columbus av cor Cedar.

Furnishing Goods, 5 Wall St., Kingston.

Losses Equitably Adjusted and Promptly Paid

Parker Nelson, Dock.
Pendergast Wm., Lackawanna.
Permann Frederick, Main n Eagle Hotel.
Platner Charles, Hasbrouck av cor Cross.
Plunkett Luke, Columbus av cor Cedar.
Quigly John, Hone ab Hunter.
Rigney Thomas, Garden n Ferry.
Rippe George, Columbus av cor Cedar.
Schenck Joseph, Dock.
Schick Casper, Wilbur.
Schnitzler J., Mill.
Schumann F. C. Dock.
Sisson F. H., Main n E Front.
Snyder Clermont, Chambers n Ravine.
Sparty Roman, Division ab Mansion House.
Stamer August, Point rd cor Jarrold.
Thiele V., Division opp Abeel.
Tiencken Siba, Wall n Bowery.
Totter Frank, John n Wall.
Traver Theodore A., Ferry House.
Trenkle Joseph, Chambers cor Cross.
Uhle Martin, Abeel cor Post.
Volke Joseph, Point rd cor Second av.
Volle C., Abeel W of Wurts.
Wagner George, Union av n Greenkill av.
Winchel Henry, Wilbur.
Zimmer C., 36 Garden.

SASH, BLINDS AND DOORS.

Burhans Albert, Hoffman n Union av.
Donaldson & Musson, Powell Dock Columbus av.
Minor Charles, Union av ab Chestnut.
Styles J. R., Furnace n Liberty.
Tillson & Brink, Union av n Elmendorf.

J. O. & G. B. MERRITT, Gloves and

At **HIRAM ROOSA'S** Agency, Rondout, N. Y.

KINGSTON BUSINESS DIRECTORY. 217

Van Gaasbeek A. E., Union av n City Hall.
Whitaker W. H., Bowery n Furnace.

SEGAR MANUFACTURERS.

Coffee J., E Front n St. James.
Forbes Alexander J., Union av bet St. James and Elmendorf.
Hardenberg C. W., Newkirk av n Division.
Zimmermann Bruno, Greenkill av n Union av.

SHIP CHANDLERS.

McMillan D. & A., Dock.

STEAMBOAT LINES.

Cornell Freight & Towing, ft Division.
Mary Powell, Powell Dock.
Romer & Tremper, Ferry.

SODA WATER MANUFACTURERS.

Cloonan & Co., Spring n Division.
Wood A., Union av cor Chester.

STAIR BUILDER.

Beutell H. M., E Front n Liberty.

SOAP AND CANDLES.

Gibson A. & Sons, 11 N Front.
McCormick P., Division n Holmes.

TANNERS AND CURRIERS.

Teller William S. & Sons, 2 N Front.

TOBACCONISTS.

Barth Ambrose, Abeel cor Hone.

Hosiery, No. 5 Wall St., Kingston.

Davidson & Krauser, John n Wall.
DuFlon J. E., Green n Pearl av.
Edmonston C. D., Garden opp Ferry.
Freer W. H., 20 Wall.
Hessert E., John cor Fair.
Liscomb G. G., Garden.
Mondschine S., Division n Ferry.
Mullen A., Lackawanna.
Mullen E., 4 N Front.
Raschke Theodore D., Abeel n Division.
Samter Alexander, Division n Garden.
Samter Morris, 21 Garden.
Samter M., 53 N Front.
Smith G. J., 45 N Front.

WATCHMAKERS AND JEWELERS.
Bond J. T., Main n E Front.
Bond J. T. Jr., Division ab Union.
Dunn Andrew Jr., Newkirk Building, Division.
Goldsmith Elizabeth, Union av n R. R.
Keller K. F., Abeel n Division.
MacMonagle William B., Winter's news store, Garden.
Martin Henry, 5 Mansion House Building.
Rahmer G., Ferry n Division.
Rice A., Division ab Mill.
Safford & Carter, 26 Wall.
Styles George B., 27 Wall.
Vignes John, 92 N Front.

WINES AND LIQUOR DEALERS.
Cullen James, Ann cor Meadow.
Johnston Theron, Fair cor N Front.
Schreiber John H., Garden and Ferry.
Weiner Samuel, 8 Garden.

Never had any Disputed Claims.

MISCELLLANEOUS.

County Officers.

Judge—Wm. Lawton ; *Justices of Sessions*—P. A. Schryver, J. D. Merrihew ; *Sheriff*—J. W. Kerr ; *County Clerk*—G. W. Deyo ; *Clerk's Deputy*—J. Bostwick ; *Surrogate*—Peter Cantine ; *District Attorney*—O. P. Carpenter ; *Treasurer*—J. M. Hasbrouck ; *Supervisor's Clerk*—H. Cockburn ; *Superintendent of the Poor*—Benjamin Winnie.

City Officers.

Mayor—James G. Lindsley ; *Aldermen*—Charles Bray, George Bug, J. H. Cordts, P. A. Canfield, Michael Cummings, John Derrenbacher, P. J. Flynn, William H. Fredenburgh, Matthew Larkin, M. J. Madden, Jacob Plough, Artemus Sahler, G. A. Shufeldt, T. H. Tremper, James Tubby, A. H. Vandling, F. L. Westbrook, W. H. Whittaker ; *Treasurer*—Grove Webster ; *Recorder*—R. F. Macauley ; *Corporation Counsel*—S. L. Stebbins ; *City Clerk*—Augustus Schepmoes.

FIRE DEPARTMENT—EASTERN DISTRICT.

Chief Engineer—George Weber ; *First Assistant Engineer*—T. J. Leonard ; *Second Assistant Engineer*—Stephen Canfield.

Embroideries, No. 5 Wall St., Kingston.

Your best interest will dictate to Insure with

KINGSTON BUSINESS DIRECTORY.

ENGINE COMPANIES.

Lackawanna Steamer No. 1., Mill. *Foreman*—L. B. Stroug.

James G. Lindsley Steamer No. 2. *Foreman*—Philip Kelly.

Ponkhockie No. 3., Columbus av. *Foreman*—Thom- Rafferty.

Protector No. 4., Hone. *Foreman*—J. T. Tubby.

Columbus Point Engine Co. No. 5. *Foreman*—Thomas Malone.

Hook and Ladder, Rescue No. 1. *Foreman*—D. Desmond.

HOSE COMPANIES.

Rapid Hose Company No. 1., Hone street. *Foreman*—George F. Stephan.

Cornell Hose Co. No. 2, Abeel street. *Foreman*—F. H. Griffiths.

Weber Hose Co. No. 3, Mill street. *Foreman*—John Legg.

FIRE DEPARTMENT—WESTERN DISTRICT.

Chief Engineer—John A. Gross ; *First Assistant Engineer*—M. T. Newkirk ; *Second Assistant Engineer*—P. Plough.

ENGINE COMPANIES.

American No. 1, E Front. *Foreman*—W. A. Lines.

Washington Steamer No. 3, Firemans' Hall, Fair street. *Foreman*—J. Bostwick.

Excelsior No. 4, John bet Crown and Green. *Foreman*.

HOSE COMPANIES.

Excelsior Hose No. 4, John. *Foreman*—D. Fisher.

J. O. & G. B. MERRITT, Ladies'

HIRAM ROOSA, Agent at Rondout, N. Y.

American Hose No. 2, E Front n St. James. Foreman—S. W. Doyle.
Wiltwyck No. 1, Fireman's Hall. Foreman—Alfred Tanner.
Hook and Ladder, Wiltwyck No. 1, Fireman's Hall. Foreman—George Lowery.

BANKS.

Kingston National Bank—Main cor Fair. Capital, $150,000. President—C. H. Van Gaasbeek ; Cashier—N. E. Brodhead ; Teller—L. B. Van Gaasbeek ; Directors—Artemas Sahler, Edward Crosby, J. O. Merritt, G. D. Crispell, Luke Noon, F. W. Ingall, Hiram Radcliff, C. H. Van Gaasbeek.

State of New York National Bank—Wall cor John. Capital, $325,000. President—E. DuBois ; Vice-President—A. Near ; Cashier—C. Burhans ; Teller—F. A. Waters ; Directors—E. DuBois, A. Near, P. Masten, C. Oliver, J. Griffith, D. Johnston, P. C. Lefever, A. H. Bruyn, J. Hasbrouck, Ira Hoffman, Cornelius Burhans, E. M. Brigham, W. Shultis, C. P. Ridenour, Hiram Davis.

National Ulster County Bank—Wall street. Capital $150,000. President—C. D. Bruyn ; Vice President—Peter Crispell, Jr. ; Cashier—B. L. Brodhead ; Teller—C. M. Eckert ; Directors—Peter Crispell, Jr., Abner Hasbrouck, C. D. Bruyn, A. H. Bruyn, James Kiersted, G. N. Van Deusen, O. Hasbrouck, A. Lefever, J. S., DeWitt, Solomon Shears.

The National Bank of Rondout—Ferry street. President—Jansen Hasbrouck ; Cashier—E. B. Newkirk ; Capital $200,000. Shares $100 each. Directors—Jansen Hasbrouck, W. B. Crane, N. Anderson, A. Sleght, G. M. Gillett, W. F. Romer, Geo. H. Sharp,

Undergarments, 5 Wall St., Kingston.

If not convenient to call, send your application by

KINGSTON BUSINESS DIRECTORY.

E. T. Van Nostrand, Cornelius Hardenbergh, James Oliver, Jacob H. Davis.

First National Bank of Rondout—President—Thomas Cornell; Vice President—S. D. Coykendall. Capital $300,000. Cashier—Charles Bray. Directors—Thomas Cornell, A. A. Crosby, E. M. Brigham, M. J. Madden, James G. Lindsley, A. S. Staples, E. K. Perkins, A. Benson, S. D. Coykendall.

Rondout Savings Bank—Garden street, Rondout. President—Thomas Cornell; Vice President—S. D. Coykendall; Secretary—A. Benson. Present rate of interest 6 per cent.

Ulster County Savings Institution—Wall street, Kingston, N. Y. Amount of Deposits $2,000,000. President—Jansen Hasbrouck; Vice President—Augustus H. Bruyn; Secretary—Caleb S. Clay; Treasurer—James E. Ostrander; Assistant Treasurer—Matthew T. Trumpbour. Present rate of interest 6 per cent. on all sums from $5,00 to $5,000.

MUSIC HALL.

John cor Fair st., Kingston. President—E. Du Bois; Vice President—A. Schoonmaker Jr.; Secretary—A. T. Newton; Treasurer—Cornelius Burhans; Directors—A. H. Bruyn, Artemas Sahler, T. B. Gates, W. S. Kenyon, F. W. Ingalls.

INCORPORATED COMPANIES.

Delaware and Hudson Canal Company, Rondout.— Perpetual franchise as a Canal and Railroad and Coal Company, granted by Pennsylvania, March 13, 1823, and incorporated by the State of New York, April 23, 1823. Capital $20,000,000.

J. O. & G. B. MERRITT, Cloths and

Mail to **HIRAM ROOSA**, Insur. Agent, Rondout.

Newark Lime and Cement Munufacturing Company—Garden street near Tompkins, Rondout. Agent—James G. Lindsley.

CHURCHES.

First Reformed Dutch Church—Organized 1660. Main street, between Wall and Fair streets. Pastor, Rev. David N. Vandeveer.

Baptist Church—Albany avenue near Union avenue. Organized 1832. Pastor, Rev. Z. Grennell, Jr.

Second Reformed Dutch Church—Organized 1849. Fair street, between Maiden Lane and Pearl. Pastor, Rev. C. H. Stitt, D. D.

Reformed (Wiltwick)—Pastor, ———— ————.

First Methodist Episcopal Church of St. James—Fair street, between Main and Pearl streets. Organized 1824–25. Pastor, Rev. A. Ostrander.

Second Methodist Episcopal Church—E Front street, corner of Liberty street. Organized 1855. Pastor, Rev. W. Mickle.

Protestant Episcopal Church of St. John—Wall, bet N Front and John streets. Organized 1832. Rector, Rev. ———— ————.

Presbyterian Church—E Front street, corner Maiden Lane. Pastor, Rev. J. D. Denniston.

Catholic Church of St. Joseph—Wall, cor of Main street. Pastor, Rev. J. Dougherty.

Jewish Synagogue—Wall street. Rev. J. Eisner, Rabbi.

Presbyterian Church—Abeel street, n Wurts street. Organized 1833. Pastor, Edward D. Ledyard.

German Evangelical Lutheran Trinity Church—Hunter street, cor Ravine street. Organized 1849. Pastor Rev. J. M. Steiner.

Cassimeres, No. 5 Wall St., Kingston.

Insure with no other Agent.

224   KINGSTON BUSINESS DIRECTORY.

Methodist Episcopal Church—Wurts street. Pastor, Rev. J. J. Dean.
Roman Catholic, St. Peter's—Adams street. Pastor, Rev. John Raufeisen.
Congregation Emanuel—Union street, near Post. Rabbi, D. Wolff.
Roman Catholic Church of St. Mary—Division st. Erected 1849. Pastor, Rev. Michael Carthage O'Farrell. Asst. Pastor, Rev. Michael Newman.
Baptist Church—Wurts street, cor Spring. Organized 1841. Pastor, Rev. James Cooper.
Protestant Episcopal Church of the Holy Spirit—Pierpont street, cor Wurts street. Organized 1850. Rector, Rev. J. B. Murray.
German Evangelical Lutheran Church—Livingston. Pastor, Rev. E. F. Stutz.
Childrens' Church—Abruyn street. D. B. Abbey, Supt. Union Sunday School.
American Union M. E. Church—Flatbush av. Pastor, Rev. Wm. Coconen.

SECRET SOCIETIES.

Kingston Lodge No. 10 F. & A. M.—Meets every Tuesday evening at their Hall, Savings Bank Building. Alex. J. Forbes, W. M. G. M. Brown, S. M. J. Roosa, J. M.
Rondout Lodge No. 343 F. & A. M.—Meets every Monday evening at 7 o'clock, at Masonic Hall, Garden street. George B. Hibbard, W. M. T. O. Taylor, S. W. A. Wood J. W.
Mount Horeb Chapter No. 75 of R. A. M.—Meets at Kingston Lodge Room Savings Bank Building, Wall street every Friday evening. H. B. Luther, H. P.
Hudson River Council No. 21 of R. and S. M.—

J. O. & G. B. MERRITT, Flannels and

HIRAM ROOSA, Gen'l Ins, Agent, Rondout, N. Y.

Regular assembly first Thursday of every month. H. B. Luther, T. I. M.

Rondout Commandry No. 53—Meets in Masonic Hall, second and fourth Wednesday evenings of each month. Abel A. Crosby, E. C. James McCausland, G. Frank J. Hecker, C. G. George B. Hibbard, P. David C. Reid, S. W. John B. Alliger, J. W. Charles Bray, T. Grove Webster, R. Thad. O. Taylor, S. B. William C. Turner, S. B. L. D. Hoornbeck, W. Daniel B. Stow, S.

ODD FELLOWS.

Kosciusko Lodge No. 86 of Northern New York, Kingston. Organized 1843. Meets at Odd Fellow's Hall N Front, every Wednesday evening. J. E. Du-Flon, N. G.

Aretas Lodge No. 172, *I. O. of O. F.*—Thos. Sturgeon, N. G.—George Drautz, V. G.—J. Johnson, Sec. —Joseph Tubby, Treas.—James Whittaker, P. S. Meets every Wednesday evening in Odd Fellows' Hall.

United German Lodge No. 303.—Meets every Thursday evening in Odd Fellows' Hall.

Franklin Lodge No. 37, *Knights of Phythias*—Meets at Odd Fellows' Hall, every Thursday evening.

Ulster Lodge No. 76, *K. of P.*—Meets every Tuesday evening, Odd Fellows' Hall, Garden, Rondout.

Wiltwick Division No. 28, *S. of T.*—Meets Monday evenings, in Romeyn's Building, Wall street.

Minnehaha Division S. of T. No. 83.—Meets every Friday evening, in Odd Fellows' Hall, Garden, Rondout.

RAIL ROADS.

New York, Kingston & S. R. R.—President, Gen. George H. Sharpe ; Vice-President, B. G. Morss ; Sec.

Blankets, No. 5 Wall St., Kingston.

HIRAM ROOSA'S Accidental, Life, Fire, Marine

and Treas., Rev. J. C. Hoes, D. D.; General Manager, W. B. Litchfield; Supt., H. P. Breed.
Wallkill Valley Railway Company—City of Kingston, (Rondout.) Robert H. Berdell, President; Artemas Sahler, Vice-President; James E. Ostrander, Secretary; J. H. Jones, General Superintendent; Wisner Murray, Treasurer.

STREET DIRECTORY.

Abeel, from Division southerly to town line.
Adams, from Pierpont to Hudson.
Albany, from Columbus Point to the River.
Albany avenue, from E. Front to town line.
Abruyn, from Mill to Rondout Creek.
Ann, from Mill to Ravine.
Beach, from Albany to Ridge.
Big Fly Road, from Linderman avenue to town line.
Bowery, from Fair to Union avenue.
Bruyn avenue, from Albany avenue to Flatbush av.
Canal, from Ferry to Lackawanna.
Catherine, from Hasbrouck avenue to Prospect.
Cedar, from Mill to Columbus avenue.
Cedar, from Union avenue to Plank road.
Chipp, from Wall south-westerly.
Chambers from Mill to Stuyvesant.
Charles, from Abruyn to Grove.
Chestnut, from Division to Cemetery.
Chestnut, from Mill to Livingston.
Columbus avenue, continuation of Garden street to Columbus Point avenue.
Columbus Point avenue, from Union avenue to Kingston Point.

J. O. & G. B. MERRITT, Notions and

Insurance and Real Estate Agency, Rondout, N. Y.

Cordts, from Columbus Point avenue to Beach.
Crane, from Mill to Grove.
Cross, from Division to Hasbrouck avenue.
Crown, from Green to N Front.
Dederick, from Union avenue to Esther avenue.
Downs, from Union avenue to Ten Broeck avenue.
Division, from Ferry to Holmes.
Dock, from Lackawanna to Ravine.
DuBois, from Maple to Newkirk avenue.
East Ravine, from Abeel to Holmes.
East Front, from North Front to Cemetery.
Elmendorf av, from Union av to Ten Broeck av.
Esther avenue, from Albany av to town line.
Elm, from First to Fourth av.
Ferry, from Canal to Garden.
First avenue, from Columbus avenue to Pine.
Fourth avenue, from Columbus avenue to Pine.
Fair, from N Front to old Wilbur road.
Flatbush avenue, from Union avenue North.
Flatbush avenue, from Albany av to town line.
Flat Rocks road, from Pearl to Linderman avenue.
Ford, from N Front to Esopus Creek.
Furnace, from Greenkill avenue to beyond Liberty.
Garden, from Union avenue to Flatbush avenue.
Garden, from Division to Tompkins.
German, from Hone to Ridge.
Grove, from Abruyn to Kingston.
Green, from N Front to St. James.
Greenkill avenue, from Union avenue to Marius.
Greenkill road, from Greenkill avenue to town line.
Grand, from Union avenue to Ten Broeck avenue.
Henry, from Wall to Union avenue.
Hurley avenue, from Bridge to town line.
Hanraty, from Point road, south

Trimmings, No. 5 Wall St., Kingston.

HIRAM ROOSA'S Agency represents a Combined

Hasbrouck avenue, from Ferry to Columbus Point avenue.
Henry, from North to Livingston.
Holmes, from Plerpont to Division.
Hone, from Abeel to Holmes.
Hudson, from Spring to Rondout Creek.
Hudson, from Jane to Rondout creek.
Hunter, from Hone to Ridge.
Hutton from Columbus Point avenue to Ridge.
Jane, from Columbus avenue to Livingston.
John, from Green to E Front.
Joy's Lane, from Lucas tp to Bridge.
Kingston, from Mill to Kingston Point.
Lackawanna, from Division to Hudson.
Livingston, from Stuyvesant to Point road.
Lord, from Wurts to Hone.
Liberty, from E Front to Union avenue.
Linderman avenue, from Wall to Flat Rocks road.
Love Lane, from Wall to Marius.
Lucas Turnpike, from Green to town line.
Maiden Lane, from Albany avenue to Green.
Marius, from Greenkill avenue to town line.
Main, from Green to E Front.
Manor Place, from Albany avenue to Esopus creek.
Mason, from Wurts to Hone.
Maple, from Newkirk avenue to DuBois.
Meadow, from Division to Hasbrouck avenue.
Mill, from Division to Hasbrouck avenue.
Montgomery, from Albany to Livingston.
North, from Henry to Rondout Creek.
North Livingston, from Columbus Point avenue to town line.
North Ridge, from Hutton to Beach.
North Front, from Bridge to E Front.

J. O. & G. B. MERRITT, Dry Goods and

Capital of $50,000,000. Rondout, N. Y.

KINGSTON BUSINESS DIRECTORY.

O'Neil, from Union avenue to Ten Broeck avenue.
Oak, from First avenue to Fourth avenue.
O'Reilley, from Union avenue to Prince.
Pierpont, from Division to Hudson.
Pine, from Maiden Lane to Greenkill avenue.
Pine Grove avenue, from Union avenue to Cemetery.
Plank road, from Pine to town line.
Prince, from Union avenue to Flatbush avenue.
Prospect, from St. James to Greenkill avenue.
Pell's Road, from Pearl to Big Fly road.
Pearl, from E Front to town line.
Pierce, from E Front to Furnace.
Pine, from Fourth to Hutton.
Pine, from Ravine to Hudson.
Ponkhockie, from Mill to G. North's residence.
Prospect, from Mill to Columbus avenue.
Post, from Abeel to Spring.
Ravine, from Division to Columbus avenue.
Ridge, from Abeel to Pine.
Rogers, from Division to Wurts.
Russell, from Pierpont to Spring.
Second avenue, from Columbus avenue to Pine.
Spring, from Division to Hudson.
Smith avenue, from Albany avenue to Prince.
St. James, from Albany av to Green.
Sterling, from Van Buren to Jacob's Valley road.
Stuyvesant, from Livingston to Division.
Suydam, from Livingston to Division.
Taylor, from Hurley av to Bridge.
Ten Broeck avenue, from Albany av to Flatbush av.
Tompkins, from Mill to Columbus avenue.
Union, from Hone to Grove.
Union avenue, from Albany av to town line.
Vine, from Albany to Livingston.

Carpets, No. 5 Wall St., Kingston.

HIRAM ROOSA Insures Vessels and Cargoes

230   KINGSTON BUSINESS DIRECTORY.

Van Buren, from Furnace to Union avenue.
Wall, from N Front to Old Wilbur road.
Water, from Grove to Kingston.
Willow, from Livingston to Ridge.
Wurts, from Abeel to Holmes.
Washington avenue, from the bridge to Greenkill rd.

J. D. DEYO,

Livery and Exchange Stables,

Office—Market Street, near Terwilliger House,

ELLENVILLE, N. Y.

☞ *HORSES AND CARRIAGES TO LET, WITH DRIVERS, IF DESIRED.*

J. O. & G. B. MERRITT, Black Silks at

ELLENVILLE DIRECTORY.

American Express Company, (E. Sanders, agent,) Canal.
Bachman Frank, saloon, Centre n Market.
Bailey & Deyo, coal and lumber, Canal.
Bautsch F., tailor, Canal.
Beers P. F., stoves, crockery, &c., Canal.
Bluenemthal I., clothing, Canal.
Bradford Madison, saloon, n Depot.
Broas J. A. Mrs., milliner, Canal n Main.
Brodhead F., lawyer, Canal cor Market.
Brodhead W., (pro. American House,) hd Canal.
BROWN J. A., druggist and chemist, Canal-st., n Main.
Butterfuss Charles, harness maker, Canal.
Campbell J. B., harness manuf., Canal.
CARLEY A. A., hairdresser and hair restorative, Canal cor Main.
Carley Charles R., baker, Market cor Centre.
Carpenter Wm., tobacconist, Canal cor Market.
Clark M. A., milliner, Canal n Main.
Coleman Nicholas, saloon, Main cor Warren.
CONSTABLE & DE GARMO, pros. Terwilliger House, Canal cor Market.
Corbin Isaac, druggist, Canal.
Cox J. L., blacksmith, Canal.
Cox Brothers, grain, flour, feed, &c., ft Centre cor tow path.
Crisman House, (J. Crisman, pro.,) Main n Canal.

Bargains, No. 5 Wall St., Kingston.

Get an Accidental Policy at

ELLENVILLE DIRECTORY.

CRISMAN J., pro. Crisman House, Main n Canal.
Crum Charles E., station agent, Depot.
Curtis & Moore, yankee notions, Canal.
Derby W. C., dentist, Canal.
DeWitt George W., small beer manuf., hd Canal.
DeWitt John T., lawyer, Main.
DEYO J. D., livery, Market n Canal.
Divine J. H. & Co., gen. merchandise, Canal.
Donaldson D. B., barrel head manuf., hd Canal.
DUTCHER & HOLMES, furniture and undertakers, Canal n Main.
Eck George, saloon, ft Centre.
Ellenville Glass Works, store and office, Canal.
ELLENVILLE JOURNAL, (S. M. Taylor, editor and publisher,) Canal n Main.
Ellenville Knife Co., M. B. Tears, supt., W. H. De Garmo, secretary and treasurer, hd Canal.
Ellenville Press, (Benedict Bros'., editors and pros.,) Canal bel Market.
Ellenville Savings Bank, Canal.
Erickson G., shoemaker, Market.
FINCH P., M. D., physician and surgeon, Canal-st. n Main.
First National Bank of Ellenville, Canal.
FOLANT, HAMMOND & ELLIOT, hardware, Canal cor Market.
FREILEWEH MARTIN, saloon and spruce beer, Canal.
Fuller Wm. D., butcher, Market cor Canal.
GEISLER BERNARD, butcher, Canal n Glass Works.
Gerrard Mary D., hotel, Market n Main.
Gonder John, shoemaker, ft Centre.
Gaernsey E. W., boots, shoes and Post Master, Canal.
Hagenow Wm., shoemaker, Centre n Market.

J. O. & G. B. MERRITT, Black Alpacas

HAIGHT A. V., book and job printer, Canal n Main.
HALE J. P., livery stables, Centre n Main.
Hanford W. S. P., brick manuf., Centre n Depot.
Hanmer J. L., physician, Centre.
Hartshorn Warren, stoves, &c., Canal.
Hartwig Henry, stoves, &c., Canal cor tow path.
Hasbrouck W. H., lawyer, Canal.
Hermance Jacob & Co., grain, flour, feed, provisions, Centre n Depot.
Hoar George, boat builder, Canal Lock.
Hoar Henry J., blacksmith, tow path.
Hogan M., dining rooms, Canal.
Home National Bank of Ellenville, Market n Canal.
Hornbeck Wm., merchant tailor, Canal.
Houston & Myers, harness, &c., Liberty sq.
Hunter & Lent, boots, shoes, &c., Canal.
Johnson A., carriage manuf., Canal.
Keeler George G., lawyer, Canal cor Main.
Keeler James B., town clerk, Canal cor Main.
Kimbark Frederick, mer. tailor, Canal cor Main.
Kindberg J., painter, Liberty sq.
Knapp D. J., carriage manuf., Canal.
Kopf Jacob, saloon, Canal.
Kuhfeldt Frederick, grocer, Canal Lock.
Lamoree H. V., fish, &c., Canal.
Lent C. H., insurance, Canal.
Losey I. H., painter and trimmer, Liberty sq.
Low J. M., gen. merchandise, hd Canal.
Lyon John, lawyer, Centre ab Main.
Lyons E. Mrs., dress making, Canal.
McMullen M., tobacconist, Canal opp Hermance.
Mance I. W., fancy goods, &c., Canal cor Main.
Meinhold Lewis, gen. merchandise, Canal n Market.
Miller H. J., carriage maker, Market n Canal.

and Brilliantines, 5 Wall St., Kingston.

Morse William & Son, grist mill, hd Canal.
Neafie & Terwilliger, insurance, Canal.
Nickason Bros., sash, blinds, &c., Canal.
Otis A., physician, Maiden Lane cor Canal.
Penrose M. Mrs., saloon, Canal.
Rockwell N., jeweler, Canal n Market.
Rose & Leopold, dry goods, clothing, &c., Canal.
Rubli H., shoemaker, Canal.
Russell Asa S., blacksmith, Canal.
Russell J. W., blacksmith, Market cor Centre.
Ryan William, grocer, Canal.
Sahler, Reynolds & DuBois, hardware, iron, steel, &c., Canal cor Main.
Saxer Lawrence, hairdresser, Canal.
Sayers A. Miss, millinery, &c., Canal.
Schoonmaker & Eaton, liquors, Canal.
Schoonover Benjamin, billiards, Canal.
Scoresby W. F., physician, Centre cor Child.
Smith Wm. B., confectioner, Canal.
Staub George, hairdresser, Canal.
Stoehr C., saloon, Canal.
Taylor J. W., grocer, Canal cor Market.
TAYLOR S. M., editor and publisher, Ellenville Journal, Canal.
TERWILLIGER HOUSE, (Constable & DeGarmo, pros.,) Canal cor Market.
Terwilliger H. H., grocer, Canal.
Terwilliger J., carpenter, Centre cor Market.
Terwilliger Nelson, gen. merchandise, Canal Lock.
Thompson Albert & Co., tanners, Canal.
Tice A. Wurts, photographer, Canal.
Ulster Seminary, (A. McIntyre, principal,) Maple av.
Van Bergan A., shoemaker, Canal.
Van Schaick G. M., confectioner, Canal.

J. O. & G. B. MERRITT, Choice Dress

operative Plan at H. ROOSA'S Agency, Rondout.

ELLENVILLE DIRECTORY.

Van Wagener J. J., gen. merchandise, Canal.
Van Wagoner & Munson, druggists, Canal.
Wallace William, blacksmith, hd Canal.
Ward John G., Market n Centre.
Webb Ira B., liquors, Canal.
Webb W. B., livery, Liberty sq.
Weber Jacob, hairdresser, Canal.
Weller A. S., gen. merchandise, Canal.
Weller David A., butcher, hd Canal.
Weston Daniel, pottery, Warren cor Market.
Whitney E. Miss, dressmaking, hd Canal.
Whittaker J. A., jeweler, Canal.
Winslow J. F., furniture, Main.
Wolf C. Mrs., butcher, Liberty sq.
Wood A. B., mer. tailor, Canal.
Wood Alice, Miss, millinery, &c., n hd Canal.
Wood L. K., livery, hd Canal.
YOUNG & REYNOLDS, foundry and machinists, Centre n Depot.
Ziegler John, shoemaker, Canal.

Goods, No. 5 Wall St., Kingston.

SAUGERTIES DIRECTORY.

Abeel David, tobacconist, Main.
Artman Benjamin, fish, saloon, &c., Partition.
Bahr H., root beer, East Bridge.
Barritt T. J., books, jewelry, &c., Main.
Bengel J. C., butcher, Partition.
Bigelow Blue Stone Co., T. Maxwell, agt., Main.
Blackwell E., butcher, Partition.
Bookstaver Jesse F., lawyer, Main.
Brainard Nelson, marble yards, Main.
Brede J. & Co., baker, &c.,, Partition.
Brink Edmund physician, Partition.
Brink Edward, sewing machines, &c., Main.
Burhans & Brainard, gen. merchandise, blue stone, &c., Main.
Burhans George, carriage manuf., Livingston.
Butzel John L' Sons, gen. merchandise, Partition.
Butzel F. S., milliner, Partition.
Cantine Peter, lawyer and surrogate, Main.
Capen Edmund, boots and shoes, Partition.
Carnright J. F. & A., flour, feed, &c., Partition cor Jane.
Chipman E. D., physician, Market.
Clark Michael, Mrs., saloon, Partition.
Cohen Albert, merchant tailor, &c., Partition.
Cole & Abeel, grocers, Main.
COON BENJAMIN M., lawyer, justice peace, notary public, Main.
Cripman D. W., hats, boots, &c., Partition.
CROWLEY DENNIS, billiard and dining saloon, 124 Partition.

J. O. & G. B. MERRITT, Kid Gloves,

Real Estate Agency, Rondout, N. Y.

SAUGERTIES DIRECTORY.

Crowley John, notions, &c., Partition.
CUNYES WM. D. W., pro. Exchange Hotel, Main cor Partition.
Curley Daniel, groceries and liquors, Partition.
Curley James, tailor and saloon, Market cor Livingston.
Davis J. W. & Son, boots and shoes, Partition cor Main.
Dawes Thomas S., physician, Market.
Deavlin M., furniture and undertaker, Partition.
Decker Bros., hardware, stoves, &c., Partition.
Dedrick & Saulpaugh, hardware, stoves, Partition.
Dedrick John, butcher, Main.
Derby Charles H., butcher, Partition.
DeWitt J. H., physician, Main.
Dixon Samuel, pro. Saugerties Hotel.
Donavan R., gen. merchandise, Partition.
Du Bois William B., cooperage, Steamboat Wharf.

EXCHANGE HOTEL,

(Wm. D. W. Cunyes, pro.,) Main cor Partition.
Eckert J. W., carpenter, &c., Partition.
Eckert P. & S., milliners, Market.
Eckert W. H. Mrs., milliner, Mill.
Elliott J. Mrs., saloon, E Bridge.
Elmendorf J. S., confectioner, Main.
Feroe A. E. & W. E., ale brewery, Steamboat wharf.
Fields Thomas, planing mills, Stone Dock.
Finger Brothers, lumber, coal, &c., Livingston.
First National Bank of Saugerties, Main.
French D. A., furniture and undertaking, Main.
Friedman David, leather, &c., Partition.
Hanson James., carriage manuf., Livingston.
HARDENBERG J. H., lunch rooms, Partition cor Jane.

No. 5 Wall Street, Kingston.

Hillas James, confectionery, Partition.
Hillas Thomas, coal and lumber, n Ferry.
Jacobs C. D., mer. tailor, Main.
James C. C., gen. merchandise, E Bridge.
Jernegan C. P., homeopathic physician, Main.
Jernegan E., photographer, 139 Partition.
Kilroy Martin, boarding house, Partition.
Kimble Warren, physician, Market.
King William, hairdresser, Partition.
Kipp William E., harness &c., Market.
Kleeber John, boots and shoes, Partition.
Knaust A. H., grocer, Partition.
Krohn Moses, tobacconist, Partition.
Laflin & Rand, powder Co., Main.
Lamb & Kipp, hardware, paints, &c., Market.
Lawless Elizabeth, saloon, Partition.
Lazarus Jacob, mer. tailor, Partition.
Legge & Lowther, carriage manufac., Livingston.
LISCOMB CHAS. G., druggist, Main.
McDonnough M., grocer, Partition.
McENROE E., grocer, hotel, also manuf. of mingo root beer and sarsaparilla, East Bridge.
McGrath & Burke, gen. merchandise, Partition.
McPherson D., painter, &c., Post.
MacCarthy R., variety store, Main.
Maines James, blacksmith, Main.
Mattes L., hairdresser, Partition.
Mattes Philip, hairdresser, Partition.
Maxwell P., news, &c., E Bridge.
Maxwell Wm. H., stationery, &c., Main.
Merchant James, tobacconist, Main.
Merclean Samuel, justice peace, Main.
Merritt J. K., dry goods and carpets, Main.
Mittrach Hermann, mer. tailor, Partition.

J. O. & G. B. MERRITT, Gent's

At **HIRAM ROOSA'S** Agency, Rondout, N. Y.

Milligan Wm. rolling mills, E Bridge.
Myer & Lockwood, dry goods and groceries, 126 Partition.
Myer J. A., carriage painter, Livingston.
Nestlen Jacob, jeweler, Partition.
Peters Gustavus, saloon, Partition.
Peters H., clothing, &c., Partition.
Preston A. & Son, general merchandise, Partition.
Pultz W. N. & A., livery, Partition.
Quick, Bros., blacksmiths, Livingston.
Quinn John, grocer, Partition.
Reinhard Joseph W., hair dresser, Phœnix Hotel.
Rice P. A., painter, Main.
Rightmyer, Peter, carpenter, Livingston.
Roosa Alfred, grocer, Market cor Livingston.
Roosa P. E., carpenter, Livingston.
Rosepaugh Isaac, undertaker, &c., Partition.
Rowe C., carriage manufac., Partition.
Rowe David, grocer &c., Main.
RUSSELL & MYERS, N. River blue stone, Livingston
Saugerties National Bank, Main.
Saugerties Savings Bank, Main.
Saugerties Telegraph, Geo. W. Elting, editor, &c., Partition.
Schoenfield Moses, clothing, &c., Main.
Searing S. G., hardware, stoves, &c., Main.
Sheffield Paper Mills, n Ferry.
Shultis C. P. & Co., gen. merchandise, Main.
Shults John, butcher, Partition.
Sinnott Catherine, grocer, E Bridge.
Smith C. H., hairdresser, Main.
Smith J., lawyer, Partition.
Snyder George K., lumber, coal, &c., Steamboat wharf.
Swart H. B. Mrs., confectionery, books, &c., Main.

Furnishing Goods, 5 Wall St., Kingston.

HIRAM ROOSA, Gen'l Ins. Agent, Rondout, N. Y.

Swart Ira, grocer, Main.
Sudderley A. J., confectioner, &c., Partition.
Sudderley L. A. Miss, milliner, Main.
Suderley C. F., grocer, bakery, &c., Partition.
Taylor John, fish, &c., Partition.
Teller & Teetsel, harness manufac., Partition.
Teller James G., hats, caps, &c., Partition.
Tepe Henry, saloon, Partition.
Turck Henry, pro. Pheonix Hotel, Partition.
Tyson J. J., mer. tailor, Market.
Underhill C. P., pro. Barclay House, n Ferry.
Van Buskirk W. E. & Co., druggist, tobacco, &c., Main cor Partition.
Van Deusen C. L., druggist, Main cor Market.
VAN HOESEN W. S. & CO., pros. Saugerties Variety Iron Works, Post.
Van Keuren & Finger, iron foundry, Livingston.
Van Nettan Uriah, lumber, &c., Partition.
Van Natten W. H., liquors, &c., Partition.
Vedder Eliza, physician, Bridge cor Jane.
Vedder John, physician, Bridge cor Jane.
Western Union Tel., (F. M. Baldwin, man.,) Partition.
Whitaker & Finger, dry goods and groceries, Partition
Whitaker E. & C., lawyers, Partition.
Whitbeck Isaac, boots and shoes, Main.
White C. E., dry goods and groceries, Main.
Wilbur G., notions, &c., Partition.
Willard Charles E., Physician, Main.
Williams C., lawyer, Partition.
Williams J. L., gen. merchandise, E Bridge cor Ann.
Winans Herman, lawyer, Main.
Wygant Harvey, dentist, Main.
Yerger Lewis, saloon, Market.
Ziegler L. Miss, milliner, Partition.
Ziegler Louis, saloon, Partition.

J. O. & G. B. MERRITT, Dry Goods.

www.ingramcontent.com/pod-product-compliance
Lightning Source LLC
Chambersburg PA
CBHW061956180426
43198CB00036B/1279